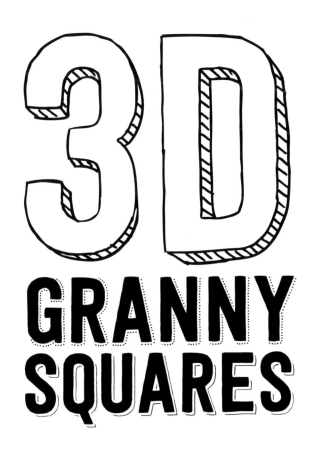

3D

GRANNY SQUARES

3D GRANNY SQUARES

100 CROCHET PATTERNS
FOR POP-UP GRANNY SQUARES

CAITIE MOORE · SHARNA MOORE · CELINE SEMAAN

DAVID & CHARLES

www.davidandcharles.com

CONTENTS

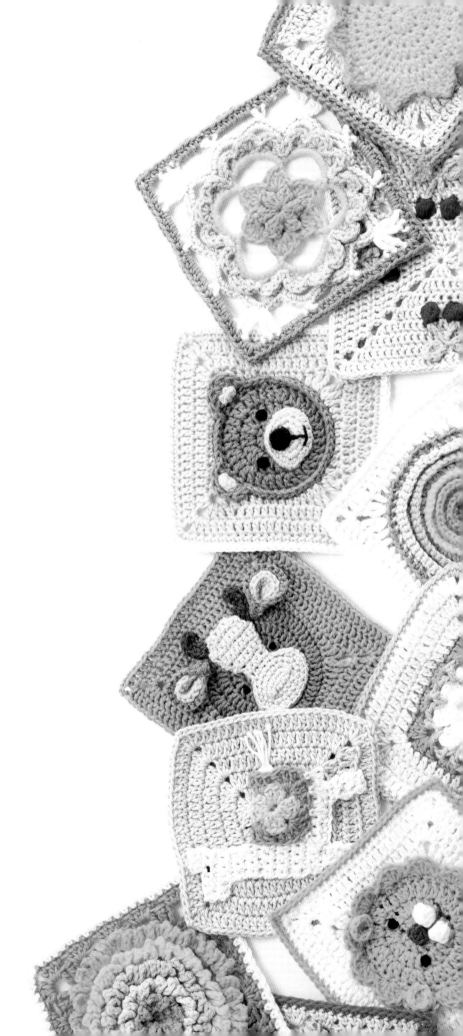

HOW TO USE THIS BOOK

Welcome to the wonderful world of three-dimensional granny squares! These little squares of loveliness just took a turn for the more tactile, as Caitie Moore, Celine Semaan and Sharna Moore present a collection of a hundred designs, each with a surface element that makes them irresistibly 3D. You can mix and match as much as you want to create impressive granny square blankets, or alternatively try some of the project ideas scattered throughout this book. Before you start, please read the following advice and information.

READING PATTERNS AND CHARTS

This book contains patterns for 100 granny squares and 10 projects. All of the square patterns are accompanied by coloured charts that show each individual layer of crochet to be made. The colours shown on the charts represent the different yarn colours used for the design, and a colour key is provided with each pattern to help you to identify the shades used (see Yarn Key). To follow the charts, refer to the symbol key (see Chart Symbols).

BASIC KIT

All you need for each granny square is some crochet hooks and yarn (see Yarn Key). Some squares require a little stuffing, and you will also need a yarn needle for weaving in ends and adding embroidery details. For the projects you may need additional supplies, but these will be listed with the instructions. Always read through the instructions carefully, checking the assembly details and any additional materials list, before you start a particular square or project to ensure that you have all of the required items.

CROCHET HOOKS

Metric sizes have been provided for crochet hooks throughout. Please refer to the following conversion chart if your hooks are labelled with imperial or US sizes instead:

MM	IMPERIAL	US
2.75	11	2/C
3	11	
3.25	10	3/D
3.5	9	4/E
3.75		5/F
4	8	6/G

TERMINOLOGY

The patterns in this book have all been written using US terms. If you are used to working with UK terms, then please note the following differences in stitch names:

US TERM	UK TERM
single crochet	double crochet
half double crochet	half treble crochet
double crochet	treble crochet
treble crochet	double treble crochet
double treble crochet	triple treble crochet
triple treble crochet	quadruple treble crochet

YARN KEY

All of the granny squares and projects in this book use Paintbox Yarns Cotton DK range, which features 50g (1.75oz) balls in a wide range of colours. You don't need to stick to the specified shades used for each design, but the following key has been provided to help you to identify the chosen colours in case you wish to replicate the design exactly:

#	COLOUR & CODE
1	Paper White (401)
2	Pure Black (402)
3	Champagne White (403)
4	Misty Grey (404)
5	Stormy Grey (405)
6	Slate Grey (406)
7	Granite Grey (407)
8	Vanilla Cream (408)
9	Light Caramel (409)
10	Soft Fudge (410)
11	Coffee Bean (411)
12	Bright Peach (412)
13	Tomato Red (413)
14	Rose Red (414)
15	Red Wine (416)
16	Melon Sorbet (417)
17	Mandarin Orange (418)
18	Blood Orange (420)
19	Banana Cream (421)
20	Daffodil Yellow (422)
21	Buttercup Yellow (423)
22	Mustard Yellow (424)
23	Pistachio Green (425)
24	Spearmint Green (426)
25	Slate Green (427)
26	Racing Green (428)
27	Lime Green (429)
28	Grass Green (430)
29	Evergreen (431)
30	Seafoam Blue (432)
31	Washed Teal (433)
32	Marine Blue (434)
33	Kingfisher Blue (435)
34	Duck Egg Blue (436)
35	Dolphin Blue (437)
36	Sky Blue (439)
37	Sailor Blue (440)
38	Dusty Rose (442)
39	Tea Rose (443)
40	Raspberry Pink (444)
41	Rich Mauve (445)
42	Pale Lilac (446)
43	Pansy Purple (448)
44	Candyfloss Pink (450)
45	Bubblegum Pink (451)
46	Lipstick Pink (452)
47	Ballet Pink (453)
48	Blush Pink (454)
49	Peach Orange (455)
50	Vintage Pink (456)

CHART SYMBOLS

Please use the following key to identify
the symbols in the crochet charts:

◄	Starting point	)	Spike stitch
◎	Magic ring		Picot
○	Chain	⋏	sc2tog
•	Slip stitch	⋏	sc3tog
+	Single crochet		hdc5tog
T	Half double crochet		dc4tog
†	Double crochet		dc5tog
‡	Treble crochet		ttr2tog
	Double treble crochet		3-dc-puff
	Triple treble crochet		5-dc-puff
⌒	Back loop		7-dc-puff
⌣	Front loop		2-dc-popcorn
ↄ	Back post		3-dc-popcorn
ↄ	Front post		4-dc-popcorn
♀	Loop stitch		5-dc-popcorn
	Puff stitch		Bobble

ABBREVIATIONS

The following abbreviations have been used
for the patterns featured in this book:

approx	approximately
BL	back loop/s
BLO	back loop/s only
bpdc	back post double crochet
bphdc	back post half double crochet
bpsc	back post single crochet
bpslst	back post slip stitch
ch	chain
ch-sp	chain space
dc	double crochet
dc4tog	double crochet 4 together
dc5tog	double crochet 5 together
dtr	double treble crochet
FL	front loop/s
FLO	front loop/s only
fpdc	front post double crochet
fpdtr	front post double treble crochet
fphdc	front post half double crochet
fpsc	front post single crochet
fpslst	front post slip stitch
fptr	front post treble crochet
fpttr	front post triple treble crochet
hdc	half double crochet
hdc5tog	half double crochet 5 together
rem	remaining
rep	repeat
Rnd(s)	round(s)
RS	right side
sc	single crochet
sc2tog	single crochet 2 together
sc3tog	single crochet 3 together
sk	skip
slst	slip stitch
sp	space(s)
st(s)	stitch(es)
tr	treble crochet
ttr	triple treble crochet
ttr2tog	triple treble crochet 2 together
WS	wrong side

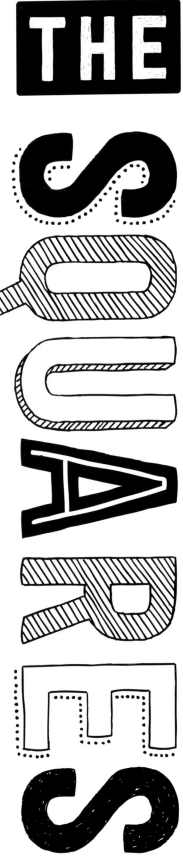

THE SQUARES

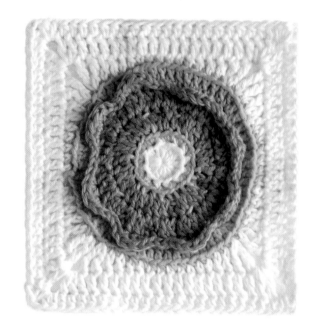

	1
	22
	45

DOUGHNUT

With a 4mm hook and **Colour 1**, make a magic ring.

Rnd 1: ch3, 11dc in ring, slst in third ch of initial ch3. [12dc]

Fasten off **Colour 1**.

Join **Colour 22** in BL of any Rnd 1 st. All sts in this rnd are made in BL of Rnd 1 sts:

Rnd 2: ch, 2sc in each st to end of rnd, slst in first sc. [24sc]

Fasten off **Colour 22**.

Join **Colour 45** in BL of any Rnd 2 st. All sts in this rnd are made in BL of Rnd 2 sts:

Rnd 3: ch3, dc in same st, dc in next st, (2dc in next st, dc in next st) 11 times, slst in initial dc. [36dc]

Rnd 4: ch3, dc in same st, dc in next 2 sts, (2dc in next st, dc in next 2 sts) 11 times. [48dc]

All sts in this rnd are made in FL of Rnd 4 sts:

Rnd 5: *slst in next 3 sts, sc in next st, 2hdc in next st, (hdc, sc) in next st**, rep from * to ** 7 times. [24hdc, 16sc, 24slst]

Fasten off **Colour 45**.

SQUARE

Join **Colour 22** in BL of any Rnd 4 st of doughnut. All sts in this rnd are made in BL of Rnd 4 sts:

Rnd 6: ch3, dc in st, dc in next 3 sts, (2dc in next st, dc in next 3 sts) 11 times, slst in initial dc. [60dc]

Fasten off **Colour 22**.

Join **Colour 1** in BL of any Rnd 6 st. All sts in this rnd are made in BL of Rnd 6 sts:

Rnd 7: ch4, tr in st, ch2, 2tr in next st, dc in next 2 sts, hdc in next 2 sts, sc in next 5 sts, hdc in next 2 sts, dc in next 2 sts, *2tr in next st, ch2, 2tr in next st, dc in next 2 sts, hdc in next 2 sts, sc in next 5 sts, hdc in next 2 sts, dc in next 2 sts**, rep from * to ** twice, slst in first ch of initial ch4. [16tr, 16dc, 16hdc, 20sc, 4ch2]

Rnd 8: slst in next st, slst in ch-2-sp, ch3, (dc, ch2, 2dc) in same ch-2-sp, dc in next 17 sts, *(2dc, ch2, 2dc) in ch-2-sp, dc in next 17 sts**, rep from * to ** twice, slst in third ch of initial ch3. [84dc, 4ch2]

Rnd 9: slst in next st, slst in ch-2-sp, ch2, (hdc, ch2, 2hdc) in same ch-2-sp, hdc in next 21 sts, *(2hdc, ch2, 2hdc) in ch-2-sp, hdc in next 21 sts**, rep from * to ** twice. [100hdc, 4ch2]

Fasten off **Colour 1**.

FINISHING

Embroider sprinkles using assorted colours.

SQUARE CHART

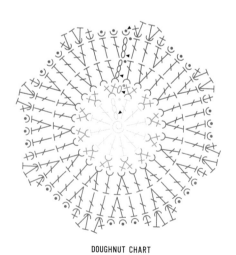

DOUGHNUT CHART

SQUARE

With a 4mm hook and **Colour 5** make a magic ring.

Rnd 1: ch3, 2dc in ring, ch2, (3dc in ring, ch2) 3 times, slst in third ch of initial ch3. [12dc, 4ch2]

Rnd 2: ch3, *dc in each st to ch-2-sp, (2dc, ch2, 2dc) in ch-2-sp**, rep from * to ** 3 times, slst in third ch of initial ch3. [28dc, 4ch2]

Rnds 3-6: ch3, *dc in each st to ch-2-sp, (2dc, ch2, 2dc) in ch-2-sp**, rep from * to ** 3 times, dc in rem sts to complete rnd, slst in third ch of initial ch3. [92dc, 4ch2]

Fasten off **Colour 5**.

Join **Colour 45** in any dc of Rnd 7.

Rnd 7: ch, *sc in each st to ch-2-sp, (sc, ch, sc) in ch-2-sp**, rep from * to ** 3 times, sc in rem sts to complete rnd, slst in first sc. [100sc, 4ch]

Fasten off **Colour 45**.

COFFEE CUP

With **Colour 31**, ch10.

Row 1: sc in second ch from hook, sc in each ch to end, ch, turn. [9sc]

Row 2: 3sc in first st, sc in next 7 sts, 3sc in last st, ch, turn. [13sc]

Row 3: sc in each to st to end, ch, turn. [13sc]

Rows 4-14: Rep Row 3. At end of last rep, do not turn; instead work sc all around sides and bottom of cup. [11sc down both sides, 10sc along bottom]

Fasten off **Colour 31**.

Join **Colour 11** to first st in Row 14.

Row 15: ch, sc in each st to end, turn. [13sc]

Row 16: ch, sc in each st to end, turn. [13sc]

Fasten off **Colour 11**.

Join **Colour 3** to first st in Row 16.

Row 17: *bobble in first st, (sc in next st, bobble in next st) 6 times. [7 bobbles, 6sc]

Fasten off **Colour 3**.

HEART

With **Colour 45**, ch2.

Row 1: (3dc, 3sc, ch2, 3sc, 3dc) in 2nd ch from hook, slst into ring to close. [6dc, 6sc, 2ch]

Fasten off **Colour 45**.

FINISHING

Stitch heart onto coffee cup, and then stitch onto centre of square.

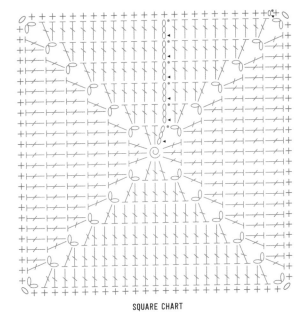

SQUARE CHART

5	■
45	■
31	■
11	■
3	■

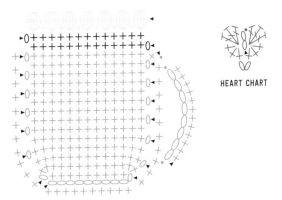

COFFEE CUP CHART

HEART CHART

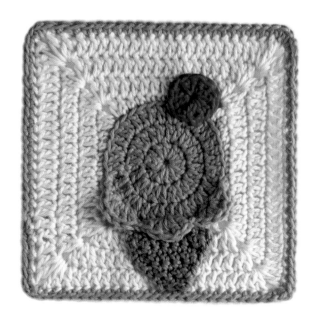

SQUARE

With a 4mm hook and **Colour 45**, make a magic ring.

Rnd 1: ch3, 11dc in ring, slst in third ch of initial ch3. [12dc]

Rnd 2: ch3, dc in same st, 2dc in each st to end of rnd, slst in third ch of initial ch3. [24dc]

Rnd 3: ch3, dc in same st, dc in next st, (2dc in next st, dc in next st) 11 times, slst in third ch of initial ch3. [36dc]

Fasten off **Colour 45**.

Join **Colour 44** in BL of any st in Rnd 3. All sts in this rnd are made in BL of Rnd 3 sts:

Rnd 4: ch3, dc in same st, ch2, 2dc in next st, hdc in next 2 sts, sc in next 3 sts, hdc in next 2 sts, *2dc in next st, ch2, 2dc in next st, hdc in next 2 sts, sc in next 3 sts, hdc in next 2 sts**, rep from * to ** twice, slst in third ch of initial ch3, slst in next st, slst in corner sp. [44sts, 4ch-2]

Rnd 5: (ch3, dc, ch2, 2dc) in corner sp, *dc in each st to next corner sp, (2dc, ch2, 2dc) in corner sp**, rep from * to ** twice, dc in each st to end, slst in third ch of initial ch3. [60dc, 4ch-2]

Rnds 6-7: Rep Rnd 5. [92dc, 4ch-2]

Fasten off **Colour 44**.

Join **Colour 45** in any st of Rnd 7.

Rnd 8: ch, *sc in each st to corner sp, (sc, ch, sc) in corner sp**, rep from * to ** 3 times, sc in rem sts to complete rnd, slst in first sc. [100sc, 4ch]

Fasten off **Colour 45**.

ICE CREAM FRILL

Join **Colour 45** in FL of Rnd 3 of square, 8 sts down from top left-hand corner sp.

Rnd 1: sc, *sk 1 st, 5dc in next st, sk 1 st, sc**, rep from * to ** twice, slst in same st as last sc. [15dc, 4sc]

Fasten off **Colour 45**.

CONE

With **Colour 11**, ch6.

Row 1: hdc in third ch from hook, hdc in each ch to end, turn. [4hdc]

Row 2: 2hdc in first st, hdc in each st to end, turn. [5hdc]

Rows 3-6: Rep Row 2. [9hdc]

Fasten off **Colour 11**.

CHERRY

With **Colour 14**, make a magic ring.

Rnd 1: ch3, 11dc in ring, slst in third ch of initial ch3. [12dc]

Fasten off **Colour 14**.

FINISHING

Stitch cherry onto ice cream as shown. Stitch cone onto square under ice cream frill.

■	11
■	45
■	44
■	14

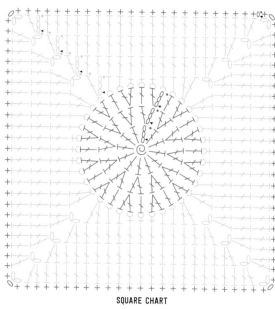

SQUARE CHART

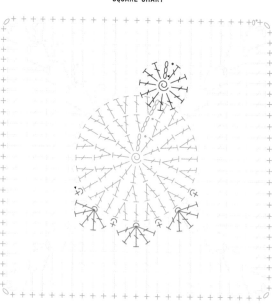

CHERRY AND ICE CREAM FRILL CHART

CONE CHART

COOKIE

With a 4mm hook and **Colour 9**, make a magic ring.

Rnd 1: ch3, 11dc in ring, slst in third ch of initial ch3. [12dc]

Rnd 2: ch3, dc in same st, 2dc in each st to end of rnd, slst in third ch of initial ch3. [24dc]

Rnd 3: ch3, dc in same st, dc in next st, (2dc in next st, dc in next st) 11 times, slst in third ch of initial ch3. [36dc]

Fasten off **Colour 9**. Rep to make a second cookie.

On RS of first cookie, make 10 random 3-dc-puffs with **Colour 11**.

Place cookies together with WS facing. Work sc in each st through both cookies to join.

SQUARE

Join **Colour 19** in any st of Rnd 3 of joined cookies.

Rnd 4: ch3, dc in same st, ch2, 2dc in next st, hdc in next 2 sts, sc in next 3 sts, hdc in next 2 sts, *2dc in next st, ch2, 2dc in next st, hdc in next 2 sts, sc in next 3 sts, hdc in next 2 sts**, rep from * to ** twice, slst in third ch of initial ch3, slst in next st, slst in corner sp. [44sts, 4ch-2]

Rnd 5: (ch3, dc, ch2, 2dc) in corner sp, *dc in each st to next corner sp, (2dc, ch2, 2dc) in corner sp**, rep from * to ** twice, dc in each st to end, slst in third ch of initial ch3. [60dc, 4ch-2]

Rnds 6-7: Rep Rnd 5. [92dc, 4ch-2]

Fasten off **Colour 19**.

Join **Colour 9** in any st of Rnd 7.

Rnd 8: ch, *sc in each st to corner sp, (sc, ch, sc) in corner sp**, rep from * to ** 3 times, sc in rem sts to complete rnd. [100sc, 4ch]

Fasten off **Colour 9**.

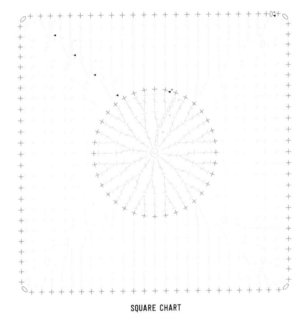

19	
9	
11	

SQUARE CHART

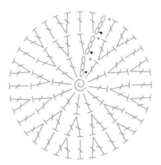

COOKIE CHART

SQUARE

With a 4mm hook and Colour 21, ch2.

Rnd 1: 6sc in second ch from hook, slst in first sc. [6sc]

Rnd 2: ch, 2sc in each st to end of rnd, slst in first sc. [12sc]

Rnd 3: ch, (2sc in next st, sc) 6 times, slst in first sc. [18sc]

Fasten off Colour 21.

Join Colour 9 in BL of any st in Rnd 3. All sts in this rnd are made in BL of Rnd 3 sts:

Rnd 4: ch, (2sc in next st, sc in next 2 sts) 6 times, slst in first sc. [24sc]

Rnd 5: ch, (2sc in next st, sc in next 3 sts) 6 times, slst in first sc. [30sc]

Rnd 6: ch, (2sc in next st, sc in next 4 sts) 6 times, slst in first sc. [36sc]

Rnd 7: ch3, dc in same st, ch2, 2dc in next st, hdc in next 2 sts, sc in next 3 sts, hdc in next 2 sts, *2dc in next st, ch2, 2dc in next st, hdc in next 2 sts, sc in next 3 sts, hdc in next 2 sts; rep from * twice more, slst in third ch of initial ch3, slst in next st, slst in corner sp. [44sts, 4ch-2]

Rnd 8: (ch3, dc, ch2, 2dc) in corner sp, *dc in each st to next corner sp, (2dc, ch2, 2dc) in corner sp**, rep from * to ** twice, dc in each st to end, slst in third ch of initial ch3. [60dc, 4ch-2]

Rnds 9-10: Rep Rnd 8. [92dc, 4ch-2]

Fasten off Colour 9.

Join Colour 11 in any st of Rnd 10.

Rnd 11: ch, *sc in each st to corner sp, (sc, ch, sc) in corner sp**, rep from * to ** 3 times, sc in rem sts to complete rnd, slst in first sc. [100sc, 4ch]

Fasten off Colour 11.

EGG WHITE

Join Colour 1 in FL of any st in Rnd 3 of square.

Rnd 1: ch, (2sc in next st, sc in next 2 sts) 6 times, slst in first sc. [24sc]

Rnd 2: ch, (2sc in next st, sc in next 3 sts) 6 times, slst in first sc. [30sc]

Rnd 3: ch, (2hdc in next st, hdc in next 4 sts) 6 times, slst in first sc. [36hdc]

Rnd 4: ch, (2hdc in next st, hdc in next 5 sts) 6 times, slst in first sc. [42hdc]

Rnd 5: ch, sc in next 4 sts, dc, 3dc in next st, dc, hdc in next 2 sts, sc in next 2 sts, hdc in next 2 sts, dc, 3dc in next st, dc, hdc in next 2 sts, sc in next 4 sts, hdc, 3hdc in next st, hdc, sc in next 4 sts, hdc, 3hdc in next st, hdc, 3hdc in next st, hdc, sc in next 8 sts, slst in first sc. [10dc, 20hdc, 22sc]

Fasten off Colour 1.

▨	1
▨	21
▨	9
■	11

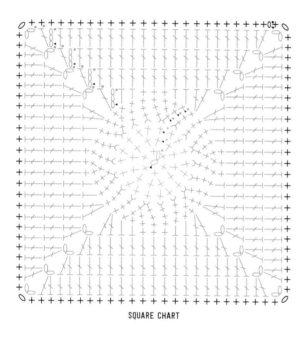

SQUARE CHART

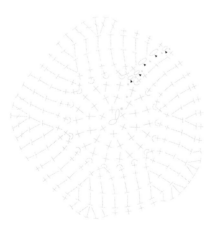

EGG WHITE CHART

FRIED EGG POT HOLDER

FRONT SQUARE

Follow instructions for Fried Egg to make 1 complete square, omitting Rnd 11 from the square pattern.

BACK SQUARE

With a 4mm hook and **Colour 9**, make a magic ring,

Rnd 1: ch3, 2dc in ring, ch2, *3dc in ring, ch2**, rep from * to ** twice, slst in third ch of initial ch3. [12dc, 4ch2]

Rnd 2: ch3, *dc in each st to ch-2-sp, (2dc, ch2, 2dc) in ch-2-sp**, rep from * to ** 3 times, slst in third ch of initial ch3. [28dc, 4ch2]

Rnds 3-6: ch3, *dc in each st to ch-2-sp, (2dc, ch2, 2dc) in ch-2-sp**, rep from * to ** 3 times, dc in rem sts to complete rnd, slst in third ch of initial ch3. [92dc, 4ch2]

Fasten off **Colour 9**.

FINISHING

Place squares together with WS facing. Join **Colour 11** to last rnd of both squares, 5 sts away from a corner sp on any side.

Work sc in each st through both squares, working (sc, ch, sc) in each corner sp. Before completing the rnd, ch20 (to form the loop), then slst to join.

Fasten off **Colour 11**.

ICE LOLLY

With a 4mm hook and Colour 14, ch12.

Row 1: sc in second ch from hook, sc in each ch to end, turn. [11sc]

Row 2: ch, sc in each st to end, turn. [11sc]

Rows 3-8: Rep Row 2. [11sc]

Fasten off Colour 14.

Join Colour 1 in last st worked of Row 8.

Rows 9-16: Rep Row 2. [11sc]

Fasten off Colour 1.

Join Colour 11 in last st worked of Row 16.

Rows 17-20: Rep Row 2. [11sc]

Row 21: ch, sk first st, sc in each st to last st, sk last st. [9sc]

Fasten off Colour 11.

Embroider sprinkles onto Rows 17-21 using assorted colours.

LOLLY STICK

Join Colour 9 in fifth ch of foundation row of ice lolly.

Row 1: ch6, dc in fourth ch, dc in next 2 ch, slst to eighth ch of start of ice lolly. [4dc]

Fasten off Colour 9.

SQUARE

With Colour 19, make a magic ring.

Rnd 1: ch3, 2dc in ring, ch2, (3dc in ring, ch2) 3 times, slst in third ch of initial ch3. [12dc, 4ch-2]

Rnd 2: ch3, *dc in each st to ch-2-sp, (2dc, ch2, 2dc) in ch-2-sp**, rep from * to ** 3 times, slst in third ch of initial ch3. [28dc, 4ch-2]

Rnd 3: Rep Rnd 2. [44dc, 4ch-2]

Attach base of ice lolly to one side of square as follows:

Rnd 4: ch3, *dc in each st to ch-2-sp, (2dc, ch2, 2dc) in ch-2-sp**, rep from * to ** twice, dc in edge st from base of ice lolly and next st from square together, (dc in next st from base of ice lolly and next st from square) 10 times, (2dc, ch2, 2dc) in ch-2-sp, dc in rem sts to end of rnd, slst in third ch of initial ch3. [60dc, 4ch-2]

Rnd 5: ch3, *dc in each st to ch-2-sp, (2dc, ch2, 2dc) in ch-2-sp**, rep from * to ** 3 times, dc in rem sts to end of rnd, slst in third ch of initial ch3. [76dc, 4ch-2]

Rnd 6: Rep Rnd 5. [92dc, 4ch-2]

Fasten off Colour 19.

Join Colour 45 in any st of Rnd 6.

Rnd 7: ch, *sc in each st to corner sp, (sc, ch, sc) in corner sp**, rep from * to ** 3 times, sc in each st to complete rnd. [100sc, 4ch]

Fasten off Colour 45.

Stitch top of ice lolly to square.

20	
1	
32	
14	
45	
11	
19	
9	

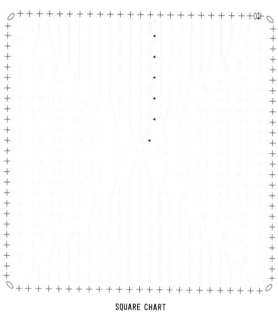

SQUARE CHART

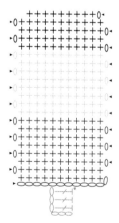

ICE LOLLY AND LOLLY STICK CHART

PIE

With a 2.75mm hook and **Colour 15**, make a magic ring.

Rnd 1: 6sc in ring, slst to close rnd. [6sc]

Rnd 2: ch3, 3dc in each of next 5 sts, 2dc in last st, slst to close rnd. [18dc]

Rnd 3: ch3, dc in next st, (dc in next st, 2dc in next st) 8 times, slst to close rnd. [26dc]

Rnd 4: ch3, (2dc in next st, 2dc in next st, dc in next st) 8 times, 3dc in last st, slst to close rnd. [44dc]

Rnd 5: ch2, (2hdc in next 2 sts, hdc in next 2 sts) 10 times, hdc in last 3 sts, invisible join. [64hdc]

Fasten off **Colour 15**.

Join **Colour 9** in any st of Rnd 5 with a standing sc.

Rnd 6: sc in each st around, slst to close rnd. [64sc]

All sts in this rnd are made in FL of Rnd 6 sts:

Rnd 7: ch, sk 1 st, 5dc in next st, sk 1 st, (sc in next st, sk 1 st, 5dc in next st, sk 1 st) 15 times, slst to close rnd. [96, 16 scallops]

Fasten off **Colour 9**.

SQUARE

Join **Colour 1** with a standing tr in BL of any st in Rnd 6 of pie.

Rnd 8: (ch2, tr) in same st, *tr in next st, dc in next 2 sts, hdc in next 2 sts, sc in next 5 sts, hdc in next 2 sts, dc in next 2 sts, tr in next st, (tr, ch2, tr) in next st**, rep from * to ** 3 times omitting (tr, ch2, tr) in last rep, slst to close rnd. [68, 4ch-2]

Rnd 9: slst in ch-2-sp, ch3, (dc, ch2, 2dc) in ch-2-sp, *dc in next 17 sts, (2dc, ch2, 2dc) in ch-2-sp**, rep from * to ** 3 times omitting (2dc, ch2, 2dc) in last rep, slst to close rnd. [84dc, 4ch-2]

Rnd 10: ch3, dc in next st, *(2dc, ch3, 2dc) in ch-2-sp, dc in next 21 sts**, rep from * to ** 3 times omitting last 2dc in last rep, slst to close rnd. [100, 4ch-3]

Rnd 11: ch3, dc in next 3 sts, *(2dc, ch3, 2dc) in ch-3-sp, dc in next 25 sts**, rep from * to ** 3 times omitting last 4dc in last rep, slst to close rnd. [116, 4ch-3]

Fasten off **Colour 1**.

LATTICE

With **Colour 9**, ch20.

Row 1: hdc in third ch from hook, hdc in each ch to end. [18hdc]

Fasten off **Colour 9**. Rep to make a total of 6 lattice strips.

Arrange 3 lattice strips evenly, in same direction, across pie. Stitch to secure in place at either end of each strip.

Add next 3 lattice strips perpendicularly to first 3 strips and secure on one side only. Weave strips together to form lattice and stitch in place.

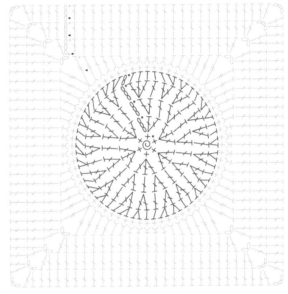

SQUARE CHART

15	■
9	▨
1	▨

PIE CHART

LATTICE CHART

WAFFLE

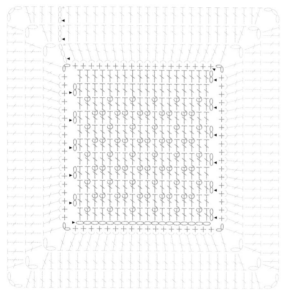

SQUARE CHART

STRAWBERRY LEAF CHART

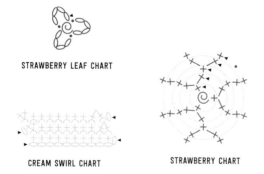

CREAM SWIRL CHART

STRAWBERRY CHART

	9
	30
	1
	46
	25

SQUARE

With a 2.75mm hook and **Colour 9**, ch20.

Row 1: dc in third ch from hook, dc in each ch to end of row. [19]

Row 2: ch2, turn, dc in next st, (fpdc in next st, dc in next 2 sts) 5 times, fpdc in next st, dc in last st. [19]

Row 3: ch2, turn, dc in next st, (dc in next st, fpdc in next 2 sts) 5 times, dc in last 2 sts. [19]

Rows 4-9: Rep Rows 2-3. [19]

Row 10: Rep Row 2. [19]

Row 11: ch2, turn, dc in each st to end of row. [19]

Fasten off and rejoin **Colour 9** at start of Row 11 between first and second sts with a standing sc.

Rnd 12: sc between sts across row a further 17 times [18sc], ch2, turn work 90 degrees, sc in side of top row, 17sc evenly along same side [18sc along side], turn 90 degrees, ch2, sc between each st along bottom edge [18sc along bottom], ch2, turn 90 degrees, sc in side of bottom row, 17sc evenly along same side to top [18sc along side]. [72sc, 4ch-2]

Fasten off **Colour 9** .

Join **Colour 30** in any ch-2-sp of Rnd 12. All sts in this rnd, apart from those in corners, are made in BL of Rnd 12 sts:

Rnd 13: ch5, dc in ch-2-sp, dc in next 18 sts, *(dc, ch2, dc) in corner sp, dc in next 18 sts**, rep from * to ** twice, slst in third ch of initial ch5. [80dc, 4ch-2]

Rnd 14: ch3, *(2dc, ch2, 2dc) in ch-2-sp, dc in next 20 sts**, rep from * to ** 3 times omitting last dc, slst to close rnd. [96dc, 4ch-2]

Rnd 15: ch3, dc in next 2 sts, *(2dc, ch3, 2dc) in ch-2-sp, dc in next 24 sts**, rep from * to ** 3 times omitting last 3 sts, slst to close rnd. [112dc, 4ch-3]

Fasten off **Colour 30**.

CREAM SWIRL

With **Colour 1**, ch11.

Row 1: sc in second ch from hook, sc in each ch to end. [10sc]

All sts in the following rows are made in BLO:

Row 2: ch, turn, 2sc in next st, sc in next 7 sts, sc2tog over last 2 sts. [10sc]

Row 3: ch, turn, sc2tog over first 2 sts, sc in next 7 sts, 2sc in next st. [10sc]

Rep Rows 2-3 until piece measures approx 7cm tall.

Fasten off **Colour 1**.

Form a tube by stitching first and last rows together with whip stitch.

Weave yarn tail through sts at one open end of tube and pull closed. Rep on other side of tube.

Gently squash tube flat to form cream swirl.

STRAWBERRY

With **Colour 46**, make a magic ring.

Rnd 1: 3sc in ring. [3sc]

Rnd 2: 2sc in each st. [6sc]

Rnd 3: sc in each st. [6sc]

Rnd 4: (2sc in next st, sc in next 2 sts) twice. [8sc]

Rnd 5: sc in each st, slst to close rnd. [8sc]

Fasten off **Colour 46**. Using yarn tail, cinch open end of strawberry closed.

STRAWBERRY LEAF

With **Colour 25**, make a magic ring.

Rnd 1: (ch4, slst in ring) 3 times, pull ring tight to close. [3 leaves]

Fasten off **Colour 25**. Using yarn tail, stitch leaf to top of strawberry.

FINISHING

Stitch strawberry to top of cream swirl and then attach to square as shown.

CUPCAKE

With a 2.75mm hook and **Colour 44**, make a magic ring.

Rnd 1: 6sc in ring, slst to close rnd. [6sc]

Rnd 2: ch3, 3dc in each of next 5 sts, 2dc in last st, slst to close rnd. [18dc]

Rnd 3: ch3, dc in next st, (dc in next st, 2dc in next st) 8 times, slst to close rnd. [26dc]

Rnd 4: ch3, (2dc in next st, 2dc in next st, dc in next st) 8 times, 3dc in last st, slst to close rnd. [44dc]

Rnd 5: Fold circle in half and sc through both layers. [22sc]

Fasten off **Colour 44**.

Add small whip stitches for sprinkles using assorted colours.

CUPCAKE FRILLS

Join **Colour 44** to one end of flat edge of folded cupcake.

The following scallops are worked across flat edge of semi-circle:

First scallop: ch2, 5dc in outer edge of Rnd 4, slst in outer edge of Rnd 3. [ch2, 5dc, slst]

Second scallop: 6dc in outer edge of Rnd 2, slst in outer edge of Rnd 1. [7]

Third scallop: 6dc in outer edge of Rnd 1, slst in outer edge of Rnd 2. [7]

Fourth scallop: 6dc in outer edge of Rnd 3, slst in outer edge of Rnd 4. [7]

Fasten off **Colour 44**.

CASE

With **Colour 42**, ch9.

Row 1: sc in second ch from hook, sc in each ch to end. [8sc]

All sts in the following rows are made in BLO:

Row 2: ch, turn, slst in next st, sc in next 4 sts, hdc in next 2 sts, dc in last st. [8sc]

Row 3: ch, turn, sc in each st. [8sc]

Rows 4-9: Rep Rows 2-3. [8sc]

Row 10: Rep Row 2. [8sc]

Fasten off **Colour 42**. Using yarn tail, stitch case to back of cupcake as shown.

CHERRY

With **Colour 45**, make a magic ring.

Rnd 1: 8sc in ring, slst in first sc. [8sc]

Fasten off **Colour 45**. Using yarn tail, stitch cherry to top of cupcake.

SQUARE

With RS of cupcake facing, join **Colour 31** to outer edge of Rnd 5 on right-hand side of cupcake. Join yarn in back of stitch and make a standing dc in same st.

All sts in this rnd are made in BLO:

Rnd 1: (2dc in next st, dc in next st) 10 times, dc in next st [end of top of cake], dc in each st down side of case [last dc will be in slst], 4dc in first ch at bottom, 2dc in next ch, 4dc in next ch, 2dc in next ch, 4dc in last ch, dc in each ch up side of case, slst to close rnd. [64dc]

Fasten off **Colour 31** and rejoin in last dc before first 4-dc cluster from Rnd 1 with a standing tr.

Rnd 2: (ch2, tr) in same st, *tr in next st, dc in next 2 sts, hdc in next 2 sts, sc in next 5 sts, hdc in next 2 sts, dc in next 2 sts, tr in next st, (tr, ch2, tr) in next st**, rep from * to ** 3 times omitting (tr, ch2, tr) in last rep, slst to close rnd. [68, 4ch-2]

Rnd 3: slst in ch-2-sp, ch3, (dc, ch2, 2dc) in ch-2-sp, *dc in next 17 sts, (2dc, ch2, 2dc) in ch-2-sp**, rep from * to ** 3 times omitting (2dc, ch2, 2dc) in last rep, slst to close rnd. [84dc, 4ch-2]

Rnd 4: ch3, dc in next st, *(2dc, ch3, 2dc) in ch-2-sp, dc in next 21 sts**, rep from * to ** 3 times omitting last 2dc in last rep, slst to close rnd. [100dc, 4ch-3]

Rnd 5: ch3, dc in next 3 sts, *(2dc, ch3, 2dc) in ch-3-sp, dc in next 25 sts**, rep from * to ** 3 times omitting last 4dc in last rep, slst to close rnd. [116dc, 4ch-3]

Fasten off **Colour 31**.

44	
31	
45	
42	

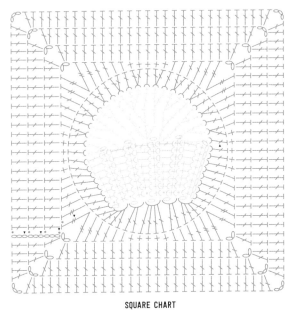

SQUARE CHART

CUPCAKE CHART

CHERRY CHART

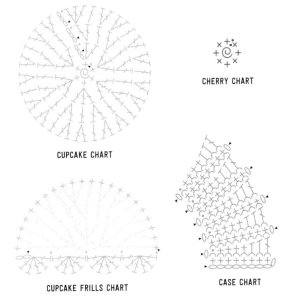

CUPCAKE FRILLS CHART

CASE CHART

30
1

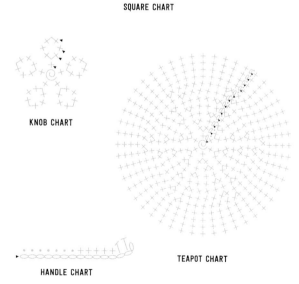

SQUARE CHART

KNOB CHART

HANDLE CHART

TEAPOT CHART

SQUARE

With a 2.75mm hook and **Colour 30**, make a magic ring.

Rnd 1: 6sc in ring, slst to close rnd. [6sc]

Rnd 2: ch3, 3dc in each of next 5 sts, 2dc in last st, slst to close rnd. [18dc]

Rnd 3: ch3, dc in next st, (dc in next st, 2dc in next st) 8 times, slst to close rnd. [26dc]

Rnd 4: ch3, (2dc in next st, 2dc in next st, dc in next st) 8 times, 3dc in last st, slst to close rnd. [44dc]

Rnd 5: ch3, (2dc in next 2 sts, dc in next 2 sts) 10 times, dc in last 3 sts, slst to close rnd. [64dc]

Fasten off **Colour 30**.

Join **Colour 1** in any st of Rnd 5 with a standing tr.

Rnd 6: (ch2, tr) in same st, *tr in next st, dc in next 2 sts, hdc in next 2 sts, sc in next 5 sts, hdc in next 2 sts, dc in next 2 sts, tr in next st, (tr, ch2, tr) in next st**, rep from * to ** 3 times omitting (tr, ch2, tr) in last rep, slst to close rnd. [68, 4ch-2]

Rnd 7: slst in ch-2-sp, ch3, (dc, ch2, 2dc) in ch-2-sp, *dc in next 17 sts, (2dc, ch2, 2dc) in ch-2-sp**, rep from * to ** 3 times omitting (2dc, ch2, 2dc) in last rep, slst to close rnd. [84dc, 4ch-2]

Rnd 8: ch3, dc in next st, *(2dc, ch3, 2dc) in ch-2-sp, dc in next 21 sts**, rep from * to ** 3 times omitting last 2dc in last rep, slst to close rnd. [100dc, 4ch-3]

Rnd 9: ch3, dc in next 3 sts, *(2dc, ch3, 2dc) in ch-3-sp, dc in next 25 sts**, rep from * to ** 3 times omitting last 4dc in last rep. [116dc, 4ch-3]

Fasten off **Colour 1**.

TEAPOT

With **Colour 30**, make a magic ring.

Rnd 1: 6sc in ring, slst to close rnd. [6sc]

Rnd 2: ch, 2sc in each st, slst to close rnd. [12sc]

Rnd 3: ch, (sc in next st, 2sc in next st) to end of rnd, slst to close rnd. [18sc]

Rnd 4: ch, (2sc in next st, sc in next 2 sts) to end of rnd, slst to close rnd. [24sc]

Rnd 5: ch, (sc in next 3 sts, 2sc in next st) to end of rnd, slst to close rnd. [30sc]

Rnd 6: ch, (2sc in next st, sc in next 4 sts) to end of rnd, slst to close rnd. [36sc]

Rnd 7: ch, (sc in next 5 sts, 2sc in next st) to end of rnd, slst to close rnd. [42sc]

Rnd 8: ch, (2sc in next st, sc in next 6 sts) to end of rnd, slst to close rnd. [48sc]

Rnds 9-12: ch, sc in each st. [48sc]

Fasten off **Colour 30**.

Embroider flowers and leaves on side of teapot using assorted colours. Add a few French knots to flowers and back stitch around top of teapot.

SPOUT

With **Colour 30**, make a magic ring.

Rnd 1: 6sc in ring, slst to close rnd. [6sc]

All sts in this rnd are made in BL of Rnd 1 sts:

Rnd 2: ch, sc in each st. [6sc]

Rnd 3: ch, sc in each st. [6sc]

Rnd 4: ch, 2sc in next 2 sts, sc2tog twice. [6sc]

Rnd 5: ch, sc in each st. [6sc]

Rnd 6: ch, 2sc in next 3 sts, sc in next 3 sts. [9sc]

Rnd 7: ch, sc in each st. [9sc]

Rnd 8: ch, sc in next 3 sts, sc2tog twice, 2sc in next 2 sts. [9sc]

Rnd 9: ch, sc in each st. [9sc]

Rnd 10: ch, sc in next 3 sts, 2hdc in next 3 sts, sc in next 3 sts. [12]

Fasten off **Colour 30**.

KNOB

With **Colour 30**, make a magic ring.

Rnd 1: 5sc, pull ring closed. [5sc]

Rnd 2: 2sc in each st. [10sc]

Rnd 3: sc in each st. [10sc]

Rnd 4: sc2tog 5 times. [5sc]

Stuff lightly. Fasten off **Colour 30**.

HANDLE

With **Colour 30**, ch15.

Row 1: hdc in second ch from hook, hdc in next st, sc in next 5 sts, slst in each ch to end of row. [14]

Fasten off **Colour 30**.

FINISHING

Attach teapot to square, whip stitching in BL of teapot and outer edge of Rnd 5 of square. Leave a gap to lightly stuff teapot and then stitch closed.

Attach spout and knob to teapot. Attach bottom of handle to teapot, curl top of handle so that open end is pointing downwards and secure in place.

TEAPOT PINCUSHION

SQUARE

With **Colour 8**, work Rnds 1-5 of square for Teapot.

Fasten off **Colour 8** and rejoin in any st of Rnd 5 with a standing tr.

Work Rnd 6 of square for Teapot.

Rnd 7: slst in ch-2-sp, ch, (sc, ch2, 2sc) in ch-2-sp, *sc in next 17 sts, (2sc, ch2, 2sc) in ch-2-sp**, rep from * to ** 3 times omitting (2sc, ch2, 2sc) in last rep, slst to close rnd. [84sc, 4ch-2]

Fasten off **Colour 8** and rejoin in any ch-2-sp of Rnd 7 with a standing dc.

Rnd 8: (dc, picot, 2dc) in same ch-2-sp, (slst in next 2 sts, (hdc, dc, hdc) in next st) 6 times, slst in next 3 sts, *(2dc, picot, 2dc) in next ch-2-sp, (slst in next 2 sts, (hdc, dc, hdc) in next st) 6 times, slst in next 3 sts**, rep from * to ** twice, slst to close rnd. [88, 4 picot]

Fasten off **Colour 8**.

TEAPOT

With **Colour 3**, follow instructions for Teapot to make 1 complete teapot, spout, knob and handle.

FINISHING

Attach teapot, spout, knob and handle to square following instructions for Teapot.

SQUARE CHART

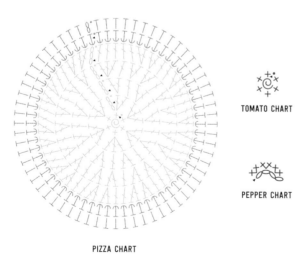

PIZZA CHART

TOMATO CHART

PEPPER CHART

20	
22	
1	
9	
13	
15	
29	

PIZZA

With a 2.75mm hook and **Colour 20**, make a magic ring.

Rnd 1: 6sc in ring, slst to close rnd. [6sc]

Rnd 2: ch3, 3dc in each of next 5 sts, 2dc in last st, slst to close rnd. [18dc]

Rnd 3: ch3, dc in next st, (dc in next st, 2dc in next st) 8 times, slst to close rnd. [26dc]

Rnd 4: ch3, (2dc in next st, 2dc in next st, dc in next st) 8 times, 3dc in last st, slst to close rnd. [44dc]

Rnd 5: ch3, (2dc in next 2 sts, dc in next 2 sts) 10 times, dc in last 3 sts, slst to close rnd. [64dc]

Fasten off **Colour 20** and join **Colour 9** in any st of Rnd 5 with a standing hdc.

All sts in this rnd are made in FLO:

Rnd 6: hdc in each st, slst to close rnd. [64hdc]

Rnd 7: ch2, hdc in each st. [64hdc]

Fasten off **Colour 9**.

SQUARE

Join **Colour 1** in BL of any st of Rnd 5 with a standing tr. All sts in this rnd are made in BLO:

Rnd 8: (ch2, tr) in same st, *tr in next st, dc in next 2 sts, hdc in next 2 sts, sc in next 5 sts, hdc in next 2 sts, dc in next 2 sts, tr in next st, (tr, ch2, tr) in next st**, rep from * to ** 3 times omitting (tr, ch2, tr) in last rep, slst to close rnd. [68, 4ch-2]

Rnd 9: slst in ch-2-sp, ch3, (dc, ch2, 2dc) in ch-2-sp, *dc in next 17 sts, (2dc, ch2, 2dc) in ch-2-sp**, rep from * to ** 3 times omitting (2dc, ch2, 2dc) in last rep, slst to close rnd. [84dc, 4ch-2]

Rnd 10: ch3, dc in next st, *(2dc, ch3, 2dc) in ch-2-sp, dc in next 21 sts**, rep from * to ** 3 times omitting last 2dc in last rep, slst to close rnd. [100dc, 4ch-3]

Rnd 11: ch3, dc in next 3 sts, *(2dc, ch3, 2dc) in ch-3-sp, dc in next 25 sts**, rep from * to ** 3 times omitting last 4dc in last rep. [116dc, 4ch-3]

Fasten off **Colour 1**.

Fold crust in half, towards centre of pizza. Using yarn tail, sew open edge of crust to outer edge of Rnd 5 with whip stitches.

Using **Colour 22**, add single long stitches from outer edge of Rnd 5 to centre of pizza to divide into 6 slices.

TOMATOES

With **Colour 13**, make a magic ring.

Rnd 1: 6sc in ring, slst to close rnd. [6sc]

Fasten off **Colour 13**.

Rep to make a total of 3 tomatoes with **Colour 13** and 3 tomatoes with **Colour 15**. Stitch onto pizza as shown.

PEPPERS

With **Colour 29**, ch4.

Rnd 1: sk first ch, 2sc in each st. [6sc]

Fasten off **Colour 29**.

Rep to make a total of 3 peppers. Stitch in place on pizza.

SQUARE

With a 2.75mm hook and **Colour 42**, ch2.

Rnd 1: (sc, hdc, dc) in second ch from hook, pull working loop and remove hook, join **Colour 31** in second ch with a standing sc, (hdc, dc) in same st, pull working loop and remove hook.

Rnd 2: working in a spiral, insert hook in **Colour 42** loop and tighten, 2dc in next 3 sts, pull working loop and remove hook, insert hook in **Colour 31** loop, 2dc in next 8 sts, pull working loop and remove hook.

Rnd 3: insert hook in **Colour 42** loop, 2dc in next 5 sts, pull working loop and remove hook, insert hook in **Colour 31** loop, 2dc in next 15 sts, pull working loop and remove hook.

Rnd 4: insert hook in **Colour 42** loop, (dc in next st, 2dc in next st) 12 times, hdc in next 3 sts, sc in next 2 sts, slst in next st, pull working loop and remove hook, insert hook in **Colour 31** loop, dc in next 11 sts, hdc in next 3 sts, sc in next 2 sts, slst in next st. [44]

Fasten off **Colours 42** and **31**.

Join **Colour 1** in BL of any st of Rnd 4 with a standing dc. All sts in this rnd are made in BLO:

Rnd 5: (2dc in next 2 sts, dc in next 2 sts) 10 times, dc in last 3 sts, slst to close rnd. [64dc]

Rnd 6: ch6, tr in same st, *tr in next st, dc in next 2 sts, hdc in next 2 sts, sc in next 5 sts, hdc in next 2 sts, dc in next 2 sts, tr in next st, (tr, ch2, tr) in next st**, rep from * to ** 3 times omitting (tr, ch2, tr) in last rep, slst to close rnd. [68, 4ch-2]

Rnd 7: slst in ch-2-sp, ch3, (dc, ch2, 2dc) in ch-2-sp, *dc in next 17 sts, (2dc, ch2, 2dc) in ch-2-sp**, rep from * to ** 3 times omitting (2dc, ch2, 2dc) in last rep, slst to close rnd. [84, 4ch-2]

Rnd 8: ch3, dc in next st, *(2dc, ch3, 2dc) in ch-2-sp, dc in next 21 sts**, rep from * to ** 3 times omitting last 2dc in last rep, slst to close rnd. [100, 4ch-3]

Rnd 9: ch3, dc in next 3 sts, *(2dc, ch3, 2dc) in ch-3-sp, dc in next 25 sts**, rep from * to ** 3 times omitting last 4dc in last rep. [116, 4ch-3]

Fasten off **Colour 1**.

WRAPPER

Join **Colour 38** in fourth dc of Rnd 4 of sweet, before ch-sp in Rnd 6 of square, with a standing sc.

Row 1: sc in next 7 sts. [8sc]

Row 2: ch8, sc in second ch from hook and sc in each ch to end of row, slst in next base st. [7sc]

All sts in the following rows are made in BLO:

Row 3: ch, sk 1, sc in next 5 sts, hdc in next 2 sts. [7]

Row 4: ch, turn, sc in next 7 sts, anchor with slst in base sc. [7]

Rep Rows 3-4 until every base sc is anchored.

Fasten off **Colour 38**.

Rep on opposite side to create a second wrapper.

1	
42	
31	
38	

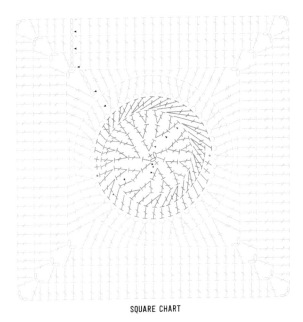

SQUARE CHART

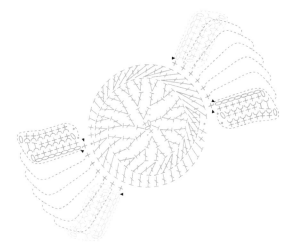

WRAPPER CHART

WATERMELON

With a 4mm hook and **Colour 46**, make a magic ring.

Rnd 1: ch3, 11dc in ring, slst in third ch of initial ch3. [12dc]

Rnd 2: ch3, dc in same st, 2dc in each st, slst in third ch of initial ch3. [24dc]

Rnd 3: ch3, dc in same st, dc in next st, (2dc in next st, dc in next st) 11 times, slst in third ch of initial ch3. [36dc]

Fasten off **Colour 46**.

Join **Colour 1** in any st of Rnd 3. All sts in this rnd are made in BLO:

Rnd 4: ch, sc in same st, sc in each st, slst in first sc. [36sc]

Fasten off **Colour 1**.

Join **Colour 25** in any st of Rnd 4.

Rnd 5: ch3, dc in same st, ch2, 2dc in next st, hdc in next 2 sts, sc in next 3 sts, hdc in next 2 sts, *2dc in next st, ch2, 2dc in next st, hdc in next 2 sts, sc in next 3 sts, hdc in next 2 sts**, rep from * to ** twice, join to top of ch3 with a slst, slst in next st, slst in corner sp. [44sts, 4ch-2]

Fasten off **Colour 25**.

Join **Colour 27** in FLO of any st in Rnd 4.

Rnd 9: ch, sc in same st, sc in next 3 sts, (2sc in next st, sc in next 3 sts) 8 times. [44sc]

Fasten off **Colour 27**.

With **Colour 2**, embroider 6 random stitches in Rnd 2 of watermelon to create pips.

SQUARE

Join **Colour 24** in any corner sp of Rnd 5 of watermelon.

Rnd 6: (ch3, dc, ch2, 2dc) in corner sp, dc in each st to next corner sp, *(2dc, ch2, 2dc) in corner sp, dc in each st to next corner sp**, rep from * to ** to end of rnd, slst in third ch of initial ch3. [60dc, 4ch-2]

Rnds 7-8: Rep Rnd 6. [92dc, 4ch-2]

Fasten off **Colour 24**.

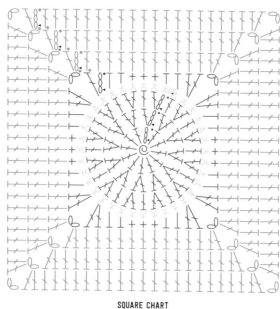

SQUARE CHART

■	46
■	27
■	25
■	24
■	1
■	2

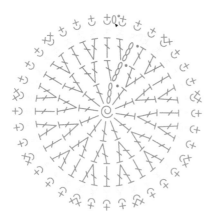

WATERMELON CHART

AVOCADO STONE

With a 4mm hook and **Colour 11**, ch4, slst in first ch to make circle.

Rnd 1: 8hdc in circle, slst in first hdc to join, working over top of 8hdc, 8dc in circle [8hdc, 8dc]

Fasten off **Colour 11**.

SQUARE

Join **Colour 11** in circle of avocado stone.

Rnd 2: working over top of 8hdc from Rnd 1 of avocado stone, 18dc in circle, working over top of 8dc from Rnd 1 of avocado stone, slst in first dc to join. [18dc]

Fasten off **Colour 11**.

Join **Colour 27** in any st of Rnd 2.

Rnd 3: ch3, dc in same st, 2hdc in next 2 sts, sc in next 12 sts, 2hdc in next 2 sts, 2dc in next st, slst to join. [4dc, 8hdc, 12sc]

Rnd 4: ch4, tr in same st, 2dc in next st, dc, hdc in next 2 sts, sc in next 4 sts, (2sc, sc in next 4 sts) twice, hdc in next 2 sts, dc, 2dc in next st, 2tr in last st, slst to join. [4tr, 6dc, 4hdc, 16sc]

Fasten off **Colour 27** and join **Colour 24** in first st of Rnd 4.

Rnd 5: ch, 2sc in first st, sc in next 4 sts, 2sc in next st, sc in next 2 sts, 2sc in next st, sc in next 8 sts, (2sc in next st, sc in next 4 sts) 3 times, 2sc in next st, sc in last 2 sts. [36sc]

Fasten off **Colour 24**.

Join **Colour 43** in ninth st from where you joined last rnd.

Rnd 6: ch3, dc in same st, ch2, 2dc in next st, hdc in next 2 sts, sc in next 3 sts, hdc in next 2 sts, 2dc in next st, ch2, (dc, hdc) in next st, sc in next 5 sts, hdc, dc, 2tr in next st, ch2, 2tr in next st, dc, hdc, sc in next 5 sts, 2dc in next st, ch2, 2dc in next st, hdc, sc in next 4 sts, hdc, dc in last st. [44]

Fasten off **Colour 43** and rejoin in any ch-2-sp.

Rnd 7: (ch3, dc, ch2, 2dc) in ch-2-sp, dc in each st to next ch-2-sp, *(2dc, ch2, 2dc) in next ch-2-sp, dc in each st to next ch-2-sp**, rep from * to ** twice, slst to third ch of starting ch, slst to ch-2-sp. [60dc, 4ch-2]

Rnds 8-9: Rep Rnd 6. [92dc, 4ch-2]

Fasten off **Colour 43**.

Join **Colour 27** in any st of Rnd 9.

Rnd 10: ch, *sc in each st to corner sp, (sc, ch, sc) in corner sp**, rep from * to ** 3 times, sc in rem sts to complete rnd. [100sc, 4ch-2]

Fasten off **Colour 27**.

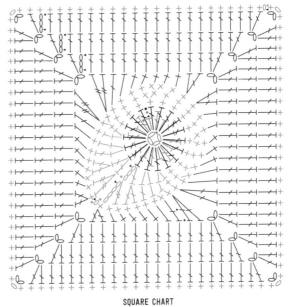

SQUARE CHART

27	
11	
43	
24	

AVOCADO STONE CHART

SQUARE

With a 2.75mm hook and **Colour 3**, make a magic ring.

Rnd 1: 6sc in ring, slst to close rnd. [6sc]

Rnd 2: ch3, 3dc in each of next 5 sts, 2dc in last st, slst to close rnd. [18dc]

Rnd 3: ch3, dc in next st, (dc in next st, 2dc in next st) 8 times, slst to close rnd. [26dc]

Rnd 4: ch3, (2dc in next st, 2dc in next st, dc in next st) 8 times, 3dc in last st, slst to close rnd. [44dc]

Fasten off **Colour 3**.

Join **Colour 15** in any st of Rnd 4 with a slst. Shape bottom of apple as follows:

Rnd 5: sc in next st, (dc, tr) in next st, (tr, dc) in next st, (dc in next 2 sts, 2dc in next 2 sts) 9 times, dc in next st, (dc, tr) in next st, (tr, dc) in next st, sc in next st, slst to close rnd. [67]

Fasten off **Colour 15**.

Join **Colour 33** in ninth st before last sc of Rnd 5 with a standing tr. All sts in this rnd are made in BLO:

Rnd 6: (ch2, tr) in same st, tr in next st, dc in next 2 sts, hdc in next 2 sts, sc in next 2 sts, sk sc, dc in same st as starting slst from Rnd 4, sk sc, sc in next 2 sts, hdc in next 2 sts, dc in next 2 sts, tr in next st, (tr, ch2, tr) in next st, *tr in next st, dc in next 2 sts, hdc in next 2 sts, sc in next 5 sts, hdc in next 2 sts, dc in next 2 sts, tr in next st, (tr, ch2, tr) in next st**, rep from * to ** twice omitting (tr, ch2, tr) in last rep, slst to close rnd. [68, 4ch-2]

Rnd 7: slst in ch-2-sp, ch3, (dc, ch2, 2dc) in ch-2-sp, *dc in next 17 sts, (2dc, ch2, 2dc) in ch-2-sp **, rep from * to ** 3 times omitting (2dc, ch2, 2dc) in last rep, slst to close rnd. [84dc, 4ch-2]

Rnd 8: ch3, dc in next st, *(2dc, ch3, 2dc) in ch-3-sp, dc in next 21 sts**, rep from * to ** 3 times omitting last 2dc in last rep, slst to close rnd. [100dc, 4ch-3]

Rnd 9: ch3, dc in next 3 sts, *(2dc, ch3, 2dc) in ch-2-sp, dc in next 25 sts**, rep from * to ** 3 times omitting last 4dc in last rep, slst to close rnd. [116dc, 4ch-3]

Fasten off **Colour 33**.

With **Colour 11**, embroider 2 seeds on either side of Rnd 1.

LEAVES

With **Colour 27**, ch6.

Row 1: slst in second ch from hook, sc in next st, (hdc, dc) in next st, (dc, hdc) in next st, slst in last st, turn to work on other side of foundation ch, ch, slst in first foundation ch, (hdc, dc) in next st, (dc, hdc) in next st, sc in next st, slst in last st. [14]

Fasten off **Colour 27**.

Rep to make a total of 2 leaves. With indent at bottom of apple, stitch leaves side by side at top of apple.

STALK

With **Colour 11**, ch6.

Row 1: sc in second ch from hook, sc in each ch to end of row. [5sc]

Fasten off **Colour 11**. Stitch stalk in place between leaves.

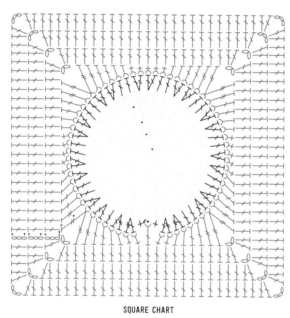

3	
15	
33	
11	
27	

SQUARE CHART

LEAF CHART

STALK CHART

APPLE COASTERS

APPLE

Follow instructions for Apple to make 1 complete apple, 2 leaves and 1 stalk.

To make a green apple, replace **Colour 15** with **Colour 27** and make leaves in **Colour 29**.

SQUARE

With **Colour 33**, work Rnd 6 of square for Apple.

Rnd 7: slst in ch-2-sp, ch, (sc, ch2, 2sc) in ch-2-sp, *sc in next 17 sts, (2sc, ch2, 2sc) in ch-2-sp**, rep from * to ** 3 times omitting (2sc, ch2, 2sc) in last rep. [84sc, 4ch-2]

Fasten off **Colour 33**.

FINISHING

Attach leaves and stalk to square following instructions for Apple.

	1
	17
	49
	27

ORANGE

With a 4mm hook and **Colour 1**, make a magic ring.

Rnd 1: ch2, 7hdc in ring, slst in second ch of initial ch2. [8hdc]

Fasten off **Colour 1**.

Join **Colour 17** in any st of Rnd 1.

Rnd 2: ch2, hdc in same st, 2hdc in each st to end, slst in second ch of initial ch2. [16hdc]

Rnd 3: ch2, hdc in same st, hdc in next st, (2hdc in next st, hdc in next st) 7 times, slst in second ch of initial ch2. [24hdc]

Rnd 4: ch2, hdc in same st, hdc in next 2 sts, (2hdc in next st, hdc in next 2 sts) 7 times, slst in FL of second ch of initial ch2. [32hdc]

All sts in this rnd are made in FLO:

Rnd 5: ch2, hdc in same st, hdc in next 3 sts, (2hdc in next st, hdc in next 3 sts) 7 times, slst in second ch of initial ch2. [40hdc]

Fasten off **Colour 17**.

Join **Colour 1** in first st of Rnd 5.

Rnd 6: ch, sc in first 5 sts, fpttr around Rnd 1 hdc (sc in next 5 sts, fpttr around Rnd 1 hdc) 7 times, slst in first sc. [8fpttr, 40sc]

Fasten off **Colour 1**.

Join **Colour 49** in any fpttr of Rnd 6.

Rnd 7: ch, sc in first 3 sts, 2sc in next st, sc in next 2 sts, *sc in next 3 sts, 2sc in next st, sc in next 2 sts**, rep from * to ** 6 times, slst in first sc. [56sc]

Fasten off **Colour 49**.

Join **Colour 17** in any st of Rnd 7.

Rnd 8: ch, sc in same st, sc in next 6 sts, (2sc in next st, sc in next 6 sts) 7 times, slst in first sc. [64sc]

Fasten off **Colour 17**.

SQUARE

Join **Colour 27** in BL of any st of Rnd 4. All sts in this rnd are made in BLO:

Rnd 9: ch8, dc in next st, hdc in next st, sc in next 4 sts, hdc in next st, *dc in next st, ch5, dc in next st, hdc in next st, sc in next 4 sts, hdc in next st**, rep from * to ** twice, slst in third ch of initial ch8. [8dc, 8hdc, 16sc, 4ch-5]

Rnd 10: slst in first ch-5-sp, ch3, (2dc, ch5, 3dc) in same sp, dc in next 3 sts, ch2, sk next 2 sts, dc in next 3 sts, *(3dc, ch5, 3dc) in next ch-5-sp, dc in next 3 sts, ch2, sk next 2 sts, dc in next 3 sts**, rep from * to ** twice, slst to close rnd. [48dc, 4ch-5, 4ch-2]

Rnd 11: slst in first 2 sts, slst in next ch-5-sp, ch3, (2dc, ch5, 3dc) in same sp, dc in next 2 sts, ch2, sk next 2 sts, dc in next 2 sts, 2dc in ch-2-sp, dc in next 2 sts, ch2, sk next 2 sts, dc in next 2 sts, *(3dc, ch5, 3dc) in same sp, dc in next 2 sts, ch2, sk next 2 sts, dc in next 2 sts, 2dc in ch-2-sp, dc in next 2 sts, ch2, sk next 2 sts, dc in next 2 sts**, rep from * to ** twice, slst to close rnd. [64dc, 4ch-5, 8ch-2]

Rnd 12: slst in first 2 sts, slst in next ch-5-sp, ch, *(2sc, ch2, 2sc) in ch-5-sp, sc in next 5 sts, 2sc in next ch-2-sp, sc in next 6 sts, 2sc in next ch-2-sp, sc in next 5 sts**, rep from * to ** 3 times. [96sc, 4ch-2]

Fasten off **Colour 27**.

Join **Colour 1** in any ch-2-sp of Rnd 12.

Rnd 13: ch, *(sc, ch2, sc) in ch-2-sp, sc in next 24 sts**, rep from * to ** 3 times. [104sc, 4ch-2]

Fasten off **Colour 1**.

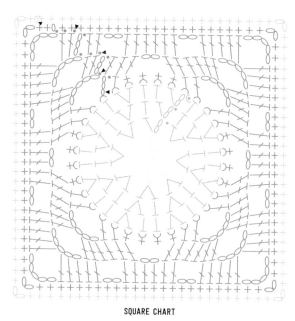

SQUARE CHART

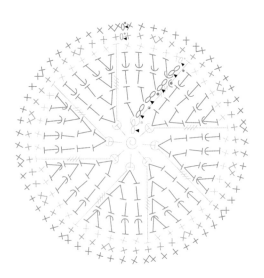

ORANGE CHART

SQUARE

With a 4mm hook and **Colour 46**, ch6, slst in first ch to make circle.

Rnd 1: ch, (puff locking with a ch, ch) 8 times in circle, slst in first puff to close rnd. [8 puffs]

Rnd 2: ch, (puff, ch, puff) in each ch-1-sp, slst in first puff. [16 puffs]

Rnd 3: slst in ch-1-sp, ch, (puff in ch-1-sp, 2 puffs between next pair of puffs) 8 times, slst to close rnd. [24 puffs]

Fasten off **Colour 46**.

Join **Colour 19** between any pair of puffs in Rnd 3.

Rnd 4: (ch3, 2dc, ch2, 3dc) in same sp, sk 3 puffs, ch2, 2sc between next pair of puffs, sk 3 puffs, ch2, *(3dc, ch2, 3dc) between next pair of puffs, sk 3 puffs, ch2, 2dc between next pair of puffs , ch2, sk 3 puffs**, rep from * to ** to end of rnd, slst to close rnd. [4-(3dc, ch2, 3dc)-sp, 4 2dc-groups]

Rnd 5: slst in next 2dc, slst in corner sp, (ch3, 2dc, ch2, 3dc) in same sp, *3dc in next ch-2-sp***, 3dc in next ch-2-sp, (3dc, ch2, 3dc) in next corner sp**, rep from * to ** to end of rnd ending last rep at ***, slst to close rnd. [4 3dc-groups per side]

Rnds 6-7: slst in 2dc, slst in corner sp, (ch3, 2dc, ch2, 3dc) in corner sp, *3dc between next 2 3dc groups**, rep from * to ** to corner sp, ((3dc, ch2, 3dc) in corner sp, ***3dc between next 2 3dc groups****, rep from *** to **** to corner sp)) 3 times, slst in ch3 to close rnd. [6 3dc-groups per side]

Fasten off **Colour 19**.

Join **Colour 5** in any corner sp of Rnd 7.

Rnd 8: ch, *(sc, ch, sc) in corner sp, sc in every st to next corner sp**, rep from * to ** 3 times, slst to close rnd. [20sc per side]

Fasten off **Colour 5**.

LEAVES

With **Colour 25**, ch6.

Row 1: sc in second ch from hook, hdc in next st, dc in next 2 sts, 5dc in last st, turn to work on other side of foundation ch, dc in next 2 sts, hdc in next 2 sts, sc in last st, slst to close row. [14]

Fasten off **Colour 25**. Rep to make a total of 2 leaves.

Stitch leaves onto square, overlapping top of raspberry.

19	
46	
25	
5	

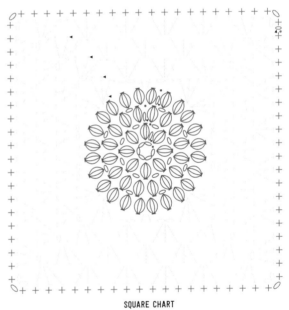

SQUARE CHART

LEAF CHART

34
27
15

SQUARE

With a 2.75mm hook and **Colour 34**, make a magic ring.

Rnd 1: ch3, 2dc, (ch3, 3dc) 3 times, ch3, slst to close rnd. [12dc, 4ch-3-sp]

Rnd 2: ch3, dc in next 2 sts, (2dc, ch3, 2dc) in ch-3-sp, *dc in next 3 sts, (2dc, ch3, 2dc) in ch-3-sp**, rep from * to ** twice, slst to close rnd. [28dc, 4 ch-3-sp]

Rnd 3: ch3, dc in next 4 sts, *(2dc, ch3, 2dc) in ch-3-sp, dc in next 7 sts**, rep from * to ** 3 times omitting last 5dc, slst to close rnd. [44dc, 4ch-3-sp]

Fasten off **Colour 34** and rejoin in any ch-3-sp of Rnd 3 with a standing dc.

Rnd 4: (dc, ch3, 2dc) in ch-3-sp, *sk 1 st, dc in next 3 sts, join and change to **Colour 15**, 7-dc-puff in next st, ch, change to **Colour 34**, dc in next 2 sts, change to **Colour 15**, 7-dc-puff in next st, ch, change to **Colour 34**, dc in next 3 sts, (2dc, ch3, 2dc) in ch-3-sp**, rep from * to ** 3 times omitting last (2dc, ch3, 2dc), slst to close rnd. [48dc, 8 puffs, 4ch-3-sp]

Fasten off **Colour 15**.

Rnd 5: ch3, dc in next st, *(2dc, ch3, 2dc) in ch-3-sp, dc in next 5 sts, dc in top of first cherry, dc in next 2 sts, dc in top of second cherry, dc in next 5 sts**, rep from * to ** 3 times omitting last 2dc, slst to close rnd. [72dc, 4ch-3-sp]

Rnd 6: ch3, dc in next 3 sts, *(2dc, ch3, 2dc) in ch-3-sp, dc in next 18 sts**, rep from * to ** 3 times omitting last 4dc, slst to close rnd. [88dc, 4ch-3-sp]

Rnd 7: ch3, dc in next 5 sts, *(2dc, ch3, 2dc) in ch-3-sp, dc in next 22 sts**, rep from * to ** 3 times omitting last 6dc, slst to close rnd. [104dc, 4ch-3-sp]

Rnd 8: ch3, dc in next 7 sts, *(2dc, ch3, 2dc) in ch-3-sp, dc in next 26 sts**, rep from * to ** 3 times omitting last 8dc, slst to close rnd. [120dc, 4ch-3-sp]

Fasten off **Colour 34**.

STALKS

Join **Colour 27** to top of cherry with slst, ch3, sc between 2 cherries in top of Rnd 7 of square, ch3, slst in second cherry.

Fasten off **Colour 27**. Rep for each pair of cherries.

LEAVES

With **Colour 27**, ch4.

Row 1: sk 1 st, sc in next st, dc in next st, slst in last st, ch, turn to work on other side of foundation ch, slst in next st, dc in next st, slst in last st. [6]

Fasten off **Colour 27**. Rep to make a total of 8 leaves.

Attach 1 leaf to either side of each cherry stalk.

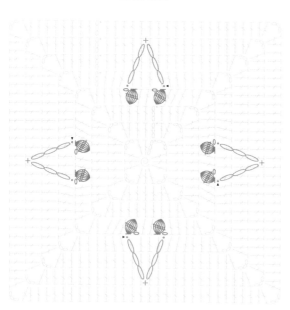

SQUARE CHART

STALKS CHART

LEAF CHART

CHERRY ENVELOPE POUCH

SQUARE

Work Rnds 1-8 of square for Cherries, replacing **Colour 34** with **Colour 31**, and replacing all ch-3-sp with ch-2-sp.

Rnd 9: ch2, hdc in next 9 sts, *(hdc, dc, tr, dc, hdc) in ch-2-sp, hdc in next 30 sts**, rep from * to ** twice, (hdc, dc, tr, dc, hdc) in next ch-2-sp, hdc in next 20 sts, slst to close rnd. [140]

Fasten off **Colour 31**.

STALKS

Follow instructions for Cherries to add stalks to the square.

LEAVES

Follow instructions for Cherries to make 8 complete leaves.

Attach 1 leaf to either side of each cherry stalk.

FINISHING

With WS of square facing, fold 3 corners toward centre of square. Join in BLO using a yarn needle.

Stitch a button where 3 corners meet. Button should fit through ch-2-sp on corner of flap.

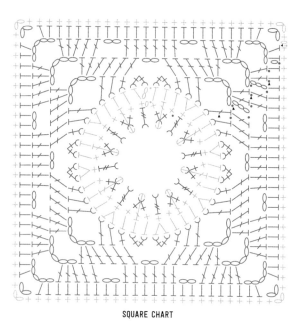

SQUARE CHART

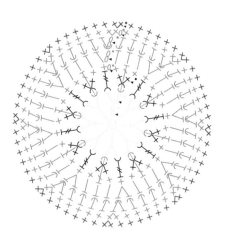

KIWI CHART

KIWI

With a 4mm hook and **Colour 19**, make a magic ring.

Rnd 1: ch2, 7hdc in ring, slst in second ch of initial ch2. [8hdc]

Rnd 2: ch2, hdc in same st, 2hdc in each st to end of rnd, slst in second ch of initial ch2. [16hdc]

Fasten off **Colour 19**.

Join **Colour 2** in BL of any Rnd 2 st. All sc in this rnd are made in BL of Rnd 2 sts:

Rnd 3: ch, 2sc in same st, tr in next st, (2sc in next st, tr in next st) 7 times. [8tr, 16sc]

Fasten off **Colour 2**.

Join **Colour 27** in any tr of Rnd 3.

Rnd 4: ch, *sc in tr, sc in next sc, dc in FL of Rnd 2 st, sc in next sc**, rep from * to ** 7 times, slst to close rnd [8dc, 24sc]

Rnd 5: ch2, hdc in same st, hdc in next 3 sts, (2hdc in next st, hdc in next 3 sts) 7 times, slst in FL of second ch of initial ch2. [40hdc]

All sts in this rnd are made in FL of Rnd 5 sts:

Rnd 6: ch2, hdc in same st, hdc in next 4 sts, (2hdc in next st, hdc in next 4 sts) 7 times, slst in second ch of initial ch2. [48hdc]

Rnd 7: ch, 2sc in same st, sc in next 5 sts, (2sc in next st, sc in next 5 sts) 7 times. [56sc]

Fasten off **Colour 27**.

Join **Colour 10** in any st of Rnd 7.

Rnd 8: ch, 2sc in first st, sc in next 6 sts, (2sc in next st, sc in next 6 sts) 7 times. [64sc]

Fasten off **Colour 10**.

SQUARE

Join **Colour 45** in any st of Rnd 5. All sts in this rnd are made in BL of Rnd 5 sts:

Rnd 9: standing dc in first st, ch5, dc in next st, hdc in next st, sc in next st, (sc2tog across next 2 sts) twice, sc in next st, hdc in next st, *dc in next st, ch5, dc in next st, hdc in next st, sc in next st, (sc2tog across next 2 sts) twice, sc in next st, hdc in next st**, rep from * to ** twice, slst to close rnd. [8dc, 8hdc, 8sc, 8sc2tog, 4ch-5]

Rnd 10: slst in next ch-5-sp, ch3, (2dc, ch5, 3dc) in same sp, dc in next 3 sts, ch2, sk next 2 sts, dc in next 3 sts, *(3dc, ch5, 3dc) in next ch-5-sp, dc in next 3 sts, ch2, sk next 2 sts, dc in next 3 sts**, rep from * to ** twice, slst to close rnd. [48dc, 4ch-5, 4ch-2]

Rnd 11: slst in next 2 sts, slst in next ch-5-sp, ch3, (2dc, ch5, 3dc) in same sp, dc in next 2 sts, ch2, sk next 2 sts, dc in next 2 sts, 2dc in ch-2-sp, dc in next 2 sts, ch2, sk next 2 sts, dc in next 2 sts, *(3dc, ch5, 3dc) in next sp, dc in next 2 sts, ch2, sk next 2 sts, dc in next 2 sts, 2dc in ch-2-sp, dc in next 2 sts, ch2, sk next 2 sts, dc in next 2 sts**, rep from * to ** twice, slst to close rnd. [64dc, 4ch-5, 8ch-2]

Rnd 12: slst in next 2 sts, slst in next ch-5-sp, ch, *(2hdc, ch2, 2hdc) in ch-5-sp, hdc in next 5 sts, 2hdc in next ch-2-sp, hdc in next 6 sts, 2hdc in next ch-2-sp, hdc in next 5 sts**, rep from * to ** 3 times. [96hdc, 4ch-2]

Fasten off **Colour 45**.

Join **Colour 44** in any ch-2-sp of Rnd 12.

Rnd 13: ch, *(sc, ch2, sc) in ch-2-sp, sc in next 24 sts**, rep from * to ** 3 times. [104sc, 4ch-2]

Fasten off **Colour 44**.

19	
2	
27	
10	
45	
44	

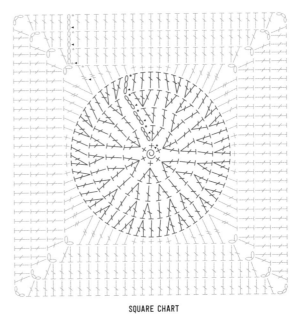

SQUARE

With a 2.75mm hook and **Colour 18**, make a magic ring.

Rnd 1: 6sc in ring, slst to close rnd. [6sc]

Rnd 2: ch3, 3dc in each of next 5 sts, 2dc in last st, slst in third ch of initial ch3. [18dc]

Rnd 3: ch3, dc in next st, (dc in next st, 2dc in next st) 8 times, slst to close rnd. [26dc]

Rnd 4: ch3, (2dc in next st, 2dc in next st, dc in next st) 8 times, 3dc in last st, slst to close rnd. [44dc]

Rnd 5: ch3, (2dc in next 2 sts, dc in next 2 sts) 10 times, dc in last 3 st, slst to close rnd. [64dc]

Fasten off **Colour 18**.

Join **Colour 8** in any st of Rnd 5 with a standing tr. All sts in this rnd are made in BLO:

Rnd 6: (ch2, tr) in same st, *tr in next st, dc in next 2 sts, hdc in next 2 sts, sc in next 5 sts, hdc in next 2 sts, dc in next 2 sts, tr in next st, (tr, ch2, tr) in next st**, rep from * to ** 3 times omitting (tr, ch2, tr) in last rep, slst to close rnd. [68, 4ch-2-sp]

Rnd 7: slst in ch-2-sp, ch3, (dc, ch2, 2dc) in ch-2-sp, *dc in next 17 sts, (2dc, ch2, 2dc) in ch-2-sp**, rep from * to ** 3 times omitting (2dc, ch2, 2dc) in last rep, slst to close rnd. [84dc, 4ch-2-sp]

Rnd 8: ch3, dc in next st, *(2dc, ch2, 2dc) in ch-2-sp, dc in next 21 sts**, rep from * to ** 3 times omitting last 2dc in last rep, slst to close rnd. [100dc, 4ch-3-sp]

Rnd 9: ch3, dc in next 3 sts, *(2dc, ch3, 2dc) in ch-3-sp, dc in next 25 sts**, rep from * to ** 3 times omitting last 4dc in last rep, slst to close rnd. [116dc, 4ch-3-sp]

Fasten off **Colour 8**.

Place a stitch marker in FL of st below third sc of any side in Rnd 6. This is centre of pumpkin, where stalk will be attached.

On opposite side of square, place a stitch marker in FL of st below third sc in Rnd 6. This is bottom of pumpkin.

PUMPKIN EDGING

Remove first stitch marker and join **Colour 18** in FL of top of pumpkin with a slst.

Rnd 10: slst in next 2 sts, sc in next 2 sts, hdc in next 3 sts, dc in next 3 sts, 2dc in next 2 sts, tr in next 4 sts, 2dc in next 2 sts, dc in next 2 sts, hdc in next 3 sts, sc in next 3 sts, slst in next 5 sts, remove second marker, slst in next st, slst in next 4 sts, sc in next 3 sts, hdc in next 3 sts, dc in next 2 sts, 2dc in next 2 sts, tr in next 4 sts, 2dc in next 2 sts, dc in next 2 sts, hdc in next 3 sts, sc in next 2 sts, slst in next 3 sts, slst to close rnd. [72]

Fasten off **Colour 18**.

Add pumpkin ridge details in back stitch with **Colour 11**, following rnds as shown.

STALK

With **Colour 11**, ch6.

Row 1: slst in second ch from hook, sc in next 2 sts, hdc in next st, dc in next 2 sts. [5]

Row 2: ch, turn, blo-hdc in next 2 sts, blo-sc in next st, blo-slst in last 2 sts. [5]

Fasten off **Colour 11**. Stitch stalk in place at top of pumpkin.

SPIRAL

With **Colour 26**, ch10.

Row 1: sc in second ch from hook, 2sc in same st, 3sc in each st to end of row. [27]

Fasten off **Colour 26**. Stitch spiral onto side of stalk as shown.

18	■
8	■
26	■
11	■

SQUARE CHART

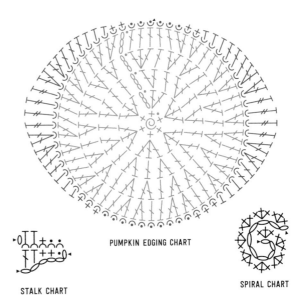

PUMPKIN EDGING CHART

STALK CHART

SPIRAL CHART

PUMPKIN

FRUIT & VEGETABLES

32
21
27

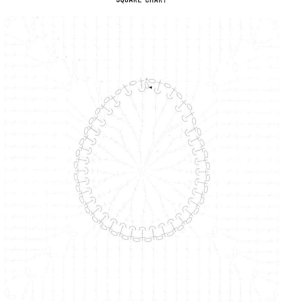

SQUARE CHART

LARGE LEAF CHART

SMALL LEAF CHART

PINEAPPLE EDGING CHART

SQUARE

With a 4mm hook and **Colour 21**, make a magic ring.

Rnd 1: ch3, 11dc in ring, slst to close rnd. [12dc]

Rnd 2: ch3, dc in same st, 2dc in each st to end of rnd, slst to close rnd. [24dc]

Rnd 3: ch3, dc in same st, 2tr in each of next 2 sts, 2dc in next st, hdc in next st, sc in each of next 2 sts, (2sc in next st, sc in next st) 8 times, sc in last st, slst to close rnd. [36 sts]

Fasten off **Colour 21**.

Join **Colour 32** in hdc of Rnd 3. All sts in this rnd are made in BL of Rnd 3 sts:

Rnd 4: ch3, dc in same st, ch2, 2dc in next st, hdc in next 2 sts, sc in next 3 sts, hdc in next 2 sts, *2dc in next st, ch2, 2dc in next st, hdc in next 2 sts, sc in next 3 sts, hdc in next 2 sts**, rep from * to ** twice, join to third ch of starting ch, slst in next dc, slst in next corner ch-2-sp. [44, 4ch-2]

Rnd 5: (ch3, dc, ch2, 2dc) in ch-2-sp, dc in each st to next ch-2-sp, *(2dc, ch2, 2dc) in next ch-2-sp, dc in each st to next ch-2-sp**, rep from * to ** twice ending last rep at starting ch, slst in next dc, slst to third ch of starting ch, slst to ch-2-sp. [60dc, 4ch-2]

Rnds 6-7: Rep Rnd 5. [92dc, 4ch-2]

Fasten off **Colour 32**.

PINEAPPLE EDGING

Join **Colour 21** in FL of any st in Rnd 3 of square. All sts in this rnd are made in FL of Rnd 3 sts.

Rnd 8: ch, (sc, ch) in each st, slst to close rnd. [36sc, 36ch-1]

Fasten off **Colour 21**.

SMALL LEAVES

With **Colour 27**, ch7.

Row 1: hdc in third ch from hook, hdc in each ch to end of row. [5hdc]

Fasten off **Colour 27**.

Rep to make a total of 3 leaves. Stitch to top of pineapple as shown.

LARGE LEAF

With **Colour 27**, ch8.

Row 1: hdc in third ch from hook, hdc in each ch to end of row. [6hdc]

Fasten off **Colour 27**.

Stitch leaf to top of pineapple.

PINEAPPLE CUSHION

SQUARE

Work Rnds 1-6 of square for Pineapple, replacing Colour 32 with Colour 48.

Fasten off Colour 48.

Join Colour 19 in any st of Rnd 6.

Rnd 7: ch, *sc in each st to corner sp, (sc, ch, sc) in corner sp**, rep from * to ** 3 times, sc in each st to end, slst to close rnd. [84sc, 4ch-1]

Fasten off Colour 19.

Join Colour 21 in FL of any st in Rnd 3.

Rnd 8: ch, (sc, ch) in each st, slst to close rnd. [36sc, 36ch-1]

Fasten off Colour 21.

Rep to make a total of 9 squares.

LEAVES

Follow instructions for Pineapple to make 27 small leaves and 9 large leaves.

Stitch 3 small leaves and 1 large leaf to top of each pineapple as shown.

ASSEMBLY

Place 2 squares together, with WS facing, and slst through BL of both squares on 1 side. Join another square to make a row of 3, and rep to make 3 rows of 3 squares. Place 2 rows together, with WS facing, and slst through BL of both rows along 1 long side. Rep to join final row to make a grid of 9 squares.

BORDER

Join Colour 19 in any outer st of the 9-square grid.

Rnd 1: *dc in each st and ch-sp to corner sp, (2dc, ch2, 2dc) in corner sp**, rep from * to ** 3 times, dc in each st to end, slst to close rnd. [284dc, 4ch-2]

Fasten off Colour 19.

Join Colour 27 in any st of Rnd 1.

Rnd 2: Rep Rnd 1. [300dc, 4ch-2]

Fasten off Colour 27.

FINISHING

Use fabric to sew an envelope backing to reverse of cushion, and stuff with cushion pad.

Alternatively, you could make 1 large granny square to back your cushion. Ensure that you leave a hole to insert cushion pad, then crochet over hole.

STRAWBERRIES

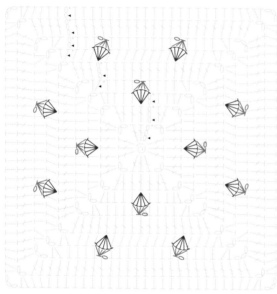

- 3
- 14
- 28

SQUARE CHART

SQUARE

With a 2.75mm hook and Colour 3, make a magic ring.

Rnd 1: ch3, 2dc, (ch2, 3dc) 3 times, ch2, slst to close rnd. [12dc, 4ch-2-sp]

Rnd 2: ch3, *dc in next 2 sts, (2dc, ch2, 2dc) in ch-2-sp, dc**, rep from * to ** 3 times omitting last dc, slst to close rnd. [28dc, 4ch-2-sp]

Rnd 3: ch2, *join and change to Colour 14, 5hdc in next st, change to Colour 3, hdc in next 3 sts, (2hdc, ch2, 2hdc) in next sp, hdc in next 3 sts**, rep from * to ** 3 times omitting last hdc, slst to close rnd. [60hdc, 4ch-2-sp]

Fasten off Colours 3 and 14.

Join Colour 3 in any ch-2-sp of Rnd 3 with a standing hdc.

Rnd 4: (hdc, ch3, 2hdc) in same sp, *sk 1 st, hdc in next 4 sts, join and change to Colour 28, hdc5tog, ch, change to Colour 3, hdc in next 4 sts, sk 1 st, (2hdc, ch3, 2hdc) in next sp**, rep from * to ** 3 times omitting last (2hdc, ch3, 2hdc), slst to close rnd. [48hdc, 4ch, 4ch-3-sp]

Fasten off Colour 28.

Rnd 5: ch3, dc in next st, *(2dc, ch2, 2dc) in ch-3-sp, dc in next 6 sts, dc in ch on top of berry, dc in next 6 sts**, rep from * to ** 3 times omitting last 2dc, slst to close rnd. [68dc, 4ch-2-sp]

Fasten off Colour 3 and rejoin in any ch-2-sp of Rnd 5 with a standing hdc.

Rnd 6: (hdc, ch2, 2hdc) in same sp, *sk 1 st, hdc in next 3 sts, join and change to Colour 14, 5hdc in next st, change to Colour 3, hdc in next 8 sts, change to Colour 14, 5hdc in next st, change to Colour 3 , hdc in next 3 sts, (2hdc, ch2, 2hdc) in next sp**, rep from * to ** 3 times omitting last (2hdc, ch2, 2hdc), slst to close rnd. [112hdc, 4ch-2-sp]

Fasten off Colour 14.

Rnd 7: ch2, sk next st, *(2hdc, ch3, 2hdc) in ch-2-sp, sk 1, hdc in next 4 sts, join and change to Colour 28, hdc5tog, ch, change to Colour 3, hdc in next 8 sts, change to Colour 28, hdc5tog, ch, change to Colour 3, hdc in next 4 sts, sk 1**, rep from * to ** 3 times omitting last 3hdc, slst to close rnd. [80hdc, 8ch, 4ch-3-sp]

Fasten off Colour 28.

Rnd 8: ch3, dc in next 2 sts, *(2dc, ch2, 2dc) in ch-3-sp, dc in next 6 sts, dc in in ch on top of berry, dc in next 8 sts, dc in ch on top of berry, dc in next 6 sts**, rep from * to ** 3 times omitting last 3dc, slst to close rnd [104dc, 4ch-2-sp]

Rnd 9: ch2, hdc in next 4 sts, *(2hdc, ch3, 2hdc) in ch-2-sp, hdc in next 26 sts**, rep from * to ** 3 times omitting last 5 sts, slst to close rnd. [120hdc, 4ch-3-sp]

Fasten off Colour 3.

STRAWBERRY TOWEL TOPPER

TRIANGLE

Work Rnds 1-7 of square for Strawberries.

Fasten off **Colours 3** and **28**.

Fold square in half diagonally to form a triangle.

Join **Colour 3** in a ch-3-sp along fold of triangle with a standing sc. This rnd is worked through both sides of triangle:

Row 8: sc in next 5 sts, sk 1 st, sc through top of both berries, sc in next 8 sts, sc through top of both berries, sc in next 6 sts. [21sc]

Row 9: ch, turn, (sk 1 st, 5dc in next st, sk 1 st, sc in next st) 5 times, slst into last st. [31]

Rep Rnds 8-9 for other side of triangle.

Fasten off **Colour 3**.

Cut a wooden skewer to match length of bottom of triangle and insert to improve stability.

STRAP

With **Colour 3**, ch36.

Row 1: sk 2 sts, hdc in third ch from hook, hdc in each st to end of row. [34hdc]

Fasten off **Colour 3**.

HANDLE

With **Colour 3**, ch36.

Row 1: sk 2 st, hdc in third ch from hook, hdc in each st to end of row. [34hdc]

Row 2: ch2, turn, hdc in next 2 sts, ch2, sk 2 sts, hdc in each st to end of row. [32hdc, 2ch]

Row 3: ch2, hdc in next 30 sts, 2hdc in ch-2-sp, hdc in last 2 sts. [34hdc]

Fasten off **Colour 3**.

FINISHING

Attach strap to either end along bottom of triangle.

Stitch handle and button in place as shown.

SHEEP

 3

 7

 24

SQUARE CHART

EAR CHART

LEG CHART

SQUARE

With a 2.75mm hook and **Colour 7**, make a magic ring.

Rnd 1: 6sc in ring, slst to close rnd. [6sc]

Rnd 2: ch3, 3dc in each of next 5 sts, 2dc in last st, slst to close rnd. [18dc]

Rnd 3: ch3, dc in next st, (dc in next st, 2dc in next st) 8 times, slst to close rnd. [26dc]

Fasten off **Colour 7**.

Join **Colour 3** with a standing dc in any st of Rnd 3.

Rnd 4: 5-dc-popcorn in same st, *ch2, sk st, 5-dc-popcorn in next st**, rep from * to ** to end of rnd, ch2, slst in back of first popcorn to close rnd. [13 popcorns, 13ch-2-sp]

Rnd 5: slst in next ch-2-sp, ch3, 4-dc-popcorn in same st, *ch2, 5-dc-popcorn in next ch-2-sp**, rep from * to ** to end of rnd, ch2, slst in back of first popcorn to close rnd. [13 popcorns, 13ch-2-sp]

For this rnd, sts are worked in both ch-2-sp and top of popcorn sts from previous rnd:

Rnd 6: ch3, 2-dc-popcorn in same st, ch2, 3-dc-popcorn in ch-2-sp, ch2, *3-dc-popcorn in back of popcorn from previous rnd, ch2, 3-dc-popcorn in ch-2-sp, ch2**, rep from * to ** 7 times, sk next popcorn, 3-dc-popcorn in ch-2-sp, rep from * to ** twice, 3-dc-popcorn in back of last popcorn, ch2, sk ch-2-sp, slst in back of first popcorn to close rnd. [24 popcorns, 24ch-2-sp]

Fasten off **Colour 3**.

Join **Colour 24** in any ch-2-sp of Rnd 6 with a standing tr. For this rnd the ch-2-sp counts as a st. Only work 1st in ch-2-sp, unless otherwise instructed:

Rnd 7: (ch3, tr) in same sp, *dc in next popcorn, hdc in next ch-sp, sc in next 7 sts, hdc in next ch-2-sp, dc in next popcorn st, (tr, ch3, tr) in next ch-2-sp**, rep from * to ** 3 times omitting (tr, ch3, tr) in last rep, slst to close rnd. [52, 4ch-3]

Rnd 8: slst in ch-3-sp, ch3, (dc, ch2, 2dc) in same sp, *dc in next 13 sts, (2dc, ch2, 2dc) in next ch-3-sp**, rep from * to ** 3 times omitting last (2dc, ch2, 2dc), slst to close rnd. [68dc, 4ch-2]

Rnd 9: ch3, dc in next st, *(2dc, ch2, 2dc) in ch-sp, dc in next 17 sts**, rep from * to ** 3 times omitting last 2dc, slst to close rnd. [84dc, 4ch-2]

Rnd 10: ch3, dc in next 3 sts, *(2dc, ch2, 2dc) in ch-sp, dc in next 21 sts**, rep from * to ** 3 times omitting last 4dc, slst to close rnd. [100dc, 4ch-2]

Fasten off **Colour 24**.

Embroider eyes and nose onto sheep's face with **Colour 3**.

LEGS

With **Colour 7**, ch8.

Row 1: hdc in third ch from hook, hdc in rem 5 sts. [6hdc]

Fasten off **Colour 7**. Rep to make a total of 2 legs.

Stitch legs between Rnds 5 and 6 of sheep, 1 popcorn apart.

EARS

With **Colour 7**, ch4.

Row 1: sc in second ch from hook, hdc in third and fourth ch from hook. [3]

Fasten off **Colour 7**. Rep to make a total of 2 ears.

Stitch ears on either side of sheep's face, 5 popcorns apart.

PIG

With a 4mm hook and **Colour 48**, make a magic ring.

Rnd 1: ch3, 11dc in ring, slst in third ch of initial ch3. [12dc]

Rnd 2: ch3, dc in same st, (2dc in next st) 11 times, slst in third ch of initial ch3. [24dc]

Rnd 3: ch3, dc in same st, dc in next st, (2dc in next st, dc in next st) 11 times, slst in third ch of initial ch3. [36dc]

Rnd 4: ch, 2sc in same st, sc in next 2 sts, (2sc in next st, sc in next 2 sts) 11 times. [48sc]

All sts in this rnd are made in FL of Rnd 4 sts:

Rnd 5: slst in next 22 sts, sc in next st, hdc in next st, (hdc, dc) in next st, (dc, hdc) in next st, hdc in next st, sc in next 2 sts, slst in next 10 sts, sc in next 2 sts, hdc in next st, (hdc, dc) in next st, (dc, hdc) in next st, hdc in next st, sc in next st, slst in next 2 sts. [4dc, 8hdc, 6sc, 34slst]

Fasten off **Colour 48**.

SQUARE

Join **Colour 1** in BL of fourth st in Rnd 4 of pig with a standing tr. All sts in this rnd are made in BL of Rnd 4 sts:

Rnd 6: tr in same st as standing tr, ch2, 2tr in next st, dc in next st, hdc in next 2 sts, sc in next 4 sts, hdc in next 2 sts, dc in next st, *2tr in next st, ch2, 2tr in next st, dc in next st, hdc in next 2 sts, sc in next 4 sts, hdc in next 2 sts, dc in next st**, rep from * to ** twice, slst to close rnd. [16tr, 8dc, 16hdc, 16sc, 4ch-2]

Rnd 7: slst in next st, slst in next ch-2-sp, ch3, (dc, ch2, 2dc) in same ch-2-sp, dc in next 14 sts, *(2dc, ch2, 2dc) in next ch-2-sp, dc in next 14 sts**, rep from * to ** twice, slst in third ch of initial ch3. [72dc, 4ch-2]

Rnd 8: slst in next st, slst in next ch-2-sp, ch3, (dc, ch2, 2dc) in same ch-2-sp, dc in next 18 sts, *(2dc, ch2, 2dc) in next ch-2-sp, dc in next 18 sts**, rep from * to ** twice, slst in third ch of initial ch3. [88dc, 4ch-2]

Rnd 9: slst in next st, slst in next ch-2-sp, ch, *(sc, ch2, sc) in ch-2-sp, sc in next 22 sts**, rep from * to ** 3 times, slst in initial sc. [96sc, 4ch-2]

Fasten off **Colour 1**.

Join **Colour 45** in any ch-2-sp of Rnd 9.

Rnd 10: ch, *(sc, ch2, sc) in next ch-2-sp, sc in next 24 sts**, rep from * to ** 3 times. [104sc, 4ch-2]

Fasten off **Colour 45**.

Embroider eyes using **Colour 2**.

EARS

Join **Colour 45** in sixth st of Rnd 5. All sts in this rnd are made in Rnd 5 sts:

Rnd 1: slst in st, ch7, slst in second ch from hook, slst in next ch, sc in next ch, hdc in next ch, dc in next ch, tr in next ch, sk next st, slst in next st. [1tr, 1dc, 1hdc, 1sc, 2slst]

Sk next 5 sts and rep Rnd 1 to make second ear.

Fasten off **Colour 45**.

Slightly fold each ear down and sew in place.

SNOUT

With a 3mm hook and **Colour 45**, make a magic ring.

Rnd 1: ch, 6sc in ring. [6sc]

Rnd 2: 3sc in next st, sc in next 2 sts, 3sc in next st, sc in next 2 sts. [10sc]

Rnd 3: sc in next st, 3sc in next st, sc in next 4 sts, 3sc in next st, sc in next 3 sts, slst in initial sc. [14sc]

Fasten off **Colour 45**.

Embroider nostrils using **Colour 2** and sew snout onto square.

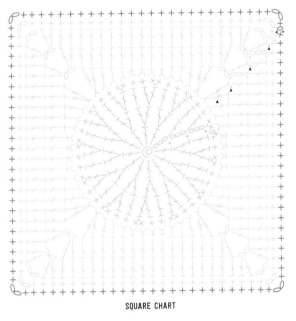

SQUARE CHART

48		
1		
45		
2		

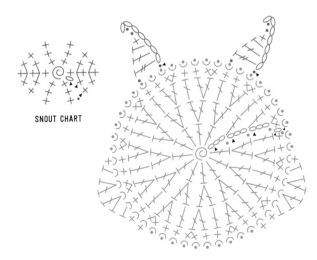

SNOUT CHART

PIG AND EARS CHART

SQUARE CHART

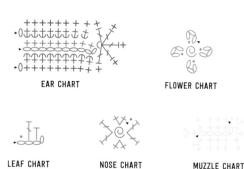

EAR CHART   FLOWER CHART

LEAF CHART   NOSE CHART   MUZZLE CHART

Colour legend: 5, 1, 48, 23, 38, 34, 20, 27, 3, 2

SQUARE

With a 2.75mm hook and **Colour 5**, make a magic ring.

Rnd 1: 6sc in ring, slst to close rnd. [6sc]

Rnd 2: ch3, 3dc in each of next 5 sts, 2dc in last st, slst to close rnd. [18sc]

Rnd 3: ch3, dc in next st, (dc in next st, 2dc in next st) 8 times, slst to close rnd. [26dc]

Rnd 4: ch3, (2dc in next st, 2dc in next st, dc in next st) 8 times, 3dc in last st, slst to close rnd. [44dc]

Rnd 5: ch3, (2dc in next 2 sts, dc in next 2 sts) 10 times, dc in last 3 sts, slst to close rnd. [64dc]

Fasten off **Colour 5**.

Join **Colour 1** in any st of Rnd 5 with a standing tr.

Rnd 6: (ch2, tr) in same st, *tr in next st, dc in next 2 sts, hdc in next 2 sts, sc in next 5 sts, hdc in next 2 sts, dc in next 2 sts, tr in next st, (tr, ch2, tr) in next st**, rep from * to ** 3 times omitting (tr, ch2, tr) in last rep, slst to close rnd. [68, 4ch-2-sp]

Rnd 7: slst in ch-2-sp, ch3, (dc, ch2, 2dc) in ch-2-sp, *dc in next 17 sts, (2dc, ch2, 2dc) in ch-2-sp**, rep from * to ** 3 times omitting (2dc, 2ch, 2dc) in last rep, slst to close rnd. [84dc, 4ch-2-sp]

Fasten off **Colour 1**.

Join **Colour 23** in any ch-2-sp of Rnd 7 with a standing sc.

Rnd 8: (sc, ch3, 2sc) in same ch-sp, *((ch, sk st, sc) in next st) 10 times, ch, sk st, (2sc, ch3, 2sc) in ch-2-sp**, rep from * to ** 3 times omitting last (2sc, ch3, 2sc), slst to close rnd. [56sc, 44ch-1-sp, 4ch-3-sp]

Fasten off **Colour 23**.

Join **Colour 1** in any ch-3-sp of Rnd 8 with a standing dc.

Rnd 9: (2dc, ch3, 3dc) in same sp, *2dc in each ch-1-sp to next ch-3-sp, (3dc, ch3, 3dc) in next ch-3-sp**, rep from * to ** 3 times omitting last (3dc, ch3, 3dc), slst to close rnd. [112dc, 4ch-3-sp]

Rnd 10: ch2, hdc in next 2 sts, *(2hdc, ch2, 2hdc) in ch-3-sp, hdc in next 28 sts**, rep from * to ** 3 times omitting last 3hdc, slst to close rnd. [128hdc, 4ch-2-sp]

Fasten off **Colour 1**.

EARS

With **Colour 48**, ch10.

Row 1: sc in second ch from hook, sc in each st to end of row. [9sc]

Fasten off **Colour 48**.

Join **Colour 5** at end of Row 1.

Row 2: ch, turn, sc in FL of next 8 sts, 5dc in FL of next st, sk turning ch, sc in FL of next 9 sts. [22]

Row 3: ch, turn, sc in each st to end of row. [22sc]

Fasten off **Colour 5**. Rep to make a total of 2 ears.

Pinch bottom of each ear and sew closed. Attach both ears to bunny's face along outer edge of Rnd 4, approx 8 sts apart.

MUZZLE

With **Colour 3**, ch5.

Rnd 1: sk first ch, sc in next 3 ch, 3sc in last ch, turn to work on other side of foundation ch, sc in next 3 ch, 3sc in next ch. [12]

Rnd 2: sc in next 4 sts, 2sc in next 2 sts, sc in next 4 sts, 2sc in next 2 sts, slst to close rnd. [16]

Fasten off **Colour 3**.

Attach muzzle to bunny's face as shown. Embroider eyes on either side of muzzle with **Colour 2**.

NOSE

With **Colour 48**, make a magic ring.

Rnd 1: 2sc, 2dc, 2sc, 2dc, slst to close rnd. [8]

Fasten off **Colour 48**.

Attach nose to top of muzzle on bunny's face.

FLOWERS

With **Colour 38**, make a magic ring.

Rnd 1: (ch3, slst into ring) 4 times. [4ch3, 4slst]

Fasten off **Colour 38**.

Rep to make a total of 2 flowers with **Colour 38** and 1 flower with **Colour 34**.

Add flower centres by creating knots using **Colour 20**. Attach flowers to square as shown.

LEAVES

With **Colour 27**, ch4.

Row 1: hdc into second ch from hook, dc into next st, slst into last st. [3]

Fasten off **Colour 27**. Rep to make a total of 3 leaves.

Stitch leaves around flowers on square as shown.

SQUARE

With a 2.75mm hook and **Colour 5**, make a magic ring.

Rnd 1: 6sc in ring, slst to close rnd. [6sc]

Rnd 2: ch3, 3dc in each of next 5 sts, 2dc in last st, slst to close rnd. [18sc]

Rnd 3: ch3, dc in next st, (dc in next st, 2dc in next st) 8 times, slst to close rnd. [26dc]

Rnd 4: ch3, (2dc in next st, 2dc in next st, dc in next st) 8 times, 3dc in last st, slst to close rnd. [44dc]

Fasten off **Colour 5**.

Join **Colour 47** in any st of Rnd 4 with a standing dc. This rnd is worked entirely in BLO:

Rnd 5: (2dc in next 2 sts, dc in next 2 sts) 10 times, dc in last 3 sts, slst to close rnd. [64]

Fasten off and rejoin **Colour 47** in any st of Rnd 5 with a standing tr.

Rnd 6: (ch2, tr) in same st, *tr in next st, dc in next 2 sts, hdc in next 2 sts, sc in next 5 sts, hdc in next 2 sts, dc in next 2 sts, tr in next st, (tr, ch2, tr) in next st**, rep from * to ** 3 times omitting (tr, ch2, tr) in last rep, slst to close rnd. [68, 4ch-2-sp]

Rnd 7: slst in ch-2-sp, ch3, (dc, ch2, 2dc) in ch-2-sp, *dc in next 17 sts, (2dc, ch2, 2dc) in ch-2-sp, rep from * to ** 3 times omitting (2dc, ch2, 2dc) in last rep, slst to close rnd. [84dc, 4ch-2-sp]

Rnd 8: ch3, dc in next st, *(2dc, ch3, 2dc) in ch-2-sp, dc in next 21 sts**, rep from * to ** 3 times omitting last 2dc in last rep, slst to close rnd. [100dc, 4ch-3-sp]

Rnd 9: ch3, dc in next 3 sts, *(2dc, ch3, 2dc) in ch-3-sp, dc in next 25 sts**, rep from * to ** 3 times omitting last 4dc in last rep, slst to close rnd. [116dc, 4ch-3-sp]

Fasten off **Colour 47**.

NOSE

With **Colour 48**, make a magic ring.

Rnd 1: 5sc in ring, slst to close rnd. [5sc]

Fasten off **Colour 48**.

Join **Colour 1** in any st of Rnd 1.

Rnd 2: 2sc in next st, sc in next 2 sts, 2sc in next st, sc in next st, slst to close rnd. [7sc]

Rnd 3: 2sc in next st, sc in next 6 sts, slst to close rnd. [8sc]

Fasten off **Colour 1**.

Join **Colour 5** in any st of Rnd 3.

Rnd 4: (2sc in next st, sc in next 3 sts) twice, slst to close rnd. [10sc]

Rnd 5: (2sc in next st, sc in next 4 sts) twice, slst to close rnd. [12sc]

Rnd 6: (2sc in next st, sc in next 5 sts) twice, slst to close rnd. [14sc]

Fasten off **Colour 5**.

Attach nose just below centre of mouse's face.

Embroider eyes on either side of nose, approx 7 sts apart, with **Colour 2**.

INNER EARS

With **Colour 48**, make a magic ring.

Rnd 1: 6sc in ring. [6sc]

Rnd 2: 2sc in each st, slst to close rnd. [12sc]

Fasten off **Colour 48**. Rep to make a total of 2 inner ears.

OUTER EARS

With **Colour 5**, make a magic ring.

Rnd 1: 6sc in ring. [6sc]

Rnd 2: 2sc in each st, slst to close rnd. [12sc]

Rnd 3: *sc in next st, 2sc in next st**, rep from * to ** to end of rnd, slst to close rnd. [18sc]

Rnd 4: *2sc in next st, sc in next 2 sts**, rep from * to ** to end of rnd, slst to close rnd. [24sc]

Fasten off **Colour 5**. Rep to make a total of 2 outer ears.

FINISHING

Place 1 inner ear on top of 1 outer ear and stitch together. Rep for second ear.

Stitch ears onto either side of head as shown, in line with ch-sp from Rnd 8.

5

47

48

1

2

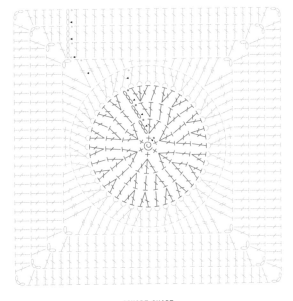

SQUARE CHART

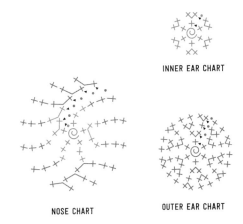

INNER EAR CHART

NOSE CHART

OUTER EAR CHART

LLAMA BODY

With a 4mm hook and **Colour 19**, ch10.

Row 1: sc in second ch from hook, sc in each ch to end of row, ch, turn. [9sc]

Row 2: 2sc in first st, sc in next 7 sts, 2sc in last st, ch, turn. [11sc]

Rows 3-9: sc in each st to end of row, ch, turn. [11sc]

Row 10: sc in next 3 sts, ch, turn. [3sc]

Rows 11-14: Rep Row 10. [3sc]

Row 15: sc in next 3 sts, ch3, turn. [3sc, 3ch]

Row 16: sc in second ch from hook, sc in next 4 sts, ch, turn. [5sc]

Rows 17-18: sc in each st, ch, turn. [5sc]

Row 19: sc in next 2 sts, ch, turn. [2sc]

Row 20: Rep Row 19. [2sc]

Fasten off **Colour 19**.

Embroider an eye onto head with **Colour 2** as shown.

LLAMA LEGS

Join **Colour 19** in bottom left corner of foundation ch of llama body.

Row 1: ch, sc, ch, turn. [2sc]

Rows 2-5: sc in next 2 sts, ch, turn. [2sc]

Fasten off **Colour 19**.

Join **Colour 19** in bottom right corner of foundation ch of llama body and rep Rows 1-5 to create second leg. Fasten off **Colour 19**.

BLANKET

With **Colour 12**, ch4.

Rnd 1: 2dc in fourth ch from hook, ch2, *(3dc, ch2) in same ch**, rep from * to ** twice, slst to top of ch4 to close rnd. [4 3dc-groups, 4ch-2-sp]

Fasten off **Colour 12**.

Join **Colour 45** in any ch-2-sp of Rnd 1.

Rnd 2: ch3, 2dc in same sp, (3dc, ch2, 3dc) in next 2 ch-2-sps, 3dc in last ch-2-sp. [6 3dc-groups]

Fasten off **Colour 45**.

SQUARE

With **Colour 5**, make a magic ring.

Rnd 1: ch3, 2dc in ring, ch2, (3dc in ring, ch2) 3 times, join to top of ch3. [12dc, 4ch-2]

Rnd 2: ch3, *dc in each st to ch-2-sp, (2dc, ch2, 2dc) in ch-2-sp**, rep from * to ** 3 times, join to top of ch3. [28dc, 4ch-2]

Rnds 3-6: ch3, *dc in each st to ch-2-sp, (2dc, ch2, 2dc) in ch-2-sp**, rep from * to ** 3 times, dc in each st to end, slst in third ch of initial ch3. [92dc, 4ch-2]

Fasten off **Colour 5**.

FINISHING

Stitch llama body onto centre of square and stitch blanket onto llama body as shown.

With **Colour 20**, make 4 tiny tassels on bottom of blanket.

With **Colour 19**, make 4 tassels on top right corner of llama body for tail.

19	
45	
12	
20	
5	
2	

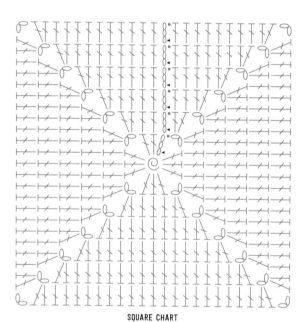

SQUARE CHART

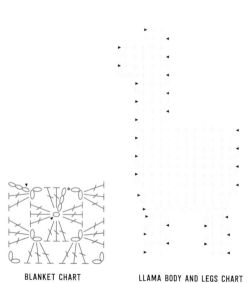

BLANKET CHART   LLAMA BODY AND LEGS CHART

LITTLE LLAMA BAG

11 ■
19 ▨
2 ■
20 ▨

LLAMA

Follow instructions for Llama to make 1 complete llama body, replacing **Colour 19** with **Colour 11**.

Embroider an eye onto head with **Colour 2** as shown.

Follow instructions for Llama to add llama legs, replacing **Colour 19** with **Colour 11**.

Follow instructions for Llama to make 1 complete blanket.

SQUARE

Work Rnds 1-6 of square for Llama, replacing **Colour 5** with **Colour 19**.

Rnds 7-8: ch3, *dc in each st to ch-2-sp, (2dc, ch2, 2dc) in ch-2-sp**, rep from * to ** 3 times, dc in each st to end, slst in third ch of initial ch3. [124dc, 4ch-2]

Fasten off **Colour 19**. Rep to make a total of 2 squares.

ASSEMBLY

Stitch llama body onto front square and stitch blanket onto llama as shown.

With **Colour 20**, make 4 tiny tassels on bottom of blanket.

With **Colour 11**, make 4 tassels on top right corner of llama body for tail.

Place both squares together. Join **Colour 19** in ch-2-sp at top left corner of Rnd 8 through both squares. Work through both squares all around to join 3 sides of bag.

Rnd 9: sc in same sp as join, sc in every st to next ch-2-sp, (sc, ch, sc) in ch-2-sp, sc in every st to next ch-2-sp, (sc, ch, sc) in next ch-2-sp, sc in every stitch to next ch-2-sp, sc in next ch-2-sp. [99sc, 2ch-1]

Fasten off **Colour 19**.

HANDLE

Join **Colour 19** in ch-2-sp at top right corner of Rnd 8 of front square.

The following rnds are worked around tops of both squares. Place a stitch marker at start of each rnd:

Row 1: sc in each st and ch-2-sp to end of rnd, slst to close rnd. [64sc]

Rnds 2-6: Rep Rnd 1. [64sc]

Rnd 7: sc in next 10 sts, ch12, sk 12 sts, sc in next 20 sts, ch12, sk 12 sts, sc in next 10 sts, slst to close rnd. [40sc, 2ch-12]

Rnd 8: sc in each st and ch to end of rnd, slst to close rnd. [64sc]

Rnd 9: Rep Rnd 8. [64sc]

Fasten off **Colour 19**.

FINISHING

Cut 36 strands of **Colour 19**, each measuring approx 15cm (6in) and use two strands of yarn for each fringe.

Fold strands in half. Use a yarn needle to thread 2 folded strands of yarn through st at left bottom corner of bag, pull yarn through loop, sk 1 st, *work another fringe, sk 1 st**, rep from * to ** to opposite corner at bottom of bag.

Trim fringe to desired length.

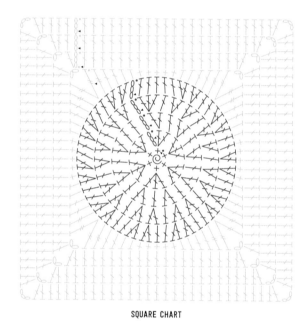

SQUARE CHART

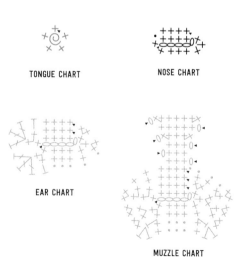

TONGUE CHART

NOSE CHART

EAR CHART

MUZZLE CHART

10	
20	
8	
2	
48	

SQUARE

With a 2.75mm hook and **Colour 10**, make a magic ring.

Rnd 1: 6sc in ring, slst to close rnd. [6sc]

Rnd 2: ch3, 3dc in each of next 5 sts, 2dc in last st, slst in third ch of initial ch3 to close rnd. [18dc]

Rnd 3: ch3, dc in next st, (dc in next st, 2dc in next st) 8 times, slst in third ch of initial ch3 to close rnd. [26dc]

Rnd 4: ch3, (2dc in next st, 2dc in next st, dc in next st) 8 times, 3dc in last st, slst in third ch of initial ch3 to close rnd. [44dc]

Rnd 5: ch3, (2dc in next 2 sts, dc in next 2 sts) 10 times, dc in last 3 st, slst in third ch of initial ch3 to close rnd. [64dc]

Fasten off **Colour 10**.

Join **Colour 20** in any st of Rnd 5 with a standing tr.

Rnd 6: (ch2, tr) in same st, *tr in next st, dc in next 2 sts, hdc in next 2 sts, sc in next 5 sts, hdc in next 2 sts, dc in next 2 sts, tr in next st, (tr, ch2, tr) in next st**, rep from * to ** 3 times omitting (tr, ch2, tr) in last rep, slst to close rnd. [68, 4ch-2]

Rnd 7: slst in ch-2-sp, ch3, (dc, ch2, 2dc) in ch-2-sp, *dc in next 17 sts, (2dc, ch2, 2dc) in ch-2-sp**, rep from * to ** 3 times omitting (2dc, ch2, 2dc) in last rep, slst to close rnd. [84dc, 4ch-2]

Rnd 8: ch3, dc in next st, *(2dc, ch3, 2dc) in ch-2-sp, dc in next 21 sts**, rep from * to ** 3 times omitting last 2dc in last rep, slst in third ch of initial ch3 to close rnd. [100dc, 4ch-3]

Rnd 9: ch3, dc in next 3 sts, *(2dc, ch3, 2dc) in ch-3-sp, dc in next 25 sts**, rep from * to ** 3 times omitting last 4dc in last rep, slst to close rnd. [116dc, 4ch-3]

Fasten off **Colour 20**.

MUZZLE

With **Colour 8**, ch5.

Rnd 1: sk first ch, sc in next 3 ch, 3sc in last ch, turn to work on other side of foundation ch, sc in next 3 ch, 3sc in next ch. [12sc]

Rnd 2: sc in next 4 sts, 2sc in next 2 sts, sc in next 4 sts, 2sc in next 2 sts. [16sc]

Rnd 3: sc in next 5 sts, 2sc in next 2 sts, (hdc, sc) in next st, slst in next 3 sts, (sc, hdc) in next st, 2sc in next 2 sts, sc in next 2 sts. [22]

Rnd 4: sc in next 6 sts, 2sc in next 3 sts, 2hdc in next st, sc in next st, slst in next 3 sts, sc in next st, 2hdc in next st, 2sc in next 3 sts, slst in next 3 sts. [30]

Continue to shape muzzle with bridge of nose as follows:

Row 1: slst in next st, ch, sc in next 3 sts. [3sc]

Row 2: ch, turn, sc in next 3 sts. [3sc]

Row 3: ch, turn, sc in next 3 sts. [3sc]

Row 4: ch, turn, 2sc in next st, sc in next st, 2sc in next st. [5sc]

Row 5: ch, turn, sc in each st to end of row. [5sc]

Row 6: ch, 2sc in next st, sc in next 3 sts, 2sc in next st. [7sc]

Fasten off **Colour 8**.

EARS

In **Colour 8**, ch5.

Rnd 1: sk first ch, sc in next 3 ch, 3sc in last ch, turn to work on other side of foundation ch, sc in next 3 ch, 3sc in next ch. [12sc]

Rnd 2: sc in next 4 sts, 2sc in next 2 sts, sc in next 4 sts, 2sc in next 2 sts. [16sc]

Rnd 3: sc in next 4 sts, hdc in next st, 3dc in next 2 sts, hdc in next st, slst in next 5 sts. [17]

Fasten off **Colour 8**. Rep to make a total of 2 ears.

NOSE

With **Colour 2**, ch5.

Rnd 1: sk first ch, sc in next 3 ch, 3sc in last ch, turn to work on other side of foundation ch, sc in next 3 ch, 3sc in next ch. [12sc]

Rnd 2: sc in next 4 sts, slst in next st. [5]

Fasten off **Colour 2**.

TONGUE

With **Colour 48**, make a magic ring.

Rnd 1: 5sc in ring, pull tight but do not slst to close rnd. [5sc]

This makes a small semi-circle. Fasten off **Colour 48**.

FINISHING

Stitch nose onto muzzle.

Stitch muzzle in place on square, with top of bridge of nose touching outer edge of Rnd 5.

Embroider eyes on either side of nose with **Colour 2**.

Stitch ears on either side of head, and stitch tongue in place as shown.

SQUARE

With a 2.75mm hook and **Colour 5**, make a magic ring.

Rnd 1: 6sc in ring, slst to close rnd. [6sc]

Rnd 2: ch3, 3dc in each of next 5 sts, 2dc in last st, slst to close rnd. [18dc]

Rnd 3: ch3, dc in next st, (dc in next st, 2dc in next st) 8 times, slst to close rnd. [26dc]

Rnd 4: ch3, (2dc in next st, 2dc in next st, dc in next st) 8 times, 3dc in last st, slst to close rnd. [44dc]

Rnd 5: ch3, (2dc in next 2 sts, dc in next 2 sts) 10 times, dc in last 3 sts, slst to close rnd. [64dc]

Fasten off **Colour 5**.

Join **Colour 1** in any st of Rnd 5 with a standing tr.

Rnd 6: (ch2, tr) in same st, *tr in next st, dc in next 2 sts, hdc in next 2 sts, sc in next 5 sts, hdc in next 2 sts, dc in next 2 sts, tr in next st, (tr, ch2, tr) in next st**, rep from * to ** 3 times omitting (tr, ch2, tr) in last rep, slst to close rnd. [68dc, 4ch-2]

Rnd 7: slst in ch-2-sp, ch3, (dc, ch2, 2dc) in ch-2-sp, *dc in next 17 sts, (2dc, ch2, 2dc) in ch-2-sp**, rep from * to ** 3 times omitting (2dc, 2ch, 2dc) in last rep, slst to close rnd. [84dc, 4ch-2]

Fasten off **Colour 1**.

Join **Colour 35** in any ch-2-sp of Rnd 7 with a standing sc.

Rnd 8: (sc, ch3, 2sc) in same ch-sp, *((ch, sk st, sc) in next st) 10 times, (ch, sk st, (2sc, ch3, 2sc) in ch-2-sp**, rep from * to ** 3 times omitting last (2sc, ch3, 2sc), slst to close rnd. [56sc, 44ch-1, 4ch-3]

Fasten off **Colour 35**.

Join **Colour 1** in any ch-3-sp of Rnd 8 with a standing dc.

Rnd 9: (2dc, ch3, 3dc) in same sp, *2dc in each ch-1-sp to next ch-3-sp, (3dc, ch3, 3dc) in next ch-3-sp**, rep from * to ** 3 times omitting last (3dc, ch3, 3dc), slst to close rnd. [112dc, 4ch-3]

Rnd 10: ch2, hdc in next 2 sts, *(2hdc, ch2, 2hdc) in ch-3-sp, hdc in next 28 sts**, rep from * to ** 3 times omitting last 3hdc, slst to close rnd. [128hdc, 4ch-2]

Fasten off **Colour 1**.

EARS

With **Colour 48**, ch10.

Row 1: sc in second ch from hook, sc in each st to end of row. [9sc]

Fasten off **Colour 48**.

Join **Colour 5** at end of Row 1.

Row 2: ch, turn, sc in FL of next 8 sts, 5 dc in FL of next st, sk turning ch, sc in FL of next 9 sts. [22]

Row 3: ch, turn, sc in each st to end of row. [22sc]

Fasten off **Colour 5**. Rep to make a total of 2 ears.

Pinch bottom of each ear and sew closed. Attach both ears to rabbit's face along outer edge of Rnd 4, approx 8 sts apart.

MUZZLE

With **Colour 3**, ch5.

Rnd 1: sk first ch, sc in next 3 ch, 3sc in last ch, turn to work on other side of foundation ch, sc in next 3 ch, 3sc in next ch. [12sc]

Rnd 2: sc in next 4 sts, 2sc in next 2 sts, sc in next 4 sts, 2sc in next 2 sts, slst to close rnd. [16sc]

Fasten off **Colour 3**.

Attach muzzle to rabbit's face as shown. Embroider eyes on either side of muzzle with **Colour 2**.

NOSE

With **Colour 48**, make a magic ring.

Rnd 1: 2sc, 2dc, 2sc, 2dc, slst to close rnd. [8]

Fasten off **Colour 48**.

Attach nose to top of muzzle on rabbit's face.

BOW TIE

With **Colour 34**, ch12.

Row 1: sk ch, hdc in next 11 sts. [11hdc]

Row 2: ch, turn, hdc in each st to end. [11hdc]

Rows 3-4: Rep Row 2. [11hdc]

Fasten off **Colour 34**.

Cut a length of **Colour 34** measuring approx 30cm (12in). Pinch top and bottom of bow tie together at centre and wind yarn around it a few times to hold shape. Secure at back.

Attach bow tie to bottom of rabbit's face as shown.

5	
1	
35	
48	
34	
3	
2	

SQUARE CHART

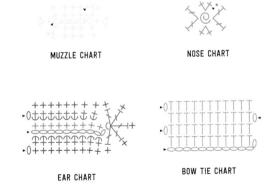

MUZZLE CHART   NOSE CHART

EAR CHART   BOW TIE CHART

SQUARE

With a 2.75mm hook and **Colour 10**, make a magic ring.

Rnd 1: 6sc, slst to close rnd. [6sc]

Rnd 2: ch3, 3dc in each of next 5 sts, 2dc in last st, slst in third ch of initial ch3 to close rnd. [18dc]

Rnd 3: ch3, dc in next st, (dc in next st, 2dc in next st) 8 times, slst in third ch of initial ch3 to close rnd. [26dc]

Rnd 4: ch3, (2dc in next st, 2dc in next st, dc in next st) 8 times, 3dc in last st, slst in third ch of initial ch3 to close rnd. [44dc]

Rnd 5: ch3, (2dc in next 2 sts, dc in next 2 sts) 10 times, dc in last 3 sts, slst in third ch of initial ch3 to close rnd. [64dc]

Fasten off **Colour 10**.

Join **Colour 24** in any st of Rnd 5 with a standing tr.

Rnd 6: (ch2, tr) in same st, *tr in next st, dc in next 2 sts, hdc in next 2 sts, sc in next 5 sts, hdc in next 2 sts, dc in next 2 sts, tr in next st, (tr, ch2, tr) in next st**, rep from * to ** 3 times omitting (tr, ch2, tr) in last rep, slst to close. rnd [68, 4ch-2-sp]

Rnd 7: slst in ch-2-sp, ch3, (dc, ch2, 2dc) in ch-2-sp, *dc in next 17 sts, (2dc, ch2, 2dc) in ch-2-sp**, rep from * to ** 3 times omitting (2dc, ch2, 2dc) in last rep, slst to close rnd. [84dc, 4ch-2-sp]

Rnd 8: ch3, dc in next st, * (2dc, ch3, 2dc) in ch-2-sp, dc in next 21 sts**, rep from * to ** 3 times omitting last 2dc in last rep, slst in third ch of initial ch3 to close rnd. [100dc, 4ch-3-sp]

Rnd 9: ch3, dc in next 3 sts, *(2dc, ch3, 2dc) in ch-3-sp, dc in next 25 sts**, rep from * to ** 3 times omitting last 4dc in last rep, slst to close rnd. [116dc, 4ch3]

Fasten off **Colour 24**.

MUZZLE

With **Colour 8**, ch5.

Rnd 1: sk first ch, sc in next 3 ch, 3sc in last ch, turn to work on other side of foundation ch, sc in next 3 ch, 3sc in next ch. [12sc]

Rnd 2: sc in next 4 sts, 2sc in next 2 sts, sc in next 4 sts, 2sc in next 2 sts. [16sc]

Rnd 3: (sc in next 5 sts, 2sc in next 2 sts) twice, sc in next 2 sts. [20sc]

Rnd 4: (sc in next 8 sts, 2sc in next 2 sts) twice. [24sc]

Continue to shape bridge of nose as follows:

Row 1: ch, sc in next 4 sts. [4sc]

Row 2: ch, turn, sc in next 4 sts. [4sc]

Row 3: ch, turn, sc in next 4 sts. [4sc]

Row 4: ch, turn, 2sc in next st, sc in next 2 sts, 2sc in next st. [6sc]

Row 5: ch, turn, sc in each st to end of row. [6sc]

Row 6: ch, turn, 2sc in next st, sc in next 4 sts, 2sc in next st. [8sc]

Row 7: ch, turn, sc in each st to end of row. [8sc]

Row 8: ch, turn, sc in each st to end of row. [8sc]

Row 9: ch, turn, sc2tog, sc in next 4 sts, sc2tog. [6sc]

Row 10: ch, turn, sc2tog, sc in next 2 sts, sc2tog. [4sc]

Fasten off **Colour 8**.

Embroider two nostrils onto nose with **Colour 48**.

HORNS

Using **Colour 7**, ch5.

Row 1: sk 1 st, sc in next st, 2hdc in next 2 sts, hdc in last st. [6]

Fasten off **Colour 7**. Rep to make a total of 2 horns.

INNER EARS

With **Colour 48**, make a magic ring.

Rnd 1: 5sc in ring. [5sc]

Rnd 2: 2sc in each st, slst to close rnd. [10sc]

Rnd 3: *sc in next st, 2sc in next st**, rep from * to ** to end of rnd, slst to close rnd. [15sc]

Fasten off **Colour 48**. Rep to make a total of 2 inner ears.

OUTER EARS

With **Colour 10**, make a magic ring.

Rnd 1: 6sc in ring. [6sc]

Rnd 2: 2sc in each st, slst to close rnd. [12sc]

Rnd 3: *2sc in next st, sc in next st**, rep from * to ** to end of rnd, slst to close rnd. [18sc]

Rnd 4: *sc in next 2 sts, 2sc in next st**, rep from * to ** to end of rnd, slst to close rnd. [24sc]

Fasten off **Colour 10**. Rep to make a total of 2 outer ears.

FINISHING

Stitch muzzle in place on square. Embroider eyes on either side of muzzle with **Colour 2**.

Place 1 inner ear on top of 1 outer ear and stitch together. Pinch circles in half, with inner circle on inside, and stitch through both layers on one edge to hold cone shape. Rep for second ear.

Stitch ears onto either side of head, and stitch horns in place.

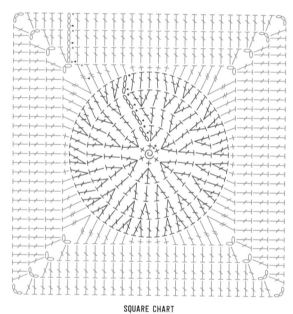

SQUARE CHART

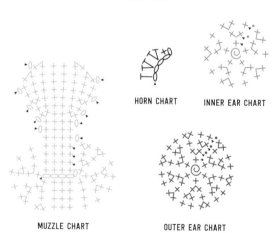

MUZZLE CHART

HORN CHART

INNER EAR CHART

OUTER EAR CHART

Colour key:
- 10
- 24
- 48
- 8
- 7
- 2

ANIMAL PLAY CUBE

SQUARE 1: CAT

Follow instructions for Cat (Rnds 1-5) to make 1 complete cat with 2 ears.

Follow instructions for Cat to make 1 muzzle and 1 nose. Assemble and embroider details following instructions for Cat.

SQUARE 2: DOG

Work Rnds 1-5 of square for Dog.

Follow instructions for Dog to make 1 muzzle, 1 nose, 1 tongue and 2 ears. Assemble and embroider details following instructions for Dog.

SQUARE 3: COW

Work Rnds 1-5 of square for Cow.

Follow instructions for Cow to make 1 muzzle, 2 horns and 2 ears. Assemble and embroider details following instructions for Cow.

SQUARE 4: PENGUIN

Work Rnds 1-5 of square for Penguin.

Follow instructions for Penguin to make 2 flippers, 1 beak, 2 feet, 2 cheeks and 1 tummy. Assemble and embroider details following instructions for Penguin.

SQUARE 5: CRAB

Work Rnds 1-5 of square for Crab, replacing **Colour 13** with **Colour 18**.

Follow instructions for Crab to make 2 legs, 2 pincers, 2 eyes and 2 eye stalks. Assemble and embroider details following instructions for Crab.

SQUARES 1-5: ASSEMBLY

Join the colour specified below in any of the 4 sts that will eventually form the corner, with a standing dc. This dc counts as first dc in Rnd 1 below:

Square 1 (Cat): **Colour 39**.
Square 2 (Dog): **Colour 20**.
Square 3 (Cow): **Colour 27**.
Square 4 (Penguin): **Colour 31**.
Square 5 (Crab): **Colour 32**.

All sts in this rnd are made in BLO:

Rnd 1: *(dc, tr, dc) in corner st, dc in next 3 sts, hdc in next 2 sts, sc in next 5 sts, hdc in next 2 sts, dc in next 3 sts**, rep from * to ** 3 times, slst to close rnd. [72]

Rnd 2: ch3, *(dc, tr, dc) in tr, dc in next 17 sts**, rep from * to ** 3 times omitting last dc, slst to close rnd. [80]

Rnd 3: ch2, hdc in next st, *(hdc, dc, tr, dc, hdc) in tr, hdc in next 19 sts**, rep from * to ** 3 times omitting last 2hdc, slst to close rnd. [96]

Fasten off.

SQUARE 6: SHEEP

Work Rnds 1-6 of square for Sheep.

Join **Colour 28** in any ch-2-sp of Rnd 6 of square with a standing st. This rnd is worked in both ch-2-sp and back of popcorn:

Rnd 7: *(dc, tr, dc) in ch-2-sp, 2dc in next popcorn, dc in next ch-2-sp, 2hdc in next popcorn, sc in next 5 sts, 2hdc in next popcorn, dc in next ch-2-sp, 2dc in next popcorn**, rep from * to ** 3 times, slst to close rnd. [72]

Rnd 8: ch3, *(dc, tr, dc) in tr, dc in next 17 sts**, rep from * to ** 3 times omitting last dc, slst to close rnd. [80]

Rnd 9: ch2, hdc in next st, *(hdc, dc, tr, dc, hdc) in tr, hdc in next 19 sts**, rep from * to ** 3 times omitting last 2hdc, slst to close rnd. [96]

Fasten off **Colour 28**.

Follow instructions for Sheep to make 2 legs and 2 ears. Assemble and embroider details following instructions for Sheep.

FINISHING

Place 2 squares together, with WS facing, and join **Colour 1** through corner tr of both squares with a standing sc.

Rnd 1: sc in each st (through both squares) along one edge, ending in dc just before corner tr. [24]

Fasten off **Colour 1**. Rep to join a total of 4 squares in a row. Join squares at end of row together with **Colour 1** to make a ring.

Join square at top of ring with **Colour 1** using sc. Insert foam block into cube and join last square to finish.

CAT

With a 2.75mm hook and **Colour 5**, make a magic ring.

Rnd 1: 6sc in ring, slst to close rnd. [6sc]

Rnd 2: ch3, 3dc in each of next 5 sts, 2dc in last st, slst in third ch of initial ch3 to close rnd. [18dc]

Rnd 3: ch3, dc in next st, (dc in next st, 2dc in next st) 8 times, slst in third ch of initial ch3 to close rnd. [26dc]

Rnd 4: ch3, (2dc in next st, 2dc in next st, dc in next st) 8 times, 3dc in last st, slst in third ch of initial ch3 to close rnd. [44dc]

Rnd 5: ch3, (2dc in next 2 sts, dc in next 2 sts) 10 times, dc in last 3 sts, slst in third ch of initial ch3 to close rnd. [64dc]

Fasten off **Colour 5**.

FIRST EAR

Join **Colour 5** in any st of Rnd 5 of cat with a slst.

Row 1: sc in FL of next 6 sts. [6sc]

Row 2: ch, turn, sc2tog, sc2tog, sc2tog. [3sc]

Row 3: ch, turn, sc2tog, sc in next st. [2sc]

Row 4: ch, turn, sc2tog. [1sc]

Fasten off **Colour 5**.

SECOND EAR

Join **Colour 5** in Rnd 5 of cat with a slst, 8 sts apart from first ear.

Rep Rows 1-5 of first ear to complete second ear.

Fasten off **Colour 5**.

SQUARE

Join **Colour 42** in BL of second sc at base of first ear with a standing tr. All sts in this rnd are made in BLO:

Rnd 6: (ch2, tr) in same st, *tr in next st, dc in next 2 sts, hdc in next 2 sts, sc in next 5 sts, hdc in next 2 sts, dc in next 2 sts, tr in next st, (tr, ch2, tr) in next st**, rep from * to ** 3 times omitting (tr, ch2, tr) in last rep, slst to close rnd. [68, 4ch-2]

Rnd 7: slst in ch-2-sp, ch3, (dc, ch2, 2dc) in ch-2-sp, *dc in next 17 sts, (2dc, ch2, 2dc) in ch-2-sp**, rep from * to ** 3 times omitting (2dc, ch2, 2dc) in last rep, slst to close rnd. [84dc, 4ch-2]

Rnd 8: ch3, dc in next st, *(2dc, ch3, 2dc) in ch-2-sp, dc in next 21 sts**, rep from * to ** 3 times omitting last 2dc in last rep, slst in third ch of initial ch3 to close rnd. [100dc, 4ch-3]

Rnd 9: ch3, dc in next 3 sts, *(2dc, ch3, 2dc) in ch-3-sp, dc in next 25 sts**, rep from * to ** 3 times omitting last 4dc in last rep, slst to close rnd. [116dc, 4ch-3]

Fasten off **Colour 42**.

MUZZLE

With **Colour 3**, make a magic ring.

Rnd 1: 6sc in ring. [6sc]

Rnd 2: 2sc in each st to end of rnd. [12sc]

Rnd 3: *sc in next st, 2sc in next st**, rep from * to ** to end of rnd. [18sc]

Rnd 4: *sc in next 2 sts, 2sc in next st**, rep from * to ** to end of rnd, slst to close rnd. [24sc]

Fasten off **Colour 3**.

NOSE

With **Colour 48**, ch4.

Row 1: sc in second ch from hook, sc in next 2 sts. [3sc]

Row 2: ch, turn, sc3tog. [1sc]

Fasten off **Colour 48**.

Stitch nose onto muzzle.

FINISHING

Stitch muzzle in place, just below centre of cat's face.

Embroider eyes onto cat's face with **Colour 2**.

Embroider mouth and ear details with **Colour 48**.

Embroider three whiskers on either side of muzzle with **Colour 7**.

■	5
■	42
■	3
■	48
■	2
■	7

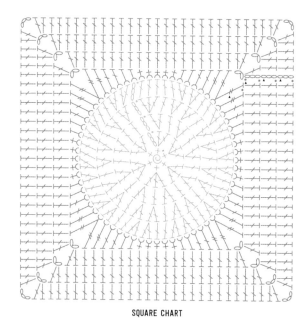

SQUARE CHART

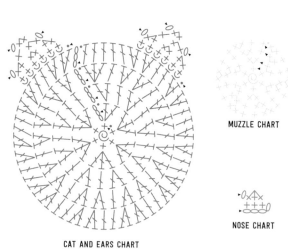

CAT AND EARS CHART

MUZZLE CHART

NOSE CHART

SQUARE

With a 4mm hook and **Colour 44**, make a magic ring.

Rnd 1: ch3, 11dc in ring, slst to close rnd. [12dc]

Rnd 2: ch3, dc in same st, 2dc in each st to end of rnd, slst to close rnd. [24dc]

Fasten off **Colour 44**.

Join **Colour 5** in any st of Rnd 2.

Rnd 3: ch3, dc in same st, dc in next st, *2dc in next st, dc in next st**, rep from * to ** to end of rnd, slst to close rnd. [36dc]

Fasten off **Colour 5**.

Join **Colour 11** in any st of Rnd 3. All sts in this rnd are made in BLO:

Rnd 4: ch3, dc in same st, ch2, 2dc in next st, hdc in next 2 sts, sc in next 3 sts, hdc in next 2 sts, *2dc in next st, ch2, 2dc in next st, hdc in next 2 sts, sc in next 3 sts, hdc in next 2 sts**, rep from * to ** twice, slst to third ch of starting ch, slst in next st, slst to ch-2-sp. [16dc, 16hdc, 12sc, 4ch-2]

Rnd 5: (ch3, dc, ch2, 2dc) in ch-2-sp, dc in each st to next ch-2-sp, *(2dc, ch2, 2dc) in next ch-2-sp, dc in each st to next ch-2-sp**, rep from * to ** twice ending last rep at initial ch3, slst to third ch of starting ch, slst in next st, slst to ch-2-sp. [60dc, 4ch-2]

Rnds 6-7: Rep Rnd 5. [92dc, 4ch-2]

Fasten off **Colour 11**.

Join **Colour 44** in any st of Rnd 7.

Rnd 8: ch, *sc in each st to corner sp, (sc, ch, sc) in corner sp**, rep from * to ** 3 times, sc in each st to end of rnd, slst to close rnd. [100sc, 4ch-1]

Fasten off **Colour 44**.

EARS

Join **Colour 5** in FL of fourth st before start of Rnd 3, with a standing sc. All sts are worked in FL in this row.

Row 1: sc in next st, 3dc in next st, sc in next 5 sts, 3dc in next st, sc in next 2 sts. [15]

Fasten off **Colour 5**.

EYES

With **Colour 2**, ch2.

Rnd 1: 6sc in second ch from hook, slst to close rnd. [6sc]

Fasten off **Colour 2**.

Join **Colour 1** in any st of Rnd 1.

Rnd 2: 2sc in each st around, slst to close rnd. [12sc]

Fasten off **Colour 1**.

Rep to make a total of 2 eyes.

Stitch eyes onto owl's head in centre of square as shown.

FINISHING

Embroider beak onto owl's head and feet onto bottom of owl's body with **Colour 22** as shown.

With **Colour 44** make two small tassels in central dc at top of owl's ears on each side.

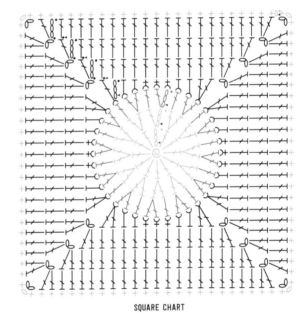

44	
5	
11	
2	
22	
1	

SQUARE CHART

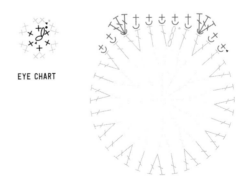

EYE CHART

EARS CHART

SQUARE

With a 4mm hook and Colour 21, ch2.

Rnd 1: 6sc in second ch, join with slst. [6sc]

Rnds 2-3: ch, sc in each st to end of rnd, slst to close rnd. [6sc]

Rnd 4: ch, 2sc in each st to end of rnd, slst to close rnd. [12sc]

Fasten off Colour 21.

Join Colour 1 in any st of Rnd 4.

Rnd 5: ch3, dc in same st, *dc in next st, 2dc in next st**, rep from * to ** to last st, dc in last st, slst to close rnd. [18dc]

Rnd 6: ch3, dc in same st, *dc in next 2 sts, 2dc in next st**, rep from * to ** to last 2 sts, dc in last 2 sts, slst to close rnd. [24dc]

Rnd 7: ch3, dc in same st, *dc in next 3 sts, 2dc in next st**, rep from * to ** to last 3 sts, dc in last 3 sts, slst to close rnd. [30dc]

Rnd 8: ch3, dc in same st, *dc in next 4 sts, 2dc in next st**, rep from * to ** to last 4 sts, dc in last 4 sts, slst to close rnd. [36dc]

Fasten off Colour 1.

Join Colour 9 in any st of Rnd 8. All sts in this rnd are made in BLO:

Rnd 9: ch3, dc in same st, ch2, 2dc in next st, hdc in next 2 sts, sc in next 3 sts, hdc in next 2 sts, *2dc in next st, ch2, 2dc in next st, hdc in next 2 sts, sc in next 3 sts, hdc in next 2 sts**, rep from * to ** twice, slst to third ch of starting ch to close rnd. [16dc, 16hdc, 12sc, 4ch-2]

Rnd 10: slst in next st, slst in ch-2-sp, (ch3, 1dc, ch2, 2dc) in ch-2-sp, dc in each st to next ch-2-sp, *(2dc, ch2, 2dc) in next ch-2-sp, dc in each st to next ch-2-sp**, rep from * to ** twice ending last rep at initial ch, slst to third ch of starting ch, slst in next st, slst to ch-2-sp. [60dc, 4ch-2]

Rnds 11-12: Rep Rnd 10. [92dc, 4ch-2]

Fasten off Colour 9.

COMB

Join Colour 14 in FL of Rnd 8 of square, 2 sts from top right corner sp in Rnd 8. All sts in this row are worked in FLO:

Row 1: sc, 5dc in next st, sc in next st, 7dc in next st, sc in next st, 5dc in next, sc in next st. [17dc, 4sc]

Fasten off Colour 14.

WADDLE

Join Colour 14 in FL of Rnd 8 of square, 3 sts from bottom left corner sp. All sts in this row are worked in FLO:

Row 1: sc, 3dc in next st, sc, 3dc in next st, sc. [6dc, 3sc]

Fasten off Colour 14.

FINISHING

With Colour 2, make 2 crochet bobble sts in Rnd 6, on either side of chicken's beak, to create eyes as shown.

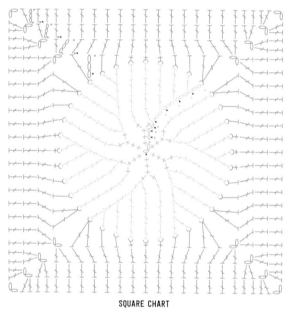

21	
1	
9	
14	
2	

SQUARE CHART

COMB AND WADDLE CHART

BEAR

With a 4mm hook and **Colour 10**, make a magic ring.

Rnd 1: ch3, 11dc in ring, slst in third ch of initial ch3. [12dc]

Rnd 2: ch3, dc in same st, (2dc in next st) 11 times, slst in third ch of initial ch3. [24dc]

Rnd 3: ch3, dc in same st, dc in next st, (2dc in next st, dc in next st) 11 times, slst in third ch of initial ch3. [36dc]

Rnd 4: ch, 2sc in st, sc in next 2 sts, (2sc in next st, sc in next 2 sts) 11 times. [48sc]

All sts in this rnd are made in FL of Rnd 4 sts:

Rnd 5: slst in next 4 sts, sk next st, 6dc in next st, sk next st, slst in next 8 sts, sk next st, 6dc in next st, sk next st, slst in next 30 sts. [12dc, 42slst]

Fasten off **Colour 10**.

SQUARE

Join **Colour 48** in BL of fifth st made in Rnd 4 of bear with a standing tr. All sts in this rnd are made in BL of Rnd 4 sts:

Rnd 6: tr in same st, ch2, 2tr in next st, dc in next st, hdc in next 2 sts, sc in next 4 sts, hdc in next 2 sts, dc in next st, *2tr in next st, ch2, 2tr in next st, dc in next st, hdc in next 2 sts, sc in next 4 sts, hdc in next 2 sts, dc in next st**, rep from * to ** twice, slst in initial tr. [16tr, 8dc, 16hdc, 16sc, 4ch-2-sp]

Rnd 7: slst in next st, slst in next ch-2-sp, ch3, (dc, ch2, 2dc) in same ch-2-sp, dc in next 14 sts, *(2dc, ch2, 2dc) in next ch-2-sp, dc in next 14 sts**, rep from * to ** twice, slst in third ch of initial ch3. [72dc, 4ch-2-sp]

Rnd 8: slst in next st, slst in next ch-2-sp, ch3, (dc, ch2, 2dc) in same ch-2-sp, dc in next 18 sts, *(2dc, ch2, 2dc) in next ch-2-sp, dc in next 18 sts**, rep from * to ** twice, slst in third ch of initial ch3. [88dc, 4ch-2-sp]

Rnd 9: slst in next st, slst in next ch-2-sp, ch, *(sc, ch2, sc) in ch-2-sp, sc in next 22 sts**, rep from * to ** 3 times. [96sc, 4ch-2]

Fasten off **Colour 48**.

Join **Colour 1** in any ch-2-sp of Rnd 9.

Rnd 10: ch, *(sc, ch2, sc) in next ch-2-sp, sc in next 24 sts**, rep from * to ** 3 times. [104sc, 4ch-2-sp]

Fasten off **Colour 1**.

INNER EARS

With a 3.5mm hook and **Colour 9**, make a magic ring.

Rnd 1: 3sc in ring. [3sc]

Fasten off **Colour 9**. Rep to make a total of 2 inner ears

Sew inner ears onto each of bear's ears on square.

SNOUT

With a 3.5mm hook and **Colour 9**, make a magic ring.

Rnd 1: 6sc in ring. [6sc]

Rnd 2: 2sc in each st to end of rnd. [12sc]

Rnd 3: sc, 3sc in next st, sc in next 5 sts, 3sc in next st, sc in next 4 sts. [16sc]

Rnd 4: sc in next 2 sts, 3sc in next st, sc in next 7 sts, 3sc in next st, sc in next 5 sts. [20sc]

Fasten off **Colour 9**.

NOSE

With a 3.5mm hook and **Colour 2**, make a magic ring.

Rnd 1: 6sc in ring. [6sc]

Fasten off **Colour 2**.

FINISHING

Sew nose onto bear's snout and attach snout to centre of square.

Embroider eyes and mouth onto bear's face with **Colour 2**.

10	■
48	■
1	■
9	■
2	■

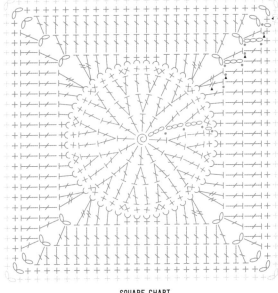

SQUARE CHART

SNOUT CHART

INNER EAR CHART

NOSE CHART

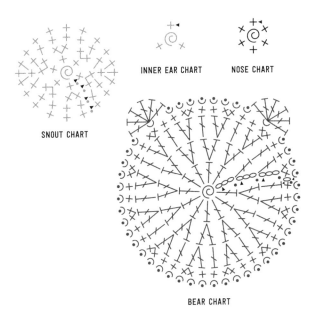

BEAR CHART

FLAMINGO

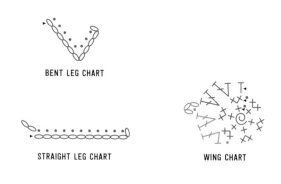

45
27
21
32
2
48
1

SQUARE CHART

BENT LEG CHART

STRAIGHT LEG CHART

WING CHART

HEAD AND NECK CHART

BEAK CHART

SQUARE

With a 2.75mm hook and **Colour 45**, make a magic ring.

Rnd 1: 6sc in ring, slst to close rnd. [6sc]

Rnd 2: ch3, 3dc in each of next 5 sts, 2dc in last st, slst in second ch of initial ch3 to close rnd. [18dc]

Rnd 3: ch3, dc in next st, (dc in next st, 2dc in next st) 8 times, invisible join to close rnd. [26dc]

Fasten off **Colour 45**.

Join **Colour 27** with a standing dc in any st of Rnd 3. This rnd is worked in BLO:

Rnd 4: (2dc in next st, 2dc in next st, dc in next st) 8 times, 3dc in last st, slst to close rnd. [44dc]

Fasten off **Colour 27**.

Join **Colour 21** in any st of Rnd 4 with a standing dc.

Rnd 5: (2dc in next 2 sts, dc in next 2 sts) 10 times, dc in last 3 sts, slst to close rnd. [64dc]

Fasten off **Colour 21**.

Join **Colour 32** in any st of Rnd 5 with a standing tr.

Rnd 6: (ch2, tr) in same st, *tr in next st, dc in next 2 sts, hdc in next 2 sts, sc in next 5 sts, hdc in next 2 sts, dc in next 2 sts, tr in next st, (tr, ch2, tr) in next st**, rep from * to ** 3 times omitting (tr, ch2, tr) in last rep, slst to close rnd. [68, 4ch-2]

Rnd 7: slst in ch-2-sp, ch3, (dc, ch2, 2dc) in ch-2-sp, *dc in next 17 sts, (2dc, ch2, 2dc) in ch-2-sp**, rep from * to ** 3 times omitting (2dc, ch2, 2dc) in last rep, slst to close rnd. [84dc, 4ch-2]

Rnd 8: ch3, dc in next st, *(2dc, ch3, 2dc) in ch-2-sp, dc in next 21 sts**, rep from * to ** 3 times omitting last 2dc in last rep, slst in third ch of initial ch3. [100dc, 4ch-3]

Rnd 9: ch3, dc in next 3 sts, *(2dc, ch3, 2dc) in ch-3-sp, dc in next 25 sts**, rep from * to ** 3 times omitting last 4dc in last rep, slst to close rnd. [116dc, 4ch-3]

Fasten off **Colour 32**.

HEAD AND NECK

With **Colour 45**, ch14.

Row 1: sc in second ch from hook, sc in next 11 sts, 7dc in last st to form head, slst in next ch on underside of foundation ch. [20]

Fasten off **Colour 45**.

BEAK

With **Colour 2**, ch5.

Row 1: slst in second ch from hook, sk next st, sc in next st, hdc in last st. [3]

Fasten off **Colour 2**.

Stitch beak onto flamingo's head.

WING

With **Colour 45**, make a magic ring.

Rnd 1: 6sc in ring, slst to close rnd. [6sc]

Rnd 2: 2sc in each st to end of rnd, slst to close rnd. [12]

Rnd 3: hdc in next st, (hdc, dc) in next st, 2dc in next st, join and change to **Colour 48**, picot, 2dc in next st, (dc, hdc) in next st, slst in next st. [15 around edge, picot]

Fasten off **Colours 45 and 48**.

STRAIGHT LEG

With **Colour 45**, ch12.

Row 1: slst in second ch from hook, slst in rem 10 sts, ch2 to create foot. [11slst, ch2]

Fasten off **Colour 45**.

BENT LEG

With **Colour 45**, ch11.

Row 1: slst in second ch from hook, slst in next 2 sts, sk 2 sts, slst in next 5 sts. [8slst]

Fasten off **Colour 45**.

FINISHING

With **Colour 1**, make a large whip stitch where beak joins head.

Embroider eye onto flamingo's head with **Colour 2**.

Pin head and neck in place on square (making sure to add a little curve) and attach.

Stitch top of straight leg to bottom of flamingo's body and secure bottom of leg in place. Stitch top of bent leg next to top of straight leg and stitch bottom of bent leg to lower half of straight leg as shown.

Stitch wing in place in centre of square, leaving tip unattached.

WILD BEASTS

SQUARE

With a 2.75mm hook and **Colour 6**, make a magic ring.

Rnd 1: 6sc in ring, slst to close rnd. [6sc]

Rnd 2: ch3, 3dc in next 5 sts, 2dc in last st, slst in third ch of initial ch3 to close rnd. [18dc]

Rnd 3: ch3, dc in first st, (dc in next st, 2dc in next st) 8 times, slst in third ch of initial ch3 to close rnd. [26dc]

Rnd 4: ch3, (2dc in next st, 2dc in next st, dc in next st) 8 times, 3dc in last st, slst in third ch of initial ch3 to close rnd. [44dc]

Rnd 5: ch3, (2dc in next 2 sts, dc in next 2 sts) 10 times, dc in last 3 sts, slst in third ch of initial ch3 to close rnd. [64dc]

Fasten off **Colour 6**.

Join **Colour 34** in circle with a standing tr.

Rnd 6: (ch2, tr) in same st, *tr in next st, dc in next 2 sts, hdc in next 2 sts, sc in next 5 sts, hdc in next 2 sts, dc in next 2 sts, tr in next st, (tr, ch2, tr) in same st**, rep from * to ** 3 times omitting (tr, ch2, tr) in last rep, slst to close rnd. [68, 4ch-2]

Rnd 7: slst in ch-2-sp, ch3, (dc, ch2, 2dc) in ch-2-sp, *dc in next 17 sts, (2dc, ch2, 2dc) in ch-2-sp**, rep from * to ** 3 times omitting (2dc, ch2, 2dc) in last rep, slst to close rnd. [84dc, 4ch-2]

Rnd 8: ch3, dc in next st, *(2dc, ch3, 2dc) in ch-2-sp, dc in next 21 sts**, rep from * to ** 3 times omitting last 2dc in last rep, slst in third ch of initial ch3 to close. [100dc, 4ch-3]

Rnd 9: ch3, dc in next 3 sts, *(2dc, ch3, 2dc) in ch-3-sp, dc in next 25 sts**, rep from * to ** 3 times omitting last 4dc in last rep, slst to close rnd. [116dc, 4ch-3]

Fasten off **Colour 34**.

TUMMY

With **Colour 1**, make a magic ring.

Rnd 1: 6sc in ring. [6sc]

Rnd 2: 2sc in each st. [12sc]

Rnd 3: *sc in next st, 2sc in next st**, rep from * to ** to end of rnd. [18sc]

Rnd 4: *2sc in next st, sc in next 2 st**, rep from * to ** to end of rnd. [24sc]

Rnd 5: *sc in next 3 sts, 2sc in next st**, rep from * to ** to end of rnd. [30sc]

Rnd 6: *2sc in next st, sc in next 4 sts**, rep from * to ** to end of rnd, slst to close rnd. [36sc]

Fasten off **Colour 1**.

FLIPPERS

With **Colour 6**, make a magic ring.

Rnd 1: 5sc in ring. [5sc]

Rnd 2: 2sc in each st to end of rnd. [10sc]

Rnd 3: *sc in next st, 2sc in next st**, rep from * to ** to end of rnd. [15sc]

Rnd 4: *2sc in next st, sc in next 2 sts**, rep from * to ** to end of rnd, slst to close rnd. [20sc]

Rnd 5: ch, fold circle in half and sc in each st around curve, through both sides of circle. [10sc]

Fasten off **Colour 6**. Rep to make a total of 2 flippers.

CHEEKS

With **Colour 44**, make a magic ring.

Rnd 1: 5sc in ring, slst to close rnd. [5sc]

Fasten off **Colour 44**. Rep to make a total of 2 cheeks.

BEAK AND FEET

With **Colour 22**, ch3.

Row 1: sk st, sc in next st, 2sc in last st. [3sc]

Fasten off **Colour 22**. Rep to make a total of 3 pieces (1 for beak and 2 for feet).

FINISHING

Stitch penguin's tummy in place on square, with outer edge of circle touching outer edge of Rnd 5 and top of circle touching outer edge of Rnd 2.

Stitch beak onto square, just above tummy, and add cheeks on either side of penguin's beak.

Embroider eyes on either side of penguin's beak with **Colour 2**.

Stitch 2 feet next to each other below penguin's tummy.

Stitch 2 flippers in place on either side of penguin's tummy.

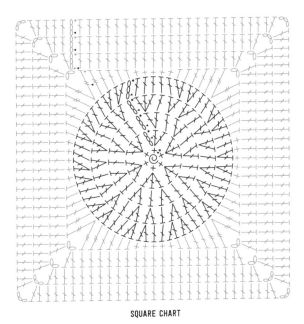

6	■
34	■
1	■
44	■
22	■
2	■

SQUARE CHART

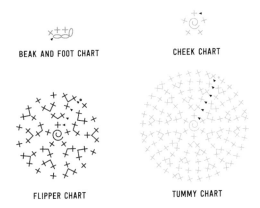

BEAK AND FOOT CHART

CHEEK CHART

FLIPPER CHART

TUMMY CHART

LION

LION

With a 4mm hook and Colour 22, make a magic ring.

Rnd 1: ch3, 11dc in ring, slst in third ch of initial ch3. [12dc]

Rnd 2: ch3, dc in same st, (2dc in next st) 11 times, slst in third ch of initial ch3. [24dc]

Rnd 3: ch3, dc in same st, dc in next st, (2dc in next st, dc in next st) 11 times, slst in third ch of initial ch3. [36dc]

Rnd 4: ch, 2sc in st, sc in next 2 sts, (2sc in next st, sc in next 2 sts) 11 times. [48sc]

Fasten off **Colour 22**.

Join **Colour 17** in any st of Rnd 4. All sts in this rnd are made in FL of Rnd 4 sts:

Rnd 5: slst in st, sk next st, 5dc in next st, sk next st, (slst in next st, sk next st, 5dc in next st, sk next st) 11 times. [60dc, 12slst]

Fasten off **Colour 17**.

SQUARE

Join **Colour 1** in BL of sixth st made in Rnd 4 with a standing tr. All sts in this rnd are made in BL of Rnd 4 sts:

Rnd 6: tr in same st, ch2, 2tr in next st, dc in next st, hdc in next 2 sts, sc in next 4 sts, hdc in next 2 sts, dc in next st, *2tr in next st, ch2, 2tr in next st, dc in next st, hdc in next 2 sts, sc in next 4 sts, hdc in next 2 sts, dc in next st**, rep from * to ** twice, slst to close rnd. [16tr, 8dc, 16hdc, 16sc, 4ch-2]

Rnd 7: slst in next st, slst in next ch-2-sp, ch3, (dc, ch2, 2dc) in same ch-2-sp, dc in next 14 sts, *(2dc, ch2, 2dc) in next ch-2-sp, dc in next 14 sts**, rep from * to ** twice, slst in third ch of initial ch3. [72dc, 4ch-2]

Rnd 8: slst in next st, slst in next ch-2-sp, ch3, (dc, ch2, 2dc) in same ch-2-sp, dc in next 18 sts, *(2dc, ch2, 2dc) in next ch-2-sp, dc in next 18 sts**, rep from * to ** twice, slst in third ch of initial ch3. [88dc, 4ch-2]

Rnd 9: slst in next st, slst in next ch-2-sp, ch, *(sc, ch2, sc) in ch-2-sp, sc in next 22 sts**, rep from * to ** 3 times. [96sc, 4ch-2]

Fasten off **Colour 1**.

Join **Colour 17** in any ch-2-sp of Rnd 9.

Rnd 10: ch, *(sc, ch2, sc) in next ch-2-sp, sc in next 24 sts,**, rep from * to ** 3 times. [104sc, 4ch-2-sp]

Fasten off **Colour 17**.

NOSE

Using a 3.5mm hook and Colour 11, make a magic ring.

Rnd 1: ch, 6sc in ring. [6sc]

Fasten off **Colour 11**.

Sew nose onto centre of square.

Embroider eyes on either side above lion's nose with **Colour 2**.

EARS

Using a 3.5mm hook and Colour 17, make a magic ring. This row is worked on WS:

Row 1: ch, 4sc in ring, turn. [4sc]

Fasten off **Colour 17** and join Colour 22.

Row 2: ch2, hdc in same st, 2hdc in each st to end of row. [8hdc]

Fasten off **Colour 22**. Rep to make a total of 2 ears.

Slightly fold ears and sew in place on square.

CHEEKS

With a 3.5mm hook and Colour 1, ch5.

Row 1: dc4tog in third ch from hook, sc in next ch, bobble in next ch. [2 bobbles, 1sc]

Fasten off **Colour 1**.

Sew cheeks onto centre of square as shown.

Embroider mouth from bottom of nose to beneath cheeks with **Colour 11**.

22	
17	
1	
11	
2	

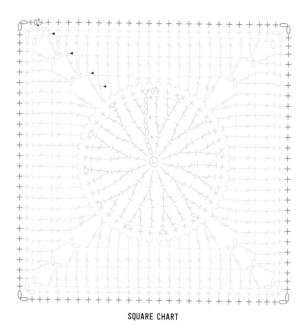

SQUARE CHART

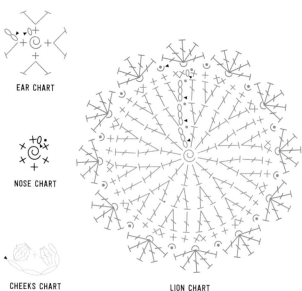

EAR CHART

NOSE CHART

CHEEKS CHART

LION CHART

FOX

With a 4mm hook and **Colour 12**, make a magic ring.

Rnd 1: ch3, 11dc in ring, slst in third ch of initial ch3. [12dc]

Rnd 2: ch3, dc in same st, (2dc in next st) 11 times, slst in third ch of initial ch3. [24dc]

Rnd 3: ch3, dc in same st, dc in next st, (2dc in next st, dc in next st) 11 times, slst in third ch of initial ch3. [36dc]

Rnd 4: ch, 2sc in st, sc in next 2 sts, (2sc in next st, sc in next 2 sts) 11 times. [48sc]

All sts in this rnd are made in FL of Rnd 4 sts:

Rnd 5: slst in next 8 sts, place stitch marker in third slst, sc in next 2 sts, hdc in next st, (hdc, dc) in next st, ch, (dc, hdc) in next st, hdc in next st, sc in next 2 sts, slst in next 16 sts, sc in next 2 sts, hdc in next st, (hdc, dc) in next st, ch, (dc, hdc) in next st, hdc in next st, sc in next 2 sts, slst in next 8 sts, place stitch marker in first slst. [4dc, 8hdc, 8sc, 32slst, 2ch]

Fasten off **Colour 12**.

EARS

Join **Colour 12** in a marked st in Rnd 5 of fox. All sts in this row are made in Rnd 5 sts:

Row 1: sc in st, sc in next 5 sts, turn. [6sc]

Row 2: ch, sc2tog across next 2 sts, sc in next 2 sts, sc2tog across next 2 sts, turn. [2sc2tog, 2sc]

Row 3: ch, (sc2tog across next 2 sts) twice, join and change to **Colour 2**, turn. [2sc2tog]

This rnd is worked on WS:

Row 4: ch, sc2tog across next 2 sts, turn. [1sc2tog]

Row 5: ch, sc. [1sc2tog]

Fasten off **Colours 12** and **2**.

Starting in the rem marked st in Rnd 5 of fox, rep Rows 1-5 to make second ear.

SQUARE

Join **Colour 27** in BL of sixth st made in Rnd 4 of fox. All sts in this rnd are made in BL of Rnd 4 sts.

Rnd 6: 2tr in st, ch2, 2tr in next st, dc in next st, hdc in next 2 sts, sc in next 4 sts, hdc in next 2 sts, dc in next st, *2tr in next st, ch2, 2tr in next st, dc in next st, hdc in next 2 sts, sc in next 4 sts, hdc in next 2 sts, dc in next st**, rep from * to ** twice, slst to close rnd. [16tr, 8dc, 16hdc, 16sc, 4ch-2]

Rnd 7: slst in next st, slst in next ch-2-sp, ch3, (dc, ch2, 2dc) in same ch-2-sp, dc in next 14 sts, *(2dc, ch2, 2dc) in next ch-2-sp, dc in next 14 sts**, rep from * to ** twice, slst in third ch of initial ch3. [72dc, 4ch-2]

Rnd 8: slst in next st, slst in next ch-2-sp, ch3, (dc, ch2, 2dc) in same ch-2-sp, dc in next 18 sts, *(2dc, ch2, 2dc) in next ch-2-sp, dc in next 18 sts**, rep from * to ** twice, slst in third ch of initial ch3. [88dc, 4ch-2]

Rnd 9: slst in next st, slst in next ch-2-sp, ch, *(sc, ch2, sc) in ch-2-sp, sc in next 22 sts**, rep from * to ** 3 times. [96sc, 4ch-2]

Fasten off **Colour 27**.

Join **Colour 1** in any ch-2-sp of Rnd 9.

Rnd 10: ch, *(sc, ch2, sc) in next ch-2-sp, sc in next 24 sts**, rep from * to ** 3 times. [104sc, 4ch-2]

Fasten off **Colour 1**.

CHEEKS

Using a 3.5mm hook and **Colour 19**, make a magic ring.

Row 1: ch3, 6dc in ring, turn. [7dc]

This row is worked on WS:

Row 2: ch3, dc in same st, *dc in next st, 2dc in next st**, rep from * to ** twice, turn. [11dc]

Row 3: ch2, hdc in same st, *hdc in next st, 2hdc in next st**, rep from * to ** 4 times. [17hdc]

Fasten off **Colour 19**. Rep to make a total of 2 cheeks.

Sew cheeks onto fox's face.

NOSE

Using a 3.5mm hook and **Colour 2**, ch4.

Row 1: 4dc in fourth ch from hook, take loop off hook and insert from front to back in third ch of initial ch3, place dropped loop on hook and pull through, ch1. [1 popcorn]

Fasten off **Colour 2**.

Sew nose onto square.

Embroider eyes onto square with **Colour 2**.

12	
27	
1	
19	
2	

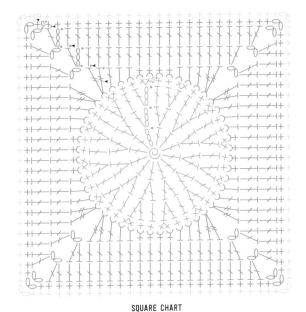

SQUARE CHART

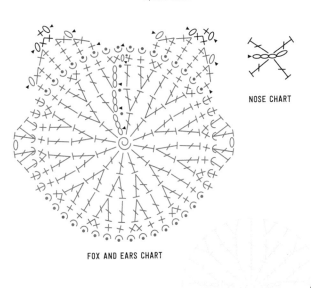

NOSE CHART

FOX AND EARS CHART

CHEEK CHART

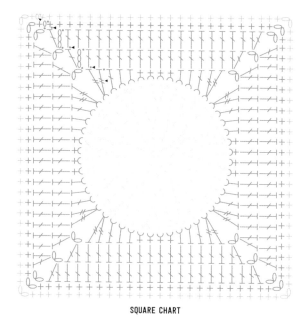

SQUARE CHART

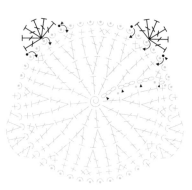

PANDA AND EARS CHART

EYE PATCH CHART

▨	1
▨	31
■	2

PANDA

With a 4mm hook and **Colour 1**, make a magic ring.

Rnd 1: ch3, 11dc in ring, slst in third ch of initial ch3. [12dc]

Rnd 2: ch3, dc in same st, (2dc in next st) 11 times, slst in third ch of initial ch3. [24dc]

Rnd 3: ch3, dc in same st, dc in next st, (2dc in next st, dc in next st) 11 times, slst in third ch of initial ch3. [36dc]

Rnd 4: ch, 2sc in st, sc in next 2 sts, (2sc in next st, sc in next 2 sts) 11 times. [48sc]

All sts in this rnd are made in FL of Rnd 4 sts:

Rnd 5: slst in next st, slst in next 20 sts, sc in next 2 sts, hdc in next st, (hdc, dc) in next st, 2dc in next st, (dc, hdc) in next st, sc in next 2 sts, slst in next 10 sts, sc in next 2 sts, (hdc, dc) in next st, (2dc) in next st, (dc, hdc) in next st, hdc in next st, sc in next 2 sts, slst in next st. [8dc, 6hdc, 8sc, 32slst]

Fasten off **Colour 1**.

EARS

Join **Colour 2** in third st made in Rnd 4 of panda.

Rnd 1: slst in st, sk next st, 6dc in next st, sk next st, slst in next st, fasten off **Colour 2**, sk next 6 sts, rejoin **Colour 2** in next st, slst in st, sk next st, 6dc in next st, sk next st, slst in next st. [12dc, 4slst]

Fasten off **Colour 2**.

SQUARE

Join **Colour 31** in BL of sixteenth st made in Rnd 4 of panda with a standing tr. All sts in this rnd are made in BL of Rnd 4 sts:

Rnd 6: tr in same st, ch2, 2tr in next st, dc in next st, hdc in next 2 sts, sc in next 4 sts, hdc in next 2 sts, dc in next st, *2tr in next st, ch2, 2tr in next st, dc in next st, hdc in next 2 sts, sc in next 4 sts, hdc in next 2 sts, dc in next st**, rep from * to ** twice, slst in initial tr. [16tr, 8dc, 16hdc, 16sc, 4ch-2]

Rnd 7: slst in next st, slst in next ch-2-sp, ch3, (dc, ch2, 2dc) in same ch-2-sp, dc in next 14 sts, *(2dc, ch2, 2dc) in next ch-2-sp, dc in next 14 sts,** rep from * to ** twice, slst in third ch of initial ch3. [72dc, 4ch-2]

Rnd 8: slst in next st, slst in next ch-2-sp, ch3, (dc, ch2, 2dc) in same ch-2-sp, dc in next 18 sts, *(2dc, ch2, 2dc) in next ch-2-sp, dc in next 18 sts,** rep from * to ** twice, slst in third ch of initial ch3. [88dc, 4ch-2]

Rnd 9: slst in next st, slst in next ch-2-sp, ch, *(sc, ch2, sc) in ch-2-sp, sc in next 22 sts**, rep from * to ** 3 times, slst in initial sc. [96sc, 4ch-2]

Fasten off **Colour 31**.

Join **Colour 1** in any ch-2-sp of Rnd 9.

Rnd 10: ch, *(sc, ch2, sc) in next ch-2-sp, sc in next 24 sts**, rep from * to ** 3 times. [104sc, 4ch-2]

Fasten off **Colour 1**.

EYE PATCHES

Using a 3mm hook and **Colour 2**, ch2.

Rnd 1: 6sc in second ch from hook. [6sc]

Rnd 2: sc in next st, (hdc, dc) in next st, (dc, hdc) in next st, sc in next st, slst in next st. [7]

Fasten off **Colour 2**. Rep to make a total of 2 eye patches.

Embroider small pupils onto eye patches with **Colour 1**.

Stitch eye patches onto panda's face as shown.

Embroider nose and mouth details beneath panda's eye patches with **Colour 2**.

JELLYFISH

With a 2.75mm hook and **Colour 48**, make a magic ring.

Rnd 1: 6sc in ring, slst to close rnd. [6sc]

Rnd 2: ch3, 3dc in each of next 5 sts, 2dc in last st, slst in third ch of initial ch3 to close rnd. [18dc]

Rnd 3: ch3, dc in next st, (dc in next st, 2dc in next st) 8 times, slst in third ch of initial ch3 to close rnd. [26dc]

Rnd 4: ch3, (2dc in next st, 2dc in next st, dc in next st) 8 times, 3dc in last st, slst to close rnd [44dc]

Fasten off **Colour 48**.

Join **Colour 39** in FL of any st of Rnd 4 with a standing dc. All sts in this row are made in FLO:

Row 5: 2dc in same st, 3dc in next 11 sts. [36dc]

Fasten off **Colour 39**.

Join **Colour 42** in any st of Rnd 4 with a standing dc. In this rnd, sts that fall below frill are made in BLO:

Rnd 6: (2dc in next 2 sts, dc in next 2 sts) 10 times, dc in last 3 sts, slst to close rnd. [64dc]

Fasten off **Colour 42**.

SQUARE

With frill of jellyfish pointing downwards, join **Colour 31** with a standing tr, in sixteenth dc from start of frill.

Rnd 7: (ch2, tr) in same st, *tr in next st, dc in next 2 sts, hdc in next 2 sts, sc in next 5 sts, hdc in next 2 sts, dc in next 2 sts, tr in next st, (tr, ch2, tr) in next st**, rep from * to ** 3 times omitting (tr, ch2, tr) in last rep, slst to close rnd. [68, 4ch-2]

Rnd 8: slst in ch-2-sp, ch3, (dc, ch2, 2dc) in ch-2-sp, *dc in next 17 sts, (2dc, ch2, 2dc) in ch-2-sp**, rep from * to ** 3 times omitting (2dc, ch2, 2dc) in last rep, slst to close rnd. [84dc, 4ch-2]

Rnd 9: ch3, dc in next st, *(2dc, ch3, 2dc) in ch-2-sp, dc in next 21 sts**, rep from * to ** 3 times omitting last 2dc in last rep, slst in third ch of initial ch3 to close. [100dc, 4ch-3]

Rnd 10: ch3, dc in next 3 sts, *(2dc, ch3, 2dc) in ch-3-sp, dc in next 25 sts**, rep from * to ** 3 times omitting last 4dc in last rep. [116dc, 4ch-3]

Fasten off **Colour 31**.

TENTACLE 1

With **Colour 48**, ch12.

Row 1: sc in second ch from hook, sc in next st, 2sc in next 2 sts, sk 2 sts, sc in next st, sk st, sc in next 3 sts. [10sc]

Fasten off **Colour 48**. Rep to make a total of 4 tentacles.

TENTACLE 2

With **Colour 42**, ch10.

Row 1: slst in second ch from hook, slst in each ch to end of row. [9slst]

Fasten off **Colour 42**. Rep to make a total of 3 tentacles.

FINISHING

Arrange tentacles under jellyfish's frill, alternating between tentacle 1 and 2 as shown. Turn some tentacles over so that they curve in different directions. Stitch the top of each tentacle in place.

Embroider eyes on outer edge of Rnd 2 of jellyfish with **Colour 2**, approx 7 sts apart.

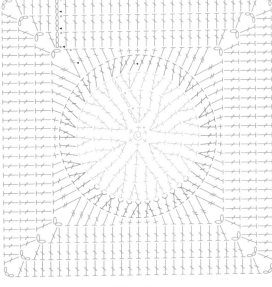

48	
39	
42	
31	
2	

SQUARE CHART

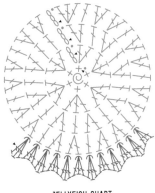

JELLYFISH CHART

TENTACLE 1 CHART

TENTACLE 2 CHART

SQUARE CHART

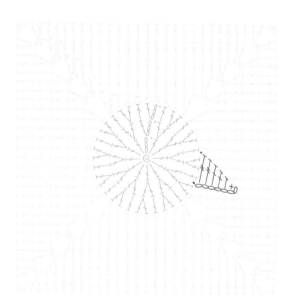

UPPER TAIL CHART

SQUARE

With a 2.75mm hook and **Colour 35**, make a magic ring.

Rnd 1: ch3, 11dc in ring, slst to close rnd. [12dc]

Rnd 2: ch3, dc in same st, 2dc in each st to end of rnd, slst to close rnd. [24dc]

Rnd 3: ch3, dc in same st, dc in next st, *2dc in next st, dc in next st**, rep from * to ** to end of rnd, slst to close rnd. [36dc]

Fasten off **Colour 35**.

Join **Colour 34** in any st of Rnd 3. All sts in this rnd are made in BLO:

Rnd 4: ch3, dc in same st, ch2, 2dc in next st, hdc in next 2 sts, sc in next 3 sts, hdc in next 2 sts, *2dc in next st, ch2, 2dc in next st, hdc in next 2 sts, sc in next 3 sts, hdc in next 2 st**, rep from * to ** twice, slst in third ch of starting ch, slst in next st, slst in ch-2-sp. [16dc, 16hdc, 12sc, 4ch-2]

Rnd 5: (ch3, dc, ch2, 2dc) in ch-2-sp, 1dc in each st to next ch-2-sp, *(2dc, ch2, 2dc) in next ch-2-sp, dc in each st to next ch-2-sp**, rep from * to ** twice ending last rep at initial ch3, slst in third ch of starting ch, slst in next st, slst in ch-2-sp. [60dc, 4ch-2]

Rnds 6-8: Rep Rnd 5. [108dc, 4ch-2]

Fasten off **Colour 34**.

Join **Colour 3** in any ch-2-sp of Rnd 8.

Rnd 9: ch, (sc, ch, sc) in ch-2-sp, *sc in each st to next ch-2-sp, (sc, ch, sc) in ch-2-sp**, rep from * to ** to end of rnd, slst to close rnd. [116sc, 4ch-1]

Fasten off **Colour 3**.

UPPER TAIL

Join **Colour 35** to right-hand lower quarter of body in st shown on chart.

Row 1: ch7, sc in second ch from hook, hdc in next st, dc in next 2 sts, tr in next 2 sts, sk 3 sts on main body, slst to next st on main body. [6]

Fasten off **Colour 35**.

LOWER TAIL

With **Colour 35**, ch6.

Row 1: sc in second ch from hook, hdc, dc in next 2 sts, 6dc in last st, turn to work on other side of foundation ch, dc in next 2 sts, hdc, sc, join with slst. [14]

Fasten off **Colour 35**. Rep to make a total of 2 lower tail sections.

SPRAY

With **Colour 3**, ch3.

Row 1: sc in second ch from hook and next st, ch, turn, sc in each st to end of row, ch4, sc in second ch from hook, 3sc in next ch, sc in next ch, sc in next sc, sc, ch4, sc in second ch from hook, 3sc in next ch, sc in next st, join with slst. [12sc on top row]

Fasten off **Colour 3**.

Stitch spray above whale's body on square.

LARGE BUBBLE

With **Colour 32**, make a magic ring.

Rnd 1: ch3, 11dc in ring, slst to join. [12dc]

Fasten off **Colour 32**.

SMALL BUBBLE

With **Colour 32**, ch2.

Row 1: 6sc in second ch from hook, slst to join. [6sc]

Fasten off **Colour 32**.

FINISHING

Stitch upper and lower tail sections to end of whale's body on square as shown.

Stitch large and small bubbles onto square next to whale's head.

Embroider eye and mouth onto whale's face with **Colour 2**.

35	
34	
3	
32	
2	

LOWER TAIL CHART

LARGE BUBBLE CHART

SMALL BUBBLE CHART

SPRAY CHART

SHARK

With a 4mm hook and **Colour 1**, make a magic ring.

Rnd 1: ch3, 5dc, join and change to **Colour 4**, 6dc, change to **Colour 1**, slst in third ch of initial ch3. [12dc]

Rnd 2: ch3, dc in same st, (2dc in next st) 5 times, change to **Colour 4**, (2dc in next st) 6 times, change to **Colour 1**, slst in third ch of initial ch3. [24dc]

Rnd 3: ch3, dc in same st, dc in next st, (2dc in next st, dc in next st) 5 times, change to **Colour 4**, (2dc in next st, dc in next st) 6 times, change to **Colour 1**, slst in third ch of initial ch3. [36dc]

Rnd 4: ch, 2sc in st, sc in next 2 sts, (2sc in next st, sc in next 2 sts) 5 times, change to **Colour 4**, (2sc in next st, sc in next 2 sts) 6 times. [48sc]

All sts in this rnd are made in FL of Rnd 4 sts:

Rnd 5: slst in next st, ch6, slst in second ch from hook, sc in next ch, hdc in next ch, dc in next ch, tr in next ch, sk next 2 sts, slst in next 20 sts, ch6, slst in second ch from hook, sc in next ch, hdc in next ch, dc in next ch, tr in next ch, sk next 2 sts, slst in next 12 sts, ch4, slst in second ch from hook, sc in next ch, hdc in next ch, slst in next 11 sts. [2tr, 2dc, 3hdc, 3sc, 44slst]

Fasten off **Colours 1** and **4**.

Embroider eyes, mouth and gills onto shark with **Colour 2**.

SQUARE

Join **Colour 33** in BL of 31st st made in Rnd 4 of shark with a standing tr. All sts in this rnd are made in BL of Rnd 4 sts:

Rnd 6: tr in same st, ch2, 2tr in next st, dc in next st, hdc in next 2 sts, sc in next 4 sts, hdc in next 2 sts, dc in next st, *2tr in next st, ch2, 2tr in next st, dc in next st, hdc in next 2 sts, sc in next 4 sts, hdc in next 2 sts, dc in next st**, rep from * to ** twice, slst to close rnd. [16tr, 8dc, 16hdc, 16sc, 4ch-2]

Rnd 7: slst in next st, slst in next ch-2-sp, ch3, (dc, ch2, 2dc) in same ch-2-sp, dc in next 14 sts, *(2dc, ch2, 2dc) in next ch-2-sp, dc in next 14 sts**, rep from * to ** twice, slst in third ch of initial ch3. [72dc, 4ch-2]

Rnd 8: slst in next st, slst in next ch-2-sp, ch3, (dc, ch2, 2dc) in same ch-2-sp, dc in next 18 sts, *(2dc, ch2, 2dc) in next ch-2-sp, dc in next 18 sts,** rep from * to ** twice, slst in third ch of initial ch3. [88dc, 4ch-2]

Rnd 9: slst in next st, slst in next ch-2-sp, ch, *(sc, ch2, sc) in ch-2-sp, sc in next 22 sts**, rep from * to ** 3 times. [96sc, 4ch-2]

Fasten off **Colour 33**.

Join **Colour 1** in any ch-2-sp of Rnd 9.

Rnd 10: ch, *(sc, ch2, sc) in next ch-2-sp, sc in next 24 sts,**, rep from * to ** 3 times. [104sc, 4ch-2]

Fasten off **Colour 1**.

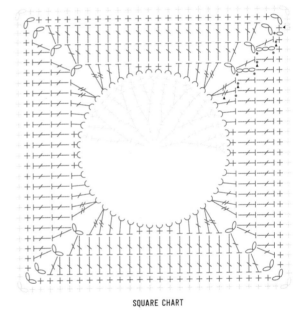

SQUARE CHART

1	
4	
33	
2	

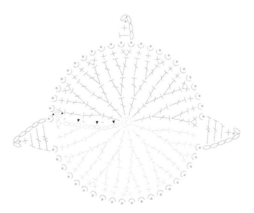

SHARK CHART

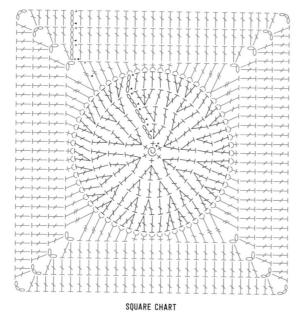

SQUARE CHART

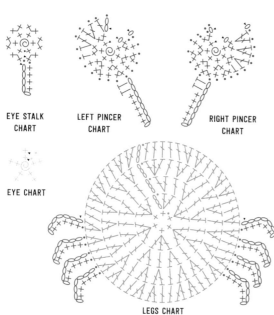

EYE STALK CHART

LEFT PINCER CHART

RIGHT PINCER CHART

EYE CHART

LEGS CHART

13
32
1
2

SQUARE

With a 2.75mm hook and **Colour 13**, make a magic ring.

Rnd 1: 6sc, slst to close rnd. [6sc]

Rnd 2: ch3, 3dc in each of next 5 sts, 2dc in last st, slst to close rnd. [18dc]

Rnd 3: ch3, dc in next st, (dc in next st, 2dc in next st) 8 times, slst to close rnd. [26dc]

Rnd 4: ch3, (2dc in next st, 2dc in next st, dc in next st) 8 times, 3dc in last st, slst in third ch of initial ch3 to close rnd. [44dc]

Rnd 5: ch3, (2dc in next 2 sts, dc in next 2 sts) 10 times, dc in last 3 sts, slst to close rnd. [64dc]

Fasten off **Colour 13**.

Join **Colour 32** in any st of Rnd 5 with a standing tr. All sts in this rnd are made in BLO:

Rnd 6: (ch2, tr) in same st, *tr in next st, dc in next 2 sts, hdc in next 2 sts, sc in next 5 sts, hdc in next 2 sts, dc in next 2 sts, tr in next st, (tr, ch2, tr) in next st**, rep from * to ** 3 times omitting (tr, ch2, tr) in last rep, slst to close rnd. [68, 4ch-2]

Rnd 7: slst in ch-2-sp, ch3, (dc, ch2, 2dc) in ch-2-sp, *dc in next 17 sts, (2dc, ch2, 2dc) in ch-2-sp**, rep from * to ** 3 times omitting (2dc, ch2, 2dc) in last rep, slst to close rnd. [84dc, 4ch-2]

Rnd 8: ch3, dc in next st, *(2dc, ch3, 2dc) in ch-2-sp, dc in next 21 sts**, rep from * to ** 3 times omitting last 2dc in last rep, slst to close rnd. [100dc, 4ch-3]

Rnd 9: ch3, dc in next 3 sts, *(2dc, ch3, 2dc) in ch-3-sp, dc in next 25 sts**, rep from * to ** 3 times omitting last 4dc in last rep, slst to close rnd. [116dc, 4ch-3]

Fasten off **Colour 32**.

RIGHT PINCER

With **Colour 13**, make a magic ring.

Row 1: 6sc in ring. [6sc]

Row 2: ch, turn, 2sc in each st. [12sc]

Row 3: ch, turn, slst in next 2 sts, (sc in next st, 2sc in next st) 3 times, hdc in next st, (hdc, dc) in next st, 2dc in next 2 sts. [18]

Row 4: ch, turn, slst in next 11 sts, ch8, turn, sk 1 ch, sc in next 5 ch, hdc in last 2 ch, slst in next st at base of ch, slst in next 7 sts. [5sc, 2hdc, 19slst]

Fasten off **Colour 13**.

LEFT PINCER

With **Colour 13**, make a magic ring.

Rnds 1-2: Rep Rnds 1-2 of Right Pincer. [12sc]

Rnd 3: ch2, turn, dc in same st, 2dc in next st, (dc, hdc) in next st, hdc in next st, (sc in next st, 2sc in next st) 3 times, sc in next st, slst in last st. [18]

Rnd 4: ch, turn, slst in next 6 sts, ch8, turn, sk 1 st, sc in next 5 sts, hdc in last 2 sts, slst in next st at base of ch, slst in next 11 sts. [5sc, 2hdc, 18hdc]

Fasten off **Colour 13**.

LEGS

Join **Colour 13** on outer edge of Rnd 5 of square, halfway up side of circle, with a slst.

Rnd 1: *ch7, turn, sk st, sc in next 2 sts, sk st, sc in next 3 sts, slst in next st of Rnd 5 to secure leg, slst in next st**, rep from * to ** 3 times, until you have 4 legs. [5sc per leg]

Fasten off **Colour 13**.

Join **Colour 13** on outer edge of Rnd 5 of square, halfway up opposite side of circle, with a slst. Rep Rnd 1 to create another 4 legs.

EYE STALKS

With **Colour 13**, make a magic ring.

Rnd 1: 6sc in ring. [6sc]

Rnd 2: 2sc in each st to end of rnd, slst to close rnd. [12sc]

Rnd 3: ch5, turn, sk st, sc in next 4 sts, slst to close rnd. [16sc]

Fasten off **Colour 13**. Rep to make a total of 2 eye stalks.

EYES

With **Colour 1**, make a magic ring.

Rnd 1: 5sc, slst to close rnd. [5sc]

Rnd 2: sc in each st to end of rnd, slst to close rnd. [5sc]

Fasten off **Colour 1**. Rep to make a total of 2 eyes.

Embroider eye detail with **Colour 2**.

FINISHING

Stitch left and right pincers in place, along outer edge of Rnd 4 of square.

Stitch eyes onto centre of eye stalks and stitch eye stalks in place along outer edge of Rnd 4 of square.

Embroider mouth under eye stalks with **Colour 1**.

SQUARE

With a 4mm hook and **Colour 28**, ch4, slst to make ring.

Rnd 1: ch3, dc in same st, ch, (2dc, ch) 5 times, slst to close rnd. [6 sets of 2dc, 6ch-1]

Fasten off **Colour 28**.

Join **Colour 27** in any ch-1-sp of Rnd 1.

Rnd 2: ch3, 2dc in same ch-1-sp, ch, (3dc in next ch-1-sp, ch) 5 times, slst to close rnd. [6 sets of 3dc, 6ch-1-sp]

Fasten off **Colour 27**.

Join **Colour 28** in initial ch3 of first set of 3dc in Rnd 2.

Rnd 3: ch, sc in same st, sc in next 2 sts, working over ch in Rnd 2, work 2dc in second group of 2dc in Rnd 1 directly below, (sc in next 3 sts from Rnd 2, working over ch in Rnd 2, work 2dc in second group of 2dc in Rnd 1 directly below) 5 times, slst to close rnd. [18sc, 12dc]

Fasten off **Colour 28**.

Join **Colour 27** in any st of Rnd 3.

Rnd 4: ch, 2sc in first st, sc in next 4 sts, (2sc in next st, sc in next 4 sts) 5 times, slst to close rnd. [36sc]

Fasten off **Colour 27**.

Join **Colour 22** in any st of Rnd 4. All sts in this rnd are made in BLO:

Rnd 5: ch3, dc in same st, ch2, 2dc in next st, hdc in next 2 sts, sc in next 3 sts, hdc in next 2 sts, *2dc in next st, ch2, 2dc in next st, hdc in next 2 sts, sc in next 3 sts, hdc in next 2 sts**, rep from * to ** twice, slst into third ch of initial ch3, slst in next st, slst in ch-2-sp. [16dc, 16hdc, 12sc, 4ch-2]

Rnd 6: (ch3, dc, ch2, 2dc) in ch-2-sp, dc in each st to next ch-2-sp, *(2dc, ch2, 2dc) in next ch-2-sp, dc in each st to next ch-2-sp**, rep from * to ** twice ending last rep at initial ch3, slst in third ch of initial ch3, slst in next st, slst in ch-2-sp. [60dc, 4ch-2]

Rnd 7: Rep Rnd 6. [76dc, 4ch-2]

Fasten off **Colour 22**.

Join **Colour 32** in any corner sp of Rnd 7.

Rnd 8: Rep Rnd 6. [92dc, 4ch-2]

Rnd 9: ch, *(sc, ch, sc) in corner sp, sc in each st to next corner sp**, rep from * to ** to end, slst in first sc. [100sc, 4ch-1]

Fasten off **Colour 32**.

HEAD

Join **Colour 28** in bottom right corner of square as shown.

Row 1: sc in next 5 sts, ch, turn. [5sc]

Row 2: sc in each st to end of row, ch, turn. [5sc]

Row 3: sc, hdc, dc, hdc, sc. [5]

Fasten off **Colour 28**.

LEGS AND TAIL

Join **Colour 28** to square, 5 sts from base of terrapin's head.

Rnd 1: *ch4, hdc in second ch from hook, hdc in next ch, join in next st with a slst, fasten off **Colour 28****, rep from * to **, sk 4 sts, rejoin **Colour 28**, rep from * to **, sk 4 sts, rejoin **Colour 28**, ch4, sc in second ch from hook, sc in next 2 ch, slst to next st, fasten off **Colour 28**, sk 4 sts, rejoin **Colour 28**, rep from * to **, sk 4 sts, rejoin **Colour 28**, rep from * to **. [2hdc per leg, 3sc for tail]

Fasten off **Colour 28**.

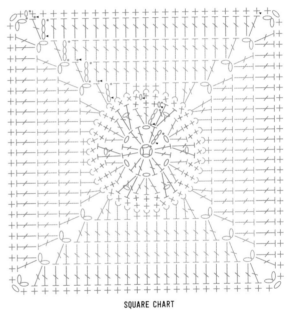

SQUARE CHART

28	▨
27	▨
22	▨
32	▨

HEAD, LEGS AND TAIL CHART

27
32
31
40
1
2
43
13

SQUARE CHART

SQUARE

With a 2.75mm hook and **Colour 27**, make a magic ring.

Rnd 1: 6sc, slst to close rnd. [6sc]

Rnd 2: ch3, 3dc in each of next 5 sts, 2dc in last st, slst to close rnd. [18dc]

Rnd 3: ch3, dc in next st, (dc in next st, 2dc in next st) 8 times, slst to close rnd. [26dc]

Rnd 4: ch3, (2dc in next st, 2dc in next st, dc in next st) 8 times, 3dc in last st, slst to close rnd. [44dc]

Fasten off **Colour 27**.

Join **Colour 32** in any st of Rnd 4 with a standing dc.

Rnd 5: (2dc in next 2 sts, dc in next 2 sts) 10 times, dc in last 3 sts, slst to close rnd. [64dc]

Fasten off **Colour 32**.

Join **Colour 31** in any st of Rnd 5 with a standing tr.

Rnd 6: (ch2, tr) in same st, *tr in next st, tr in next st, 2dc in next 2 sts, hdc in next 2 sts, sc in next 5 sts, hdc in next 2 sts, dc in next 2 sts, tr in next st, (tr, ch2, tr) in next st**, rep from * to ** 3 times omitting (tr, ch2, tr) in last rep, slst in first tr. [68, 4ch-2]

Rnd 7: slst in ch-2-sp, ch3, (dc, ch2, 2dc) in ch-2-sp, *dc in next 17 sts, (2dc, ch2, 2dc) in ch-2-sp**, rep from * to ** 3 times omitting (2dc, ch2, 2dc) in last rep, slst to close rnd. [84dc, 4ch-2]

Rnd 8: ch3, dc in next st, *(2dc, ch3, 2dc) in ch-2-sp, dc in next 21 sts**, rep from * to ** 3 times omitting last 2dc in last rep, slst to close rnd. [100dc, 4ch-3]

Rnd 9: ch3, dc in next 3 sts, *(2dc, ch3, 2dc) in ch-3-sp, dc in next 25 sts**, rep from * to ** 3 times omitting last 4dc in last rep, slst to close rnd. [116dc, 4ch-3]

Fasten off **Colour 31**.

TAIL

With **Colour 40**, ch6.

Row 1: slst in second ch from hook, sc in next 2 sts, hdc in next st, dc in next st. [5]

Row 2: ch, turn, sc in FL of next 4 sts, slst. [5]

Row 3: ch, turn, slst in BL of next st, sc in BL of next 2 sts, hdc in BL of next st, dc in BL of next st. [5]

Row 4: ch, turn, sc in FL of next 4 sts, slst. [5]

Row 5: ch, turn, slst in BL of next st, sc in BL of next 2 sts, hdc in BL of next st, dc in BL of next st. [5]

Fasten off **Colour 40**.

SIDE FIN

With **Colour 40**, ch4.

Row 1: slst in second ch from hook, sc in next st, hdc in last st. [3]

Row 2: ch, turn, sc in FL of next 2 sts, slst in FL of last st. [3]

Row 3: ch, turn, slst in BL of next st, sc in BL of next st, hdc in BL of last st. [3]

Fasten off **Colour 40**.

LIPS

With **Colour 13**, ch4.

Row 1: sk 1 st, hdc in next st, slst in next st, hdc in next st. [3]

Fasten off **Colour 13**.

EYE

With **Colour 1**, make a magic ring.

Rnd 1: 5sc, slst to close rnd. [5sc]

Fasten off **Colour 1**.

Embroider pupil in centre of eye with **Colour 2**.

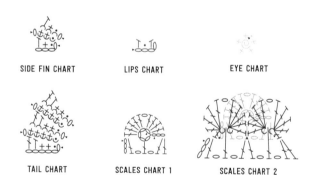

SIDE FIN CHART

LIPS CHART

EYE CHART

TAIL CHART

SCALES CHART 1

SCALES CHART 2

SCALES CHART 3

SCALES

With **Colour 43**, ch5, slst to make ring.

Rnd 1: ch3, 4dc in ring, ch, 5dc in ring. [1 scale]

This rnd sets up posts for next row of scales:

Rnd 2: ch3, dc in same st, ch, dc in ring sp from Rnd 1, ch, 2dc in third ch of ch3 from Rnd 1. [2 double posts, 1 single post]

Rnd 3: 5bpdc in st at bottom of first post on right from Rnd 1, ch, 5bpdc in back of same st, slst in top of centre single post from Rnd 1, 5bpdc in st at bottom of left hand post from Rnd 1, ch, 5bpdc in back of same st, slst to top of left hand post. [2 scales]

This rnd sets up posts for last row of scales:

Rnd 4: (ch3, dc) in same st, ch, dc in centre of scale below, ch, 2dc in single dc-post of Rnd 2, ch, dc in centre of scale below, ch, 2dc at outer edge of scale below. [3 double posts, 2 single posts]

Rnd 5: 5bpdc in st at bottom of first post on right from Rnd 4, ch, 5bpdc in back of same st, slst in top of next post from Rnd 4, (5bpdc in st at bottom of next post from Rnd 4, ch, 5bpdc in back of same st, slst to top of next post) twice. [3 scales]

Fasten off **Colour 43**.

FINISHING

Stitch scales onto square, lining up with outer edge of Rnd 4.

Stitch tail onto square, slightly tucked underneath scales.

Stitch side fin, eye and lips in place on square as shown.

SHELL

With a 4mm hook and **Colour 12**, make a magic ring.

Rnd 1: 2sc, 2hdc, 8dc in ring. [12]

All sts in this rnd are made in BLO:

Rnd 2: 2sc in next 4 sts, 2dc in next 6 sts, 2tr in next 2 sts. [8sc, 12dc, 4tr]

Rnd 3: 2tr in next 8 sts. [16tr]

Fasten off **Colour 12**.

CIRCLE

With **Colour 19**, make a magic ring.

Rnd 1: ch3, 11dc in ring, slst to join. [12dc]

Rnd 2: ch3, dc in same st, 2dc in each st to end of rnd, slst to join. [24dc]

Rnd 3: ch3, dc in same st, dc in next st, *2dc in next st, dc in next st**, rep from * to ** to end of rnd, slst to join. [36dc]

Fasten off **Colour 19**.

Place shell on top of circle, join **Colour 12** to right most st in Rnd 3 where shell fully overlaps circle, through both pieces and sc around edge to secure together.

Fasten off **Colour 12**.

SQUARE

Join **Colour 31** in any st on outer edge of joined circles. All sts in this round are made in BLO:

Rnd 4: ch3, dc in same st, ch2, 2dc in next st, hdc in next 2 sts, sc in next 3 sts, hdc in next 2 sts, *2dc in next st, ch2, 2dc in next st, hdc in next 2 sts, sc in next 3 sts, hdc in next 2 sts**, rep from * to ** twice, slst into third ch of initial ch3 to join, slst in next st, slst in ch-2-sp. [16dc, 16hdc, 12sc, 4ch-2]

Rnd 5: (ch3, dc, ch2, 2dc) in ch-2-sp, dc in each st to next ch-2-sp, *(2dc, ch2, 2dc) in next ch-2-sp, dc in each st to next ch-2-sp**, rep from * to ** twice ending last rep at initial ch3, slst into third ch of initial ch3, slst in next st, slst in ch-2-sp. [60sc, 4ch-2]

Rnds 6-7: Rep Rnd 5. [92dc, 4ch-2]

Fasten off **Colour 31**.

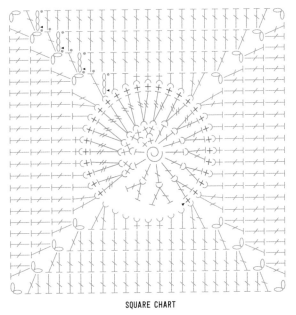

SQUARE CHART

12	
19	
31	

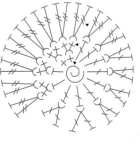

SHELL CHART

CIRCLE CHART

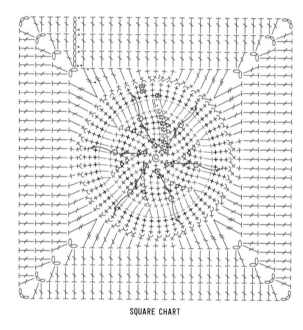

SQUARE CHART

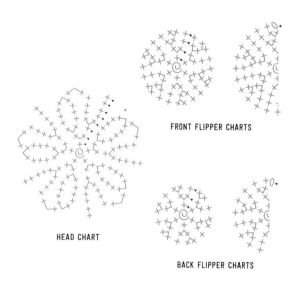

HEAD CHART

FRONT FLIPPER CHARTS

BACK FLIPPER CHARTS

■	29
■	11
■	28
■	33
■	27
■	2

SQUARE

With a 2.75mm hook and **Colour 29**, make a magic ring.

Rnd 1: 6sc, slst to close rnd. [6sc]

Rnd 2: ch, 2sc in each st to end of rnd, slst to close rnd. [12sc]

Fasten off **Colour 29**. Join **Colour 11** in any st of Rnd 2 with a standing sc.

Rnd 3: *sc in next st, 2sc in next st**, rep from * to ** to end of rnd, slst to close rnd. [18sc]

Fasten off **Colour 11**. Join **Colour 28** in any st of Rnd 3 with a standing sc.

Rnd 4: *sc in next 2 sts, 2sc in next st**, rep from * to ** to end of rnd, slst to close rnd. [24sc]

Fasten off **Colour 28**. Join **Colour 29** in any st of Rnd 4 with a standing sc.

Rnd 5: *sc in next 3 sts, 2sc in next st**, rep from * to ** to end of rnd, slst to close rnd. [30sc]

Fasten off **Colour 29**. Join **Colour 11** in any st of Rnd 5 with a standing st.

Rnd 6: *sc in next 4 sts, 2sc in next st**, rep from * to ** to end of rnd, slst to close rnd. [36sc]

Fasten off **Colour 11**. Join **Colour 29** in any st of Rnd 6 with a standing sc.

Rnd 7: *sc in next 3 sts, fptr in Rnd 2 st directly below, sk st, sc in next st, 2sc in next st**, rep from * to ** 5 times, skipping 1 sc in Rnd 2 between each fptr, slst to close rnd. [42]

Fasten off **Colour 29**. Join **Colour 28** in any st of Rnd 7 with a standing sc.

Rnd 8: *sc in next 6 sts, 2sc in next st**, rep from * to ** to end of rnd, slst to close rnd. [48sc]

Rnd 9: ch2, *hdc in next 7 sts, 2hdc in next st**, rep from * to ** to end of rnd, slst to close. [54hdc]

Fasten off **Colour 28**. Join **Colour 11** in any st of Rnd 9 with a standing sc.

Rnd 10: sc in each st to end of rnd, slst to close rnd. [54sc]

Fasten off **Colour 11**. Join **Colour 29** in Rnd 10, 1 st to right of fptr in Rnd 7, with a standing sc.

Rnd 11: *fptr in fptr directly below in Rnd 7, sk st, sc in next 8 sts**, rep from * to ** 5 times omitting last sc, slst to close rnd. [54sc]

Rnd 12: ch, sc in each st to end of rnd, slst to close rnd. [54sc]

Fasten off **Colour 29**. Join **Colour 33** in BL of any st of Rnd 12 with a standing sc. All sts in this rnd are made in BLO:

Rnd 13: *2sc in next st, sc in next 5 sts**, rep from * to ** 8 times, work 1 more sc in last st, slst to close rnd. [64sc]

Fasten off and rejoin **Colour 33** in any st of Rnd 13 with a standing tr.

Rnd 14: (ch2, tr) in same st, *tr in next st, dc in next 2 sts, hdc in next 2 sts, sc in next 5 sts, hdc in next 2 sts, dc in next 2 sts, tr in next st, (tr, ch2, tr) in next st**, rep from * to ** 3 times omitting (tr, ch2, tr) in last rep, slst to close rnd. [68, 4ch-2]

Rnd 15: slst in ch-2-sp, ch3, (dc, ch2, 2dc) in ch-2-sp, *dc in next 17 sts, (2dc, ch2, 2dc) in ch-2-sp**, rep from * to ** 3 times omitting (2dc, ch2, 2dc) in last rep, slst to close rnd. [84dc 4ch-2]

Rnd 16: ch3, dc in next st, *(2dc, ch3, 2dc) in ch-2-sp, dc in next 21 sts**, rep from * to ** 3 times omitting last 2dc in last rep, slst to close rnd. [100dc, 4ch-3]

Rnd 17: ch3, dc in next 3 sts, *(2dc, ch3, 2dc) in ch-3-sp, dc in next 25 sts**, rep from * to ** 3 times omitting last 4dc in last rep, slst to close rnd. [116dc, 4ch-3]

Fasten off **Colour 33**.

HEAD

With **Colour 27**, make a magic ring.

Rnd 1: 5sc in ring. [5sc]

Rnd 2: 2sc in each st to end. [10sc]

Rnd 3: *sc in next st, 2sc in next st**, rep from * to ** to end. [15sc]

Rnd 4: *2sc in next st, sc in next 2 sts**, rep from * to ** to end. [20]

Rnds 5-6: sc in each st to end. [20sc]

Rnd 7: *sc in next 2 sts, sc2tog**, rep from * to ** to end. [15]

Rnd 8: *sc2tog, sc in next st**, rep from * to ** to end, slst to join. [10sc]

Fasten off **Colour 27**.

Stuff head lightly, and stitch eye details with **Colour 2**. Attach head to one side of turtle's shell.

FRONT FLIPPERS

With **Colour 27**, make a magic ring.

Rnd 1: 6sc in ring. [6sc]

Rnd 2: 2sc in each st to end. [12sc]

Rnd 3: *sc in next st, 2sc in next st**, rep from * to ** to end. [18sc]

Rnd 4: *sc in next st, 2sc in next st, sc in next st**, rep from * to ** to end of rnd, slst to close rnd. [24sc]

Rnd 5: Fold circle in half, ch, sc in each st around curved edge. [12sc]

Fasten off **Colour 27**. Rep to make a total of 2 front flippers.

Stitch front flippers onto either side of turtle's head.

BACK FLIPPERS

With **Colour 27**, make a magic ring.

Rnds 1-3: Rep Rnds 1-3 of Front Flippers. [18sc]

Rnd 4: Rep Rnd 5 of Front Flippers. [9sc]

Fasten off **Colour 27**. Rep to make a total of 2 back flippers.

Stitch back flippers opposite turtle's head, approx 7 sts apart.

SQUARE

With a 4mm hook and **Colour 18**, ch4.

Rnd 1: 19dc in fourth ch from hook, slst to close rnd. [20dc]

Fasten off **Colour 18**.

Join **Colour 32** in BL of any st in Rnd 1. All sts in this rnd are worked in BLO:

Rnd 2: (ch3, 2dc, ch2, 3dc) in same st, ch3, sk 4 sts, *(3dc, ch2, 3dc) in next st, ch3, sk 4 sts**, rep from * to ** twice, slst to close rnd. [4 6-dc corner groups]

Fasten off and rejoin **Colour 32** in any corner sp of Rnd 2.

Rnd 3: (ch3, 2dc, ch2, 3dc) in ch-2-sp, 3dc in next sp, *(3dc, ch2, 3dc) in ch-2-sp, 3dc in next sp**, rep from * to ** twice, slst in third ch of initial ch3. [3 3dc-groups per side]

Rnd 4: slst in next 2 sts, (ch3, 2dc, ch2, 3dc) in corner sp, 3dc between each group of 3dc in previous rnd to corner sp, *(3dc, ch2, 3dc) in corner sp, 3dc between each group of 3dc in previous rnd to corner sp**, rep from * to ** to end, slst in third ch of initial ch3. [4 3dc-groups per side]

Rnds 5-7: Rep Rnd 4. [7 3dc-groups per side]

Fasten off **Colour 32**.

Join **Colour 18** in any corner sp of Rnd 7.

Rnd 8: ch, (sc, ch, sc) in corner sp, sc in each st to next corner sp**, rep from * to ** 3 times, slst to close rnd. [92sc, 4ch-1]

Fasten off **Colour 18**.

STARFISH

Join **Colour 18** in any dc of Rnd 1 of square.

Rnd 1: *ch6, sc in second ch from hook, hdc, dc, 2tr, sk next 3 sts, slst in next st**, rep from * to ** 4 times. [5, 6ch per point]

Fasten off **Colour 18**.

Join **Colour 12** in any st of Rnd 1.

Rnd 2: sc in each st and ch to end of rnd, slst to join. [55sc]

Fasten off **Colour 12**.

12	■
32	■
18	■

SQUARE CHART

STARFISH CHART

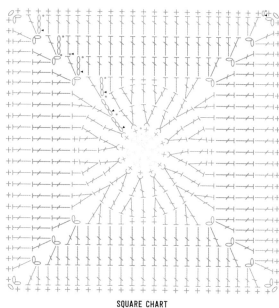

SQUARE CHART

HAT BASE CHART

BOW CHART

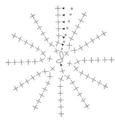

HAT CHART

HAT

With a 4mm hook and **Colour 9**, ch2.

Rnd 1: 6sc in second ch from hook, slst to close rnd. [6sc]

Rnd 2: 2sc in each st to end of rnd, slst to close rnd. [12sc]

Rnd 3: sc in each st to end of rnd, slst to close rnd. [12sc]

Rnds 4-6: Rep Rnd 3. [12sc]

Fasten off **Colour 9**.

Join **Colour 48** in any st of Rnd 6.

Rnd 7: Rep Rnd 3. [12sc]

Fasten off **Colour 48**.

SQUARE

Join **Colour 34** in any st of Rnd 7 of hat. All sts in this rnd are made in BLO:

Rnd 8: ch3, dc in same st, 2dc in each st to end of rnd, slst to close rnd. [24dc]

Rnd 9: 3ch, dc in same st, dc in next st, *2dc in next st, dc in next st**, rep from * to ** to end of rnd, slst to close rnd. [36dc]

Rnd 10: ch3, dc in same st, ch2, 2dc in next st, hdc in next 2 sts, sc in next 3 sts, hdc in next 2 sts, *2dc in next st, ch2, 2dc in next st, hdc in next 2 sts, sc in next 3 sts, hdc in next 2 sts**, rep from * to ** twice, slst into third ch of starting ch to join, slst into ch-2-sp. [16dc, 16hdc, 12sc, 4ch-2]

Fasten off **Colour 34**.

Join **Colour 48** in any ch-2-sp of Rnd 10.

Rnd 11: (ch3, dc, ch2, 2dc) in ch-2-sp, dc in each st to next ch-2-sp, *(2dc, ch2, 2dc) in next ch-2-sp, dc in each st to next ch-2-sp**, rep from * to ** twice ending last rep at initial ch3, slst in third ch of initial ch3, slst in next st, slst in ch-2-sp. [60dc, 4ch-2]

Rnd 12: Rep Rnd 11. [76dc, 4ch-2]

Fasten off **Colour 48**.

Join **Colour 34** in any ch-2-sp of Rnd 12.

Rnd 13: Rep Rnd 11 omitting last 2slst. [92dc, 4ch-2]

Fasten off **Colour 34**.

Join **Colour 9** in any ch-2-sp of Rnd 13.

Rnd 14: ch, *(sc, ch, sc) in ch-2-sp, sc in each st to next ch-2-sp**, rep from * to ** 3 times, slst to close rnd. [100sc, 4ch-1]

Fasten off **Colour 9**.

HAT BASE

Join **Colour 9** in FL of any st in Rnd 7 of hat.

Rnd 1: 2dc in each st to end of rnd, slst to close rnd. [24dc]

Fasten off **Colour 9**.

BOW

With **Colour 48**, ch7.

Row 1: sc in second ch from hook, sc in next 5 sts. [6sc]

Fasten off **Colour 48**.

Wrap a long strand of **Colour 48** around centre of bow, pull tight and secure in place.

Stitch bow onto hat as shown.

9

48

34

SUN

With a 4mm hook and **Colour 21**, make a magic ring.

Rnd 1: ch2, 9hdc in ring, slst in second ch of initial ch2. [10hdc]

Rnd 2: ch2, hdc in same st, 2hdc in each st to end of rnd, slst in second ch of initial ch2. [20hdc]

Rnd 3: ch2, hdc in same st, hdc in next st, *2hdc in next st, hdc in next st**, rep from * to ** 8 times, slst in second ch of initial ch2. [30hdc]

Rnd 4: ch2, hdc in same st, hdc in next 2 sts, *2hdc in next st, hdc in next 2 sts**, rep from * to ** 8 times, slst in second ch of initial ch2. [40hdc]

Rnd 5: ch2, hdc in same st, hdc in next 3 sts, *2hdc in next st, hdc in next 3 sts**, rep from * to ** 8 times. [50hdc]

Fasten off **Colour 21**.

Join **Colour 17** in FL of any Rnd 5 st. All sts in this rnd are made in FL of Rnd 5 sts:

Rnd 6: sc in st, (hdc, dc) in next st, ch2, (dc, hdc) in next st, sc in next st, slst in next st, *sc in next st, (hdc, dc) in next st, ch2, (dc, hdc) in next st, sc in next st, slst in next st**, rep from * to ** 8 times, slst in initial sc. [20dc, 20hdc, 20sc, 10slst, 10ch-2]

Rnd 7: slst in next 2 sts, (slst, ch, slst) in next ch-2-sp, slst in next 3 sts, slst over Rnd 6 slst and in FL of Rnd 5 st, *slst in next 3 sts, (slst, ch, slst) in next ch-2-sp, slst in next 3 sts, slst over Rnd 6 slst and in FL of Rnd 5 st**, rep from * to ** 8 times. [90slst, 10ch]

Fasten off **Colour 17**.

SQUARE

Join **Colour 1** in BL of any st in Rnd 5 of sun with a standing dc. All sts in this rnd are made in BL of Rnd 5 sts:

Rnd 8: dc in same st, dc in next 4 sts, *2dc in next st, dc in next 4 sts**, rep from * to ** 8 times, slst in first dc. [60dc]

Fasten off **Colour 1**.

Join **Colour 31** in any st of Rnd 8 with a standing tr.

Rnd 9: tr in same st, ch2, 2tr in next st, dc in next 2 sts, hdc in next 3 sts, sc in next 3 sts, hdc in next 3 sts, dc in next 2 sts, *2tr in next st, ch2, 2tr in next st, dc in next 2 sts, hdc in next 3 sts, sc in next 3 sts, hdc in next 3 sts, dc in next 2 sts**, rep from * to ** twice, slst in initial tr. [16tr, 16dc, 24hdc, 12sc, 4ch-2]

Rnd 10: slst in next st, slst in ch-2-sp, ch3, (dc, ch2, 2dc) in same ch-2-sp, dc in next 17 sts, *(2dc, ch2, 2dc) in ch-2-sp, dc in next 17 sts**, rep from * to ** twice, slst in third ch of initial ch3. [84dc, 4ch-2]

Fasten off **Colour 31**.

Join **Colour 39** in any ch-2-sp of Rnd 10. All sts in this rnd are made in BLO:

Rnd 11: ch, *(sc, ch2, sc) in ch-2-sp, sc in next 21 sts**, rep from * to ** 3 times. [92sc, 4ch-2]

Fasten off **Colour 39**.

Join **Colour 45** in any ch-2-sp of Rnd 11. All sts in this rnd are made in BLO:

Rnd 12: ch, *(sc, ch2, sc) in ch-2-sp, sc in next 23 sts**, rep from * to ** 3 times. [100sc, 4ch-2]

Fasten off **Colour 45**.

21	
17	
1	
31	
39	
45	

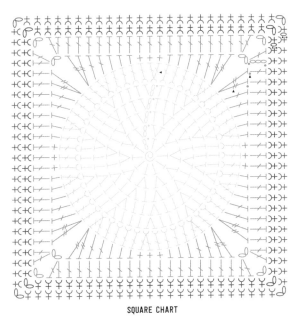

SQUARE CHART

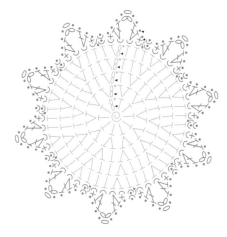

SUN CHART

PALM TREE

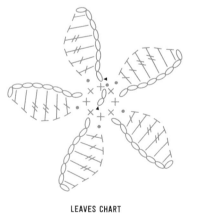

- 24
- 32
- 3
- 11

SQUARE CHART

LEAVES CHART

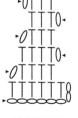

TRUNK CHART

LEAVES

With a 4mm hook and **Colour 24**, ch2.

Rnd 1: 8sc in second ch from hook, slst to close rnd. [8sc]

Rnd 2: *ch8, hdc in second ch from hook, hdc, tr in next 2 sts, dc in next 2 sts, slst in next sc**, rep from * to ** 4 times, slst to close rnd. [5 leaves]

Fasten off and rejoin **Colour 24** in BL of any st in Rnd 1. This rnd is worked on WS:

Rnd 3: *ch3, sk st, slst in next st**, rep from * to ** 3 times. [4 loops]

Fasten off **Colour 24**.

SQUARE

Join **Colour 32** in any loop in Rnd 3 of leaves.

Rnd 1: ch3, 5dc in loop, (6dc in next loop) 3 times, slst in third ch of initial ch3. [24dc]

Rnd 2: ch3, dc in same st, dc in next st, *2dc in next, dc in next st**, rep from * to ** to end of rnd. [36dc]

Rnd 3: ch3, dc in same st, ch2, 2dc in next st, hdc in next 2 sts, sc in next 3 sts, hdc in next 2 sts, *2dc in next st, ch2, 2dc in next st, hdc in next 2 sts, sc in next 3 sts, hdc in next 2 sts**, rep from * to ** twice, slst in third ch of initial ch3, slst in next st, slst in ch-2-sp. [16dc, 16hdc, 12sc, 4ch-2]

Rnd 4: (ch3, dc, ch2, 2dc, dc) in ch-2-sp, dc in each st to next ch-2-sp, *(2dc, ch2, 2dc) in next ch-2-sp, dc in each st to next ch-2-sp**, rep from * to ** twice, slst in third ch of initial ch3, slst in next st, slst in ch-2-sp. [60dc, 4ch-2]

Rnd 5: Rep Rnd 4. [76dc, 4ch-2]

Fasten off **Colour 32**.

Join **Colour 3** in any ch-2-sp of Rnd 5.

Rnd 6: rep Rnd 4. [92dc, 4ch-2]

Fasten off **Colour 3**.

Secure palm leaves onto square by stitching tips in place.

TRUNK

With **Colour 11**, ch8.

Row 1: hdc in third ch from hook, hdc in each ch to end of row. [6hdc]

Row 2: ch, turn, sk first st, hdc in next 4 sts. [4hdc]

Row 3: ch, turn, hdc in next 4 sts. [4hdc]

Row 4: ch, turn, sk first st, hdc in next 3 sts. [3hdc]

Row 5: ch, turn, hdc in next 3 sts. [3hdc]

Row 6: Rep Row 5. [3hdc]

Fasten off **Colour 11**.

Sew trunk onto bottom of square as shown.

SQUARE

With a 4mm hook and **Colour 9**, make a magic ring.

Rnd 1: ch3, 2dc in ring, ch2, *3dc in ring, ch2**, rep from * to ** twice, join to top of ch3. [12dc, 4ch-2]

Rnd 2: ch3, *dc in each st to ch-2-sp, (2dc, ch2, 2dc) in ch-2-sp**, rep from * to ** 3 times, join to top of ch3. [28dc, 4ch-2]

Rnds 3-6: ch3, *dc in each st to ch-2-sp, (2dc, ch2, 2dc) in ch-2-sp**, rep from * to ** 3 times, dc in rem sts to complete rnd, join to top of ch3. [92dc, 4ch-2]

Fasten off **Colour 9**.

Join **Colour 21** in any st of Rnd 6.

Rnd 7: ch, sc in each st to ch-2-sp, (sc, ch, sc) in ch-2-sp, rep from * to ** 3 times, slst to close rnd. [100sc, 4ch-2]

Fasten off **Colour 21**.

SANDCASTLE

With **Colour 22**, ch17.

Row 1: sc in second ch from hook, sc in each ch to end, ch, turn. [16sc]

Rows 2-10: sc in each st to end of row, ch, turn. [16sc]

Row 11: sc in next 4 sts, ch, turn. [4sc]

Rows 12-13: rep Row 11.

Fasten off **Colour 22**.

Join **Colour 21** in last st of Row 13.

Rows 14-15: ch2, join to top of Row 13 by working sc in next 4 sts, ch3, turn, sc in second ch from hook, sc in each st to end of row, ch, turn. [8sc]

Row 16: sc in each st to end of row. [8sc]

Fasten off **Colour 21**.

Join **Colour 22** to fourth st from end on other side of Row 10.

Rows 17-22: rep Rows 11-16. [8sc]

Fasten off and rejoin **Colour 22** in seventh st from start of Row 10.

Row 23: sc in next 4 sts, ch, turn. [4sc]

Rows 24-25: Rep Row 23. [4sc]

Fasten off **Colour 22**.

Stitch castle to centre of square.

FLAG

With **Colour 3**, ch5.

Fasten off **Colour 3**.

Join **Colour 18** in end of ch.

Row 1: sc in next 3 ch, ch, turn, sc in next 3 sts. [3sc]

Fasten off **Colour 18**.

Attach flag to top of sandcastle.

DOOR

With **Colour 21**, ch5.

Row 1: sc in second ch from hook, sc in next 3 ch, ch, turn. [4sc]

Row 2: sc in each st to end, ch, turn. [4sc]

Row 3: Rep Row 2. [4sc]

Fasten off **Colour 21**.

Attach door to bottom of sandcastle.

22	
21	
9	
3	
18	

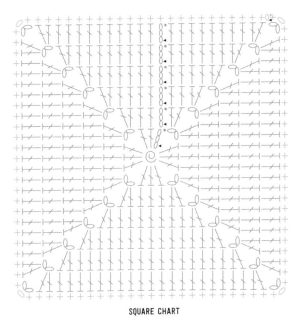

SQUARE CHART

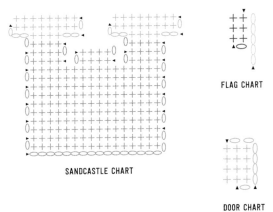

SANDCASTLE CHART

FLAG CHART

DOOR CHART

SQUARE

With a 4mm hook and **Colour 31**, make a magic ring.

Rnd 1: ch3, 2dc in ring, ch2, *3dc in ring, ch2**, rep from * to ** twice, slst in third ch of initial ch3. [12dc, 4ch-2]

Rnd 2: ch3, *dc in each st to ch-2-sp, (2dc, ch2, 2dc) in ch-2-sp**, rep from * to ** 3 times, slst in third ch of initial ch3. [28dc, 4ch-2]

Rnds 3-6: ch3, *dc in each st to ch-2-sp, (2dc, ch2, 2dc) in ch-2-sp**, rep from * to ** 3 times, dc in rem sts to complete rnd, slst in third ch of initial ch3. [92sc, 4ch-2]

Fasten off **Colour 31**.

FLIP FLOPS

With **Colour 12**, ch9.

Rnd 1: 3sc in second ch from hook, sc in next 3 ch, hdc, dc in next 2 ch, 6dc in last ch, turn to work on other side of foundation ch, dc in next 2 sts, hdc, sc in next 3 sts, join with slst. [21]

Rnd 2: ch, 2sc in next 3 sts, sc in next 7 sts, 2sc in next 4 sts, sc in next 7 sts, join with slst. [28sc]

Rnd 3: ch, sc in BL of each st to end of rnd, slst to close rnd [28sc]

Fasten off **Colour 12**. Rep to make a total of 2 flip flops.

STRINGS

With **Colour 32**, ch14.

Row 1: sc in second ch from hook, sc in next 5 ch, 3sc in next ch, sc in next 6 ch. [15sc]

Fasten off **Colour 32**. Rep to make a total of 2 strings.

Stitch strings to top of each flip flop as shown.

Attach both flip flops to centre of square.

■	12
▨	32
▨	31

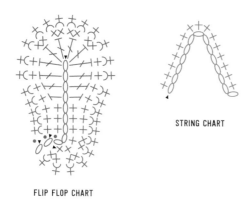

SQUARE CHART

FLIP FLOP CHART

STRING CHART

SQUARE

With a 2.75mm hook and **Colour 7**, make a magic ring.

Rnd 1: 6sc, slst to close rnd. [6sc]

Rnd 2: ch3, 3dc in each of next 5 sts, 2dc in last st, slst in third ch of initial ch3 to close rnd. [18dc]

Rnd 3: ch3, dc in next st, (dc in next st, 2dc in next st) 8 times, slst in third ch of initial ch3 to close rnd. [26dc]

Rnd 4: ch3, (2dc in next st, 2dc in next st, dc in next st) 8 times, 3dc in last st, slst to close rnd. [44dc]

Fasten off **Colour 7**.

Join **Colour 27** in any st of Rnd 4 with a standing dc. All sts in this rnd are made in BLO:

Rnd 5: (2dc in next 2 sts, dc in next 2 sts) 10 times, dc in last 3 st, slst in first dc. [64dc]

Rnd 6: ch6, tr in same st, *tr in next st, dc in next 2 sts, hdc in next 2 sts, sc in next 5 sts, hdc in next 2 sts, dc in next 2 sts, tr in next st, (tr, ch2, tr) in next st**, rep from * to ** 3 times omitting (tr, ch2, tr) in last rep, slst in fourth ch of initial ch6 to close. [68, 4ch-2]

Rnd 7: slst in ch-2-sp, ch3, (dc, ch2, 2dc) in ch-2-sp, *dc in next 17 sts, (2dc, ch2, 2dc) in ch-2-sp**, rep from * to ** 3 times omitting (2dc, ch2, 2dc) in last rep, slst to close rnd. [84dc, 4ch-2]

Rnd 8: ch3, dc in next st, *(2dc, ch3, 2dc) in ch-2-sp, dc in next 21 sts**, rep from * to ** 3 times omitting last 2dc in last rep, slst in third ch of initial ch3 to close. [100dc, 4ch-3]

Rnd 9: ch3, dc in next 3 sts, *(2dc, ch3, 2dc) in ch-3-sp, dc in next 25 sts**, rep from * to ** 3 times omitting last 4dc in last rep, slst to close rnd. [116dc, 4ch-3]

Fasten off **Colour 27**.

HEAD

With **Colour 7**, make a magic ring.

Rnd 1: 6sc, slst to close rnd. [6sc]

Rnd 2: ch3, 3dc in each of next 5 sts, 2dc in last st, slst in third ch of initial ch3 to close rnd. [18dc]

Rnd 3: ch3, dc in same st, (dc in next st, 2dc in next st) 8 times, slst to close rnd. [26dc]

Fasten off **Colour 7**.

LEGS

Join **Colour 7** to outer edge of Rnd 4 of square with a slst, lined up with a ch-sp from Rnd 6.

Rnd 1: *ch12, sc in second ch from hook, sc in next 3 sts, sk 2 sts, sc in next 5 sts, slst in next st of Rnd 4 to secure leg, slst in next 2 sts of Rnd 4**, rep from * to ** 3 times, until you have 4 legs. [9sc per leg]

Fasten off **Colour 7**.

Join **Colour 7** to outer edge of Rnd 4 of square with a slst, lined up with a ch-sp from Rnd 6 on opposite side.

Rep Rnd 1 to create another 4 legs.

Fasten off **Colour 7**.

EYES

With **Colour 1**, make a magic ring.

Rnd 1: 5sc, slst to close rnd. [5sc]

Fasten off **Colour 1**. Rep to make a total of 2 eyes.

Embroider a pupil onto each eye with **Colour 2**.

Stitch eyes onto spider's head.

FINISHING

Stitch head onto spider's body, with top of head touching outer edge of Rnd 2 of square.

Stitch a line from back of spider to top edge of square with **Colour 1**.

7	■
27	▨
1	▫
2	■

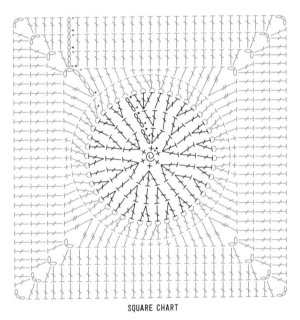

SQUARE CHART

EYE CHART

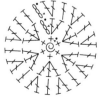

HEAD CHART

LEGS CHART

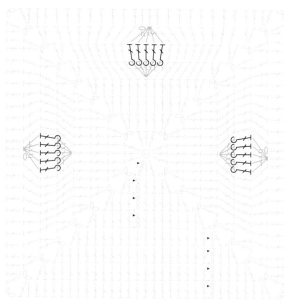

SQUARE CHART

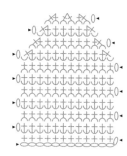

BEEHIVE CHART

WING CHART

SQUARE

With a 2.75mm hook and **Colour 3**, make a magic ring.

Rnd 1: ch3, 2dc, (ch2, 3dc) 3 times, ch2, slst in third ch of initial ch3 to close. [12dc, 4ch-2]

Rnd 2: ch3, dc in next 2 sts, *(2dc, ch2, 2dc) in ch-2-sp, dc in next 3 sts**, rep from * to ** twice, (2dc, ch2, 2dc) in ch-2-sp, slst in third ch of initial ch3 to close rnd. [28dc, 4ch-2]

Rnd 3: ch3, dc in next 4 sts, *(2dc, ch2, 2dc) in ch-2-sp, dc in next 7 sts**, rep from * to ** twice, (2dc, ch2, 2dc) in ch-2-sp, dc in last 2 sts, slst in third ch of initial ch3 to close rnd. [44dc, 4ch-2]

Rnd 4: ch3, dc in next 6 sts, *(2dc, ch2, 2dc) in ch-2-sp, dc in next 11 sts**, rep from * to ** twice, (2dc, ch2, 2dc) in ch-2-sp, dc in last 4 sts, slst to close rnd. [60dc, 4ch-2]

Fasten off and rejoin **Colour 3** in any ch-2-sp of Rnd 4 with a standing dc.

Rnd 5: (dc, ch2, 2dc) in ch-2-sp, *sk st, dc in next 6 sts, join and change to **Colour 21**, 5dc in next st, change to **Colour 3**, dc in next 6 sts, sk st, (2dc, ch2, 2dc) in ch-2-sp**, rep from * to ** twice, dc in next 15 sts, fasten off **Colour 21**, slst **Colour 3** in first st to close rnd. [82dc, 4ch-2]

Rnd 6: ch3, dc in next st, *(2dc, ch2, 2dc) in ch-2-sp, sk st, dc in next 7 sts, join and change to **Colour 2**, fpdc in next 5 sts, change to **Colour 3**, dc in next 7 sts, sk st**, rep from * to ** twice, (2dc, ch2, 2dc) in ch-2-sp, dc in next 17 sts, fasten off **Colour 2**, slst in third ch of initial ch3 to close. [92dc, 4ch-2]

Rnd 7: ch3, dc in next 3 sts, *(2dc, ch2, 2dc) in ch-2-sp, sk st, dc in next 8 sts, change to **Colour 21**, dc5tog, ch, change to **Colour 3**, dc in next 8 sts, sk st**, rep from * to ** twice, (2dc, ch2, 2dc) in ch-2-sp, dc in next 19 sts, slst in third ch of initial ch3 to close. [90dc, 3ch, 4ch-2]

Fasten off **Colour 21**.

Rnd 8: ch3, dc in next 4 sts, *(2dc, ch2, 2dc) in ch-2-sp, dc in next 10 sts, 2dc in top ch of bee, dc in next 10 sts**, rep from * to ** twice, (2dc, ch2, 2dc) in ch-2-sp, dc in next 21 sts, slst to close rnd. [109dc, 4ch-2]

Fasten off **Colour 3**.

WINGS

With **Colour 1**, make a magic ring.

Rnd 1: sc, hdc, 3dc, hdc, sc, pull tight, slst to close rnd. [7]

Fasten off **Colour 1**. Rep to make a total of 6 wings.

Stitch a wing on either side of each bee.

BEEHIVE

With **Colour 9**, ch13.

Row 1: sc in second ch from hook, sc in each st to end of row. [12sc]

Row 2: ch, turn, sc in FL of each st to end of row. [12sc]

Row 3: ch, turn, sc in BL of each st to end of row. [12sc]

Row 4: Rep Row 2. [12sc]

Row 5: Rep Row 3. [12sc]

Row 6: Rep Row 2. [12sc]

Row 7: Rep Row 3. [12sc]

Row 8: ch, turn, sc2tog in FL over next 2 sts, sc in FL of next 8 sts, sc2tog in FL over last 2 sts. [10sc]

Row 9: ch, turn, sc2tog in BL over next 2 sts, sc in BL of next 6 sts, sc2tog in BL ove next 2 sts. [8sc]

Row 10: ch, turn, sc2tog in FL over next 2 sts, sc in FL of next 4 sts, sc2tog in FL over next 2 sts. [6sc]

Row 11: ch, turn, (sc2tog in BL over next 2 sts) 3 times. [3sc]

Fasten off **Colour 9**.

Embroider door onto beehive with **Colour 10**.

Stitch beehive onto centre of square.

3
21
2
1
9
10

BUTTERFLY

With a 4mm hook and **Colour 48**, ch4.

Rnd 1: (dc ch) in fourth ch from hook, *(2dc, ch) in same st**, rep from * to ** 6 times, slst to close rnd. [18dc, 8ch-1]

Fasten off **Colour 48**.

Join **Colour 49** in any ch-1-sp of Rnd 1 with a standing dc.

Rnd 2: (ch2, 2dc) in same ch-1-sp, (2dc, ch2, 2dc) in every ch-1-sp to end, slst to close rnd. [32dc, 8 ch-2-sp]

Fasten off **Colour 49**.

Join **Colour 45** in any ch-2-sp of Rnd 2 with a standing dc.

Rnd 3: 6dc in same ch-2-sp, sk 2dc, sc in sp between 2dc-groups, *7dc in ch-2-sp, sk 2dc, sc in sp between 2dc-groups**, rep from * to ** to end of rnd, slst to close rnd. [8 7dc-groups, 8sc]

Fasten off **Colour 45**.

Join **Colour 12** in any st of Rnd 3.

Rnd 4: sc in each st to end of rnd, slst to close rnd. [64sc]

Fasten off **Colour 12**.

Fold piece in half to make butterfly shape.

With **Colour 45**, ch16. Fasten off.

With **Colour 45**, ch12. Fasten off.

Tie knot on each end of chain, pull tight and close knot.

Wrap long ch around centre of butterfly's body, catching smaller ch at top. Attach to butterfly as shown.

SQUARE

Join **Colour 44** at top right wing of butterfly with a standing dc, into sc at fold point.

Rnd 1: (2dc, ch2, 3dc) in same st, ch3, 2dc into st behind butterfly's head, ch3, (3dc, ch2, 3dc) in sc at top left wing, ch3, 2dc in sc between next 2 7dc-groups, ch3, (3dc, ch2, 3dc) in centre of bottom left 7dc-group, ch3, 2dc in sc behind tail, ch3, (3dc, ch2, 3dc) in centre of bottom right 7dc-group, ch3, 2dc in sc between 7dc-groups, ch3, join to first dc, slst in next 2 dc, slst in ch-2-sp. [32dc, 8ch-3, 4ch-2]

Rnd 2: (ch3, 2dc, ch2, 3dc) in same ch-2-sp, 3dc in each of next 2 ch-3-sp, *(3dc, ch2, 3dc) in ch-2-sp, 3dc in each of next ch-3-sp**, rep from * to ** to end of row, slst to close rnd. [16 3dc-groups]

Rnds 3–5: slst in next 2 dc, slst in ch-2-sp, (ch2, 2dc, ch2, 3dc) in ch-2-sp, 3dc between 3dc-group of previous rnd to corner, *(3dc, ch2, 3dc) in ch-2-sp, 3dc between 3dc-groups in previous rnd to corner**, rep from * to ** to end of rnd, slst in first dc. [28 3dc-groups]

Fasten off **Colour 44**.

Join **Colour 45** in any st of Rnd 5.

Rnd 6: ch, sc in each st, (sc, ch, sc) in each corner sp to complete rnd. [92sc, 4ch-2]

Fasten off **Colour 45**.

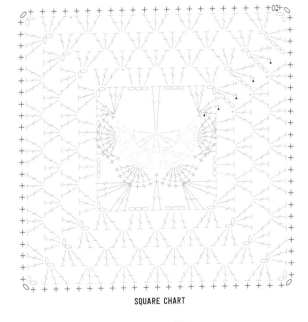

48	
49	
45	
12	
44	

SQUARE CHART

BUTTERFLY CHARTS

■	43
■	33
■	31

SQUARE

With a 4mm hook and **Colour 43**, make a magic ring,

Rnd 1: ch3, 11dc in ring. [12dc]

Fasten off **Colour 43**.

Join **Colour 33** in any st of Rnd 1. All sts in this rnd are made in BLO:

Rnd 2: ch3, dc in same st, 2dc in each st to end of rnd, slst to close rnd. [24dc]

Rnd 3: ch3, dc in same st, dc in next st, *2dc in next st, dc in next st**, rep from * to ** to end of rnd, slst to close rnd. [36dc]

Rnd 4: ch3, dc in same st, ch2, 2dc in next st, hdc in next 2 sts, sc in next 3 sts, hdc in next 2 sts, *2dc in next st, ch2, 2dc in next st, hdc in next 2 sts, sc in next 3 sts, hdc in next 2 sts**, rep from * to ** twice, , slst in third ch of initial ch3, slst in next dc, slst in ch-2-sp. [44, 4ch-2]

Rnd 5: (ch3, dc, ch2, 2dc) in ch-2-sp, dc in each st to next ch-2-sp, *(2dc, ch2, 2dc) in next ch-2-sp, dc in each st to next ch-2-sp**, rep from * to ** twice, slst in third ch of initial ch3, slst in next dc, slst in ch-2-sp. [60dc, 4ch-2]

Rnd 6: Rep Rnd 5. [76dc, 4ch-2]

Fasten off **Colour 33**.

WINGS

Join **Colour 43** in FL of Rnd 1 of square at top of rnd.

Rnd 1: sc in next 3 sts, *ch12, dc in third ch from hook, dc in next 7 ch, hdc in next 2 ch, slst to next st of Rnd 1**, rep from * to **, sc in next 4 sts, rep from * to ** twice, sc in last st. [10sts per wing]

Fasten off **Colour 43**.

BODY

With **Colour 31**, ch16.

Row 1: sc in second ch from hook, sc in next 8 sts, hdc in next 2 sts, dc in next 3 sts, 4dc in last st, turn to work on other side of foundation ch, dc in next 3 sts, hdc in next 2 sts, sc in next 9 sts, 2sc in turning ch, join. [34]

Fasten off **Colour 31**.

ANTENNAE

Join **Colour 31** on one side of head at top of dragonfly's body

Row 1: ch4, sc in second ch from hook.

Fasten off and rejoin **Colour 31** on other side of dragonfly's head. Rep Row 1 to make second antenna.

Fasten off **Colour 31**.

Sew body onto centre of square at an angle as shown.

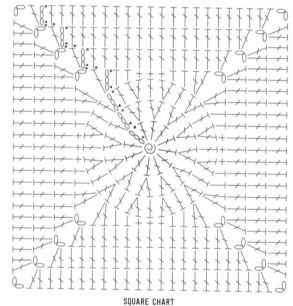

SQUARE CHART

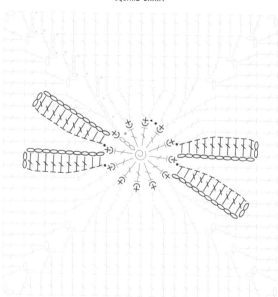

WINGS CHART

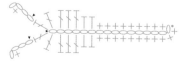

BODY AND ANTENNAE CHART

LADYBIRD

With a 2.75mm hook and **Colour 7**, make a magic ring.

Rnd 1: 6sc, slst to close rnd. [6sc]

Rnd 2: ch3, 3dc in each of next 5 sts, 2dc in last st, slst in third ch of initial ch3 to close rnd. [18dc]

Rnd 3: ch3, dc in next st, (dc in next st, 2dc in next st) 8 times, slst in third ch of initial ch3 to close rnd. [26dc]

Rnd 4: ch3, (2dc in next st, 2dc in next st, dc in next st) 8 times, 3dc in last st, slst in third ch of initial ch3 to close rnd. [44dc]

The following rows shape the ladybird's head and antennae. All sts in these rows are made in FLO:

Row 5: ch, sc in next st, hdc in next st, dc in next st, 2tr in next st, 2tr in next st, dc in next st, hdc in next st, sc in next st, slst in next st. [11]

Row 6: ch, turn, slst in next 5 sts, ch4, slst in second ch from hook, slst in next 2 sts down ch, slst in base of ch, slst in next 2 sts across top of head, ch4, slst in second ch from hook, slst in next 2 sts down ch, slst in base of ch, slst in next 5 sts. [20slst, 2ch-4]

Fasten off **Colour 7**.

SQUARE

Join **Colour 27** in BL of any st of Rnd 4 of ladybird with a standing dc. All sts in this rnd are made in BLO:

Rnd 1: (2dc in next 2 sts, dc in next 2 sts) 10 times, dc in last 3 sts, slst in third ch of initial ch3 to close rnd. [64dc]

Fasten off **Colour 27**.

With head of ladybird at top of square, join **Colour 29** in Rnd 1 with a standing tr, 2 sts to left of edge of head. This forms top left hand corner of square.

Rnd 2: (ch2, tr) in same st, *tr in next st, dc in next 2 sts, hdc in next 2 sts, sc in next 5 sts, hdc in next 2 sts, dc in next 2 sts, tr in next st, (tr, ch2, tr) in next st**, rep from * to ** 3 times omitting (tr, ch2, tr) in last rep, slst to close rnd. [68, 4ch-2]

Rnd 3: slst in ch-2-sp, ch3, (dc, ch2, 2dc) in ch-2-sp, *dc in next 17 sts, (2dc, ch2, 2dc) in ch-2-sp**, rep from * to ** 3 times omitting (2dc, ch2, 2dc) in last rep, slst to close rnd. [84dc, 4ch-2]

Rnd 4: ch3, dc in next st, *(2dc, ch3, 2dc) in ch-2-sp, dc in next 21 sts**, rep from * to ** 3 times omitting last 2dc in last rep, slst to close rnd. [100dc, 4ch-3]

Rnd 5: ch3, dc in next 3 sts, *(2dc, ch3, 2dc) in ch-3-sp, dc in next 25 sts**, rep from * to ** 3 times omitting last 4dc in last rep, slst to close rnd. [116dc, 4ch-3]

Fasten off **Colour 29**.

WINGS

With **Colour 14**, make a magic ring.

Rnd 1: 6sc, slst to close rnd. [6sc]

Rnd 2: ch3, 3dc in each of next 5 sts, 2dc in last st, slst in third ch of initial ch3 to close rnd. [18dc]

Rnd 3: ch3, dc in next st, (dc in next st, 2dc in next st) 8 times, slst in third ch of initial ch3 to close rnd. [26dc]

Rnd 4: Fold circle in half, ch, sc in each st around semi-circle through both sides. [12sc]

Fasten off **Colour 14**. Rep to make a total of 2 wings.

SPOTS

With **Colour 2**, make a magic ring.

Rnd 1: 4sc, pull tight, slst to close rnd. [4sc]

Fasten off **Colour 2**. Rep to make a total of 6 spots.

FINISHING

Stitch 3 spots onto each wing.

Stitch top of each wing below ladybird's head on both sides.

7	■
27	■
29	■
14	■
2	■

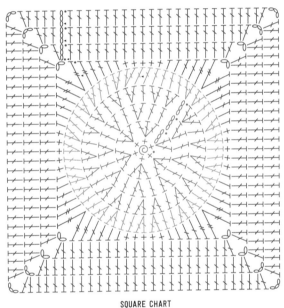

SQUARE CHART

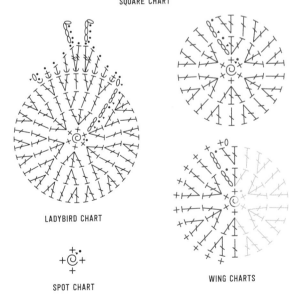

LADYBIRD CHART

SPOT CHART

WING CHARTS

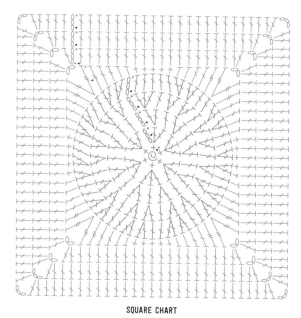

SQUARE CHART

FOOT CHART **EYELID CHART** **EYE CHART**

27	
31	
1	
2	
48	

SQUARE

With a 2.75mm hook and **Colour 27**, make a magic ring.

Rnd 1: 6sc, slst to close rnd. [6sc]

Rnd 2: ch3, 3dc in each of next 5 sts, 2dc in last st, slst to close rnd. [18dc]

Rnd 3: ch3, dc in next st, (dc in next st, 2dc in next st) 8 times, slst to close rnd. [26dc]

Rnd 4: ch3, (2dc in next st, 2dc in next st, dc in next st) 8 times, 3dc in last st, slst to close rnd. [44dc]

Rnd 5: ch3, (2dc in next 2 sts, dc in next 2 sts) 10 times, dc in last 3 sts, slst to close rnd. [64dc]

Fasten off **Colour 27**. Join **Colour 31** to Rnd 5 with a standing tr.

Rnd 6: (ch2, tr) in same st, *tr in next st, dc in next 2 sts, hdc in next 2 sts, sc in next 5 sts, hdc in next 2 sts, dc in next 2 sts, tr in next st, (tr, ch2, tr) in next st**, rep from * to ** 3 times omitting (tr, ch2, tr) in last rep, slst to close rnd. [68, 4ch-2]

Rnd 7: slst in ch-2-sp, ch3, (dc, ch2, 2dc) in ch-2-sp, *dc in next 17 sts, (2dc, ch2, 2dc) in ch-2-sp**, rep from * to ** 3 times omitting (2dc, ch2, 2dc) in last rep, slst to close rnd. [84dc, 4ch-2]

Rnd 8: ch3, dc in next st, *(2dc, ch3, 2dc) in ch-2-sp, dc in next 21 sts**, rep from * to ** 3 times omitting last 2dc in last rep, slst to close rnd. [100dc, 4ch-3]

Rnd 9: ch3, dc in next 3 sts, *(2dc, ch3, 2dc) in ch-3-sp, dc in next 25 sts**, rep from * to ** 3 times omitting last 4dc in last rep, slst to close rnd. [116dc, 4ch-3]

Fasten off **Colour 31**.

BACK LEGS

With **Colour 27**, make a magic ring.

Rnd 1: 6sc in ring. [6sc]

Rnd 2: 2sc in each st to end. [12sc]

Rnds 3-5: sc in each st to end. [12sc]

Rnd 6: (sc2tog, sc in next 4 sts) twice. [10sc]

Rnds 7-8: sc in each st to end. [10sc]

Rnd 9: (sc2tog, sc in next 3 sts) twice. [8sc]

Rnds 10-12: sc in each st to end. [8sc]

Rnd 13: (sc2tog, sc in next 2 sts) twice. [6sc]

Rnd 14: (sc2tog, sc in next st) twice. [4sc]

Rnd 15: sc in each st to end. [4]

Fasten off **Colour 27**. Rep to make a total of 2 back legs.

Stitch back legs in place on square, with bottom of legs angled slightly inwards.

FEET

With **Colour 27**, ch6.

Row 1: sc in second ch from hook, hdc in next 2 sts, dc in next 2 sts. [5]

Row 2: ch, turn, dc in FL of next 2 sts, hdc in FL of next 2 sts, sc in FL of last st. [5]

Fasten off **Colour 27**. Rep to make a total of 2 feet.

Attach feet to bottom of each back leg, pointing outwards.

FRONT LEGS

With **Colour 27**, make a magic ring.

Rnd 1: 4sc in ring. [4sc]

Rnd 2: 2sc in each st to end of rnd. [8sc]

Rnds 3-4: sc in each st to end of rnd. [8sc]

Rnd 5: (sc2tog, sc in next 2 sts) twice. [6sc]

Rnds 6-8: sc in each st to end of rnd. [6sc]

Rnd 9: hold both sides of open end together, sc in next 2 sts through both sides. [2sc]

Rnd 10: ch4, slst in second ch from hook, slst in next 2 ch, slst back in base of ch. [4slst]

Rnd 11: ch5, slst in second ch from hook, slst in next 3 ch, slst back in sc at bottom of leg. [5slst]

Rnd 12: ch4, slst in second ch from hook, slst in next 2 ch, slst back in next sc at bottom of leg. [4slst]

Fasten off **Colour 27**. Rep to make a total of 2 front legs.

Stitch front legs, side by side, on either side of Rnd 1 of square.

EYELIDS

With **Colour 27**, make a magic ring.

Rnd 1: ch3, 9dc, pull tight, slst to close rnd. [10dc]

Fasten off **Colour 27**. Rep to make a total of 2 eyelids.

EYES

With **Colour 1**, make a magic ring.

Rnd 1: 6sc, pull tight, slst to close rnd. [6sc]

Fasten off **Colour 1**. Rep to make a total of 2 eyes.

Embroider pupils onto eyes with **Colour 2**. Place eyes onto eyelids and secure in place.

Attach assembled eyes to head, approx 5 sts apart. Stitch bottom half of eyelid to head.

Embroider mouth onto frog's head below eyes with **Colour 48**.

SQUARE

With a 4mm hook and **Colour 32**, make a magic ring,

Rnd 1: ch3, 11dc in ring. [12dc]

Rnd 2: ch3, dc in same st, 2dc in each st to end of rnd. [24dc]

Rnd 3: ch3, dc in same st, dc in next st, *2dc in next st, dc in next st**, rep from * to ** to end of rnd. [36dc]

Fasten off **Colour 32**.

Join **Colour 31** in any st of Rnd 3. All sts in this rnd are made in BLO:

Rnd 4: ch3, dc in same st, ch2, 2dc in next st, hdc in next 2 sts, sc in next 3 sts, hdc in next 2 sts, *2dc in next st, ch2, 2dc in next st, hdc in next 2 sts, sc in next 3 sts, hdc in next 2 sts**, rep from * to ** twice, slst in third ch of initial ch3, slst in next dc, slst in ch-2-sp. [44sts, 4ch-2]

Rnd 5: (ch3, dc, ch2, 2dc) in ch-2-sp, dc in each st to next ch-2-sp, *(2dc, ch2, 2dc) in next ch-2-sp, dc in each st to next ch-2-sp**, rep from * to ** twice ending last rep at initial ch3, slst in third ch of initial ch3, slst in next dc, slst in ch-2-sp. [60sc, 4-ch-2]

Rnds 6-7: Rep Rnd 5. [92sc, 4ch-2]

Fasten off **Colour 31**.

Embroider 3 French knots on centre of square with **Colour 42** as shown.

BODY

With **Colour 45**, ch4.

Join in fifth st down from corner sp on left side of Rnd 3 of square with an sc, All sts in this rnd are made in FL of Rnd 3 of square:

Row 1: sc in next 18 sts. [19sc, 4ch]

Row 2: ch, turn, sc in next 23 sts. [23sc]

Row 3: ch, turn, sc in next 20 sts, hdc in next st, 3dc in next st, hdc in last st. [25]

Fasten off **Colour 45**.

ANTENNAE

Join **Colour 45** in top of snail's head.

Row 1: ch4, slst in third ch. [1slst, 4ch]

Fasten off **Colour 45**. Rep to make a total of 2 antennae.

Attach antennae to square and snail's head.

32	
31	
45	
42	

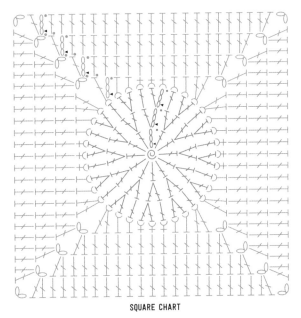

SQUARE CHART

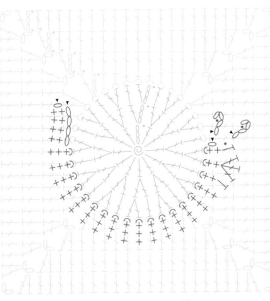

BODY AND ANTENNAE CHART

FLOWER

With a 4mm hook and **Colour 45**, make a magic ring.

Rnd 1: ch, work 8sc in ring, slst in FL of initial sc. [8sc]

All sts in this rnd are made in FLO:

Rnd 2: ch3, slst in same st, *(slst, ch3, slst) in next st**, rep from * to ** 6 times. [16slst, 8ch-3]

Fasten off **Colour 45**.

Join **Colour 17** in any st of Rnd 2. This rnd is worked on WS in leftover Rnd 1 BLO:

Rnd 3: 2 loop sts in each st to end of rnd. [16 loops]

Fasten off **Colour 17**.

Join **Colour 21** in any st of Rnd 3. All sts in this rnd are made in FLO:

Rnd 4: 2tr in st, tr in next st, (2tr in next st, tr in next st) 7 times, slst in BL of initial tr. [24tr]

All sts in this rnd are made in BL of Rnd 3, also working though BL of corresponding Rnd 4 tr made in FL of same Rnd 3 st.

Rnd 5: ch, 2sc in same st, sc in next st, (2sc in next st, sc in next st) 7 times. [24sc]

Fasten off **Colour 21**.

Join **Colour 1** in any st of Rnd 5.

Rnd 6: sc in next st, ch3, sk 2 sts, (sc in next st, ch3, sk 2 sts) 7 times, slst in initial sc. [8sc, 8ch-3]

Rnd 7: *ch2, 7tr in next ch-3-sp, ch2, slst in next sc**, rep from * to ** 7 times. [56tr, 8slst, 16ch-2]

Fasten off **Colour 1**.

SQUARE

Join **Colour 27** in any sc of Rnd 6.

Rnd 8: (bpslst around Rnd 6 sc, ch4) 8 times, slst in initial bpslst. [8bpslst, 8ch-4]

Rnd 9: slst in next ch-4-sp, ch, *(sc, ch2, dc, ch2, dc, ch2) in ch-4-sp**, rep from * to ** 7 times, slst in initial sc. [16dc, 8sc, 24ch-2]

All sts in this rnd are made in ch-sp only:

Rnd 10: slst in ch-2-sp, ch, *sc in ch-2-sp, ch2, (dc, ch2, dc) in next ch-2-sp, ch2, sc in next ch-2-sp, ch2**, rep from * to ** 7 times, slst in first sc. [16dc, 16sc, 32ch-2]

Fasten off **Colour 27**.

Join **Colour 31** in ch-2-sp between any 2dc sts in Rnd 10 with a standing dc. This counts as first dc in next rnd. All sts in this rnd are made in ch-sp only:

Rnd 11: *(3dc, ch2, 3dc) in ch-2-sp, ch3, sk next ch-2-sp, sc in next ch-2-sp, ch3, sk next ch-2-sp, slst in next ch-2-sp, ch3, sk next ch-2-sp, sc in next ch-2-sp, ch3, sk next ch-2-sp**, rep from * to ** 3 times, slst in first dc. [24dc, 8sc, 4slst, 16ch3, 4ch-2]

Fasten off **Colour 31**.

Join **Colour 38** in any ch-2-sp of Rnd 11 with a standing dc. This counts as first dc in next rnd. All sts in this rnd are made in ch-sp only:

Rnd 12: *(3dc, ch2, 3dc) in ch-2-sp, ch3, (sc in next ch-3-sp, ch3) 4 times**, rep from * to ** 3 times, slst in first dc. [24dc, 16sc, 20ch3, 4ch-2]

Fasten off **Colour 38**.

Join **Colour 39** in any ch-2-sp of Rnd 12 with a standing dc. This counts as first dc in next rnd. All sts in this rnd are made in ch-sp only:

Rnd 13: *(3dc, ch2, 3dc) in ch-2-sp, 3dc in next 5 ch-3-sp**, rep from * to ** 3 times, slst in first dc. [84dc, 4ch-2]

Fasten off **Colour 39**.

SQUARE CHART

45	
17	
21	
1	
27	
31	
38	
39	

FLOWER CHART

SQUARE

With a 2.75mm hook and **Colour 23**, make a magic ring.

Rnd 1: 6sc, slst to close rnd. [6sc]

Rnd 2: ch3, 3dc in each of next 5 sts, 2dc in last st, slst in third ch of initial ch3 to close rnd. [18dc]

Rnd 3: ch3, dc in next st, (dc in next st, 2dc in next st) 8 times, slst to close rnd. [26dc]

Fasten off **Colour 23**.

Join **Colour 10** in any st of Rnd 3 with a slst.

Rnd 4: ch3, 3-dc-puff in same st, (ch2, 3-dc-puff in next st) 25 times, ch2, slst in first puff of rnd to close. [26 3-dc-puffs, 26ch-2]

Rnd 5: slst in next ch-2-sp, ch3, 4-dc-popcorn, (ch2, 4-dc-popcorn in next st) 25 times, ch2, slst to close rnd. [26 4-dc-popcorns, 26ch-2]

Fasten off **Colour 10**.

Join **Colour 5** in any ch-2-sp of Rnd 5 with a standing tr. In this rnd, ch-2-sp are considered a st.

Rnd 6: (ch2, tr) in same st, *tr in next st, 2dc in next st, 2hdc in next st, sc in next 5 sts, hdc in next 2 sts, 2dc in next st, tr in next st, (tr, ch2, tr) in next st**, rep from * to ** 3 times omitting (tr, ch2, tr) in last rep, slst to close rnd. [68, 4ch-2]

Rnd 7: slst in ch-2-sp, ch3, (dc, ch2, 2dc) in ch-2-sp, *dc in next 17 sts, (2dc, ch2, 2dc) in ch-2-sp**, rep from * to ** 3 times omitting (2dc, ch2, 2dc) in last rep, slst to close rnd. [84dc, 4ch-2]

Rnd 8: ch3, dc in next st, *(2dc, ch3, 2dc) in ch-2-sp, dc in next 21 sts**, rep from * to ** 3 times omitting last 2dc in last rep, slst in third ch of initial ch3 to close. [100dc, 4ch-3]

Rnd 9: ch3, dc in next 3 sts, *(2dc, ch3, 2dc) in ch-3-sp, dc in next 25 sts**, rep from * to ** 3 times omitting last 4dc in last rep, slst to close rnd. [116dc, 4ch-3-sp]

Fasten off **Colour 5**.

SUCCULENT

Join **Colour 23** to any sc in outer edge of Rnd 1 of square.

Rnd 1: *slst, hdc in same st, ch, (hdc, slst) in next st**, rep from * to ** twice to make a total of 3 petals, slst to close rnd. [3 petals, each with 2slst, 2hdc, 1ch]

Fasten off and rejoin **Colour 23** in a post that is in line with tallest point of any petal from Rnd 1 with a standing st. This rnd is worked around posts of dc from Rnd 2 of square.

Rnd 2: *sc in next st, (hdc, dc, picot) in next st, (dc, hdc) in next st**, rep from * to ** 5 times to make a total of 6 petals, slst in first sc of rnd to close. [6 petals, each with 1sc, 2hdc, 2dc, 1 picot]

Fasten off and rejoin **Colour 23** in a post that is in line with tallest point of any petal from Rnd 2 with a standing st. This rnd is worked in outer edge of Rnd 2 of square. Fold Rnd 2 petals downwards to see more clearly.

Rnd 3: *(hdc, dc) in next st, (dc, picot, dc) in next st, (dc, hdc) in next st**, rep from * to ** 5 times to make a total of 6 petals, slst to close rnd. [6 petals, each with 2hdc, 4dc, 1 picot]

Fasten off and rejoin **Colour 23** in a post that is in line with tallest point of any petal from Rnd 3 with a standing sc. This rnd is worked in outer edge of Rnd 3 of square.

Rnd 4: sc in next 21 sts, sc2tog in next 2 sts, slst to close rnd. [24sc]

Rnd 5: (ch, hdc) in same st, (2dc, picot, 2dc) in next st, (hdc, sc) in next st, *(sc, hdc) in next st, (2dc, picot, 2dc) in next st, (hdc, sc) in next st**, rep from * to ** 6 times, slst to close rnd. [8 petals, each with 2sc, 2hdc, 4dc, 1 picot]

Fasten off **Colour 23**.

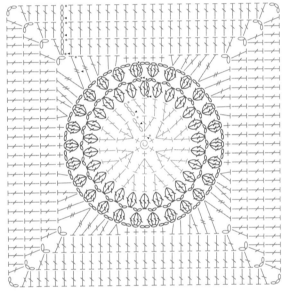

SQUARE CHART

SUCCULENT CHART

23

10

5

21

44

45

19

SQUARE CHART

SQUARE

With a 4mm hook and **Colour 21**, make a magic ring.

Rnd 1: ch3, 11dc in ring. [12dc]

Fasten off **Colour 21**.

Join **Colour 44** in FL of any st in Rnd 1. All sts in this rnd are made in FL of Rnd 1 sts:

Rnd 2: (slst, ch3, dc, ch3, slst) in each st to end of rnd. [12dc, 24slst, 24ch-3]

Fasten off **Colour 44**.

Join **Colour 45** in BL of any st in Rnd 1. All sts in this rnd are made in BL of Rnd 1 sts:

Rnd 3: (slst, ch6, ttr2tog, ch6, slst) in each st to end of rnd. [12ttr2tog, 24slst, 24ch-6]

Fasten off **Colour 45**.

Join **Colour 19** in any ttr2tog of Rnd 3.

Rnd 4: *sc in ttr2tog, ch4**, rep from * to ** 11 times. [12sc, 12ch-4]

Rnd 5: *slst in next sc, ch3, (2dc, 2hdc) in next ch-4-sp, sk next sc, 5sc in next ch-4-sp, sk next sc, (2hdc, 2dc) in next ch-4-sp, ch3**, rep from * to ** 3 times, slst to close rnd. [16dc, 16hdc, 20sc, 8ch-3, 4slst]

Rnd 6: slst in next ch-3-sp, ch, sc in same ch-3-sp, *hdc in next 2 sts, dc in next 2 sts, ch3, sk next 2 sts, slst in next st, ch3, sk next 2 sts, dc in next 2 sts, hdc in next 2 sts, sc in next ch-3-sp, ch6, sc in next ch-3-sp**, rep from * to ** 3 times, slst to close rnd. [16dc, 16hdc, 8sc, 4ch6, 8ch-3, 4slst]

Rnd 7: ch2, hdc in next 4 sts, sc in next ch-3-sp, ch4, sc in next ch-3-sp, hdc in next 5 sts, 7hdc in next ch-6-sp, *hdc in next 5 sts, sc in next ch-3-sp, ch4, sc in next ch-3-sp, hdc in next 5 sts, 7hdc in next ch-6-sp**, rep from * to ** twice. [68hdc, 8sc, 4ch-4]

Fasten off **Colour 19**.

Join **Colour 44** in fourth hdc in any 7hdc-group from Rnd 7.

Rnd 8: ch, *(sc, ch2, sc) in fourth hdc in 7hdc-group, ch, sk next st, (sc, ch, sk next st) 3 times, (sc in next st, ch) 3 times in ch-4-sp, (sc in next st, ch, sk next st) 4 times**, rep from * to ** 3 times. [52sc, 48ch, 4ch-2]

Fasten off **Colour 44**.

Join **Colour 45** in any ch-2-sp of Rnd 8.

Rnd 9: ch, *(sc, ch2, sc) in ch-2-sp, sk next st, ch, (sc in next ch, sk next st, ch) 12 times**, rep from * to ** 3 times. [56sc, 4ch-2, 52ch]

Fasten off **Colour 45**.

Join **Colour 19** in any ch-2-sp of Rnd 9.

Rnd 10: ch, *(sc, ch2, sc) in ch-2-sp, sk next st, ch, (sc in next ch, sk next st) 13 times**, rep from * to ** 3 times. [60sc, 4ch-2, 56ch]

Fasten off **Colour 19**.

SQUARE

With a 4mm hook and **Colour 39**, make a magic ring.

Rnd 1: ch, 8sc in ring, slst in FL of initial sc. [8sc]

All sts in this rnd are made in FL of Rnd 1 sts:

Rnd 2: (ch3, dc, ch3, slst) in st, *(slst, ch3, dc, ch3, slst) in next st**, rep from * to ** 6 times. [8dc, 16slst, 16ch3]

Fasten off **Colour 39**.

Join **Colour 31** in BL of any Rnd 1 st with a standing dc. All sts in this rnd are made in BL of Rnd 1 sts:

Rnd 3: dc in same st, 2dc in each st to end of rnd, slst in FL of initial dc. [16dc]

All sts in this rnd are made in FL of Rnd 3 sts:

Rnd 4: (ch3, dc, ch3, slst) in st, *(slst, ch3, dc, ch3, slst) in next st**, rep from * to ** 14 times. [16dc, 32slst, 32ch-3]

Fasten off **Colour 31**.

Join **Colour 27** in BL of any Rnd 3 st with a standing dc. All sts in this rnd are made in BL of Rnd 3 sts:

Rnd 5: dc in same st, dc in next st, *2dc in next st, dc in next st**, rep from * to ** 6 times, slst in FL of initial dc. [24dc]

All sts in this rnd are made in FL of Rnd 5 sts:

Rnd 6: (ch3, dc, ch3, slst) in st, *(slst, ch3, dc, ch3, slst) in next st**, rep from * to ** 22 times. [24dc, 48slst, 48ch-3]

Fasten off **Colour 27**.

Join **Colour 21** in BL of any Rnd 5 st with a standing dc. All sts in this rnd are made in BL of Rnd 5 sts:

Rnd 7: dc in same st, dc in next 2 sts, *2dc in next st, dc in next 2 sts**, rep from * to ** 6 times, slst in FL of initial dc. [32dc]

All sts in this rnd are made in FL of Rnd 7 sts:

Rnd 8: (ch3, dc, ch3, slst) in st, *(slst, ch3, dc, ch3, slst) in next st**, rep from * to ** 30 times. [32dc, 64slst, 64ch-3]

Fasten off **Colour 21**.

Join **Colour 17** in BL of any Rnd 7 st with a standing dc. All sts in this rnd are made in BL of Rnd 7 sts:

Rnd 9: dc in same st, dc in next 3 sts, *2dc in next st, dc in next 3 sts**, rep from * to ** 6 times, slst in FL of initial dc. [40dc]

All sts in this rnd are made in FL of Rnd 9 sts:

Rnd 10: (ch3, dc, ch3, slst) in st, *(slst, ch3, dc, ch3, slst) in next st**, rep from * to ** 38 times. [40dc, 80slst, 80ch-3]

Fasten off **Colour 17**.

Join **Colour 45** in BL of any Rnd 9 st with a standing tr. All sts in this rnd are made in BL of Rnd 9 sts:

Rnd 11: 2tr in same st, ch2, 3tr in next st, sk next 2 sts, (3dc in next st, sk next 2 sts) twice, *3tr in next st, ch2, 3tr in next st, sk next 2 sts, (3dc in next st, sk next 2 sts) twice**, rep from * to ** twice, slst in initial tr. [24tr, 24dc, 4ch-2]

Rnd 12: slst in next 2 sts, slst in next ch-2-sp, ch3, (2dc, ch2, 3dc) in same ch-2-sp, sk next 3 sts, (4dc in next st, sk next 3 sts) 3 times, *(3dc, ch2, 3dc) in next ch-2-sp, sk next 3 sts, (4dc in next st, sk next 3 sts) 3 times**, rep from * to ** twice, slst in third ch of initial ch3. [72dc, 4ch-2]

Fasten off **Colour 45**.

Join **Colour 1** in any ch-2-sp of Rnd 12.

Rnd 13: ch, *(2hdc, ch2, 2hdc) in ch-2-sp, hdc in next 18 sts**, rep from * to ** 3 times. [88hdc, 4ch-2]

Fasten off **Colour 1**.

SQUARE CHART

39	
31	
27	
21	
17	
45	
1	

GRANNY FLOWER

SQUARE CHART

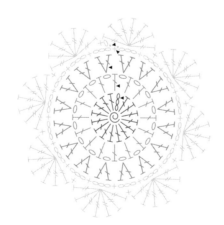
FLOWER CHART

Colour key:
- 39
- 31
- 27
- 1
- 21
- 17
- 13
- 45

FLOWER

With a 4mm hook and **Colour 39**, make a magic ring.

Rnd 1: ch3, work 15dc in ring. [16dc]

Fasten off **Colour 39**.

Join **Colour 31** in any sp between 2 sts in Rnd 1 with a standing dc. This counts as first dc in Rnd 2. All sts in this rnd are made in st sp only:

Rnd 2: (dc in st sp, ch) 16 times. [16dc, 16ch1]

Fasten off **Colour 31**.

Join **Colour 27** in any ch-sp with a standing dc. This counts as first dc in Rnd 3. All sts in this rnd are made in ch-sp only:

Rnd 3: (2dc in ch-1-sp) 16 times. [32dc]

Fasten off **Colour 27**.

Join **Colour 1** in sp between any pair of 2-dc groups with a standing sc. This counts as first sc in Rnd 4.

Rnd 4: *sc in sp between dc pair, ch3, sk 2dc**, rep from * to ** 15 times, slst in initial sc. [16sc, 16ch-3]

Rnd 5: slst in next ch-3-sp, ch, *sc in ch-3-sp, sk sc, 7tr in next ch-3-sp, sk sc**, rep from * to ** 7 times, slst in initial sc. [56tr, 8sc]

Fasten off **Colour 1**.

SQUARE

Join **Colour 21** around any sc of Rnd 4 of flower.

Rnd 6: *bpslst around Rnd 4 sc, ch3**, rep from * to ** 15 times, slst in initial bpslst. [16bpslst, 16ch-3]

Rnd 7: slst in next ch-3-sp, ch4, (2tr, ch2, 3tr) in same ch-3-sp, (3dc in next ch-3-sp) 3 times, *(3tr, ch2, 3tr) in next ch-3-sp, (3dc in next ch-3-sp) 3 times**, rep from * to ** twice, slst in fourth ch of initial ch4. [24tr, 36dc, 4ch-2]

Fasten off **Colour 21**.

Join **Colour 17** in any ch-2-sp with a standing dc. This counts as first dc in Rnd 8.

Rnd 8: *(3dc, ch2, 3dc) in ch-2-sp, sk next 3 sts, (3dc in next st sp, sk next 3 sts) 4 times**, rep from * to ** 3 times. [72dc, 4ch-2]

Fasten off **Colour 17**.

Join **Colour 13** in any ch-2-sp of Rnd 8 with a standing dc. This counts as first dc in Rnd 9.

Rnd 9: *(3dc, ch2, 3dc) in ch-2-sp, sk next 3 sts, (3dc in next st sp, sk next 3 sts) 5 times**, rep from * to ** 3 times. [84dc, 4ch-2]

Fasten off **Colour 13**.

Join **Colour 45** in any ch-2-sp of Rnd 9.

Rnd 10: ch, *(sc, ch2, sc) in ch-2-sp, sc in next 21 sts**, rep from * to ** 3 times. [92sc, 4ch-2]

Fasten off **Colour 45**.

SQUARE

With a 4mm hook and **Colour 21**, make a magic ring.

Rnd 1: ch2, 7hdc in ring, slst in second ch of initial ch2. [8hdc]

Fasten off **Colour 21**.

Join **Colour 1** in any st of Rnd 1.

Rnd 2: ch3, popcorn in st, ch2, (popcorn in next st, ch2) 7 times, slst in initial popcorn. [8 popcorns, 8ch2]

Fasten off **Colour 1**.

Join **Colour 45** in any ch-2-sp of Rnd 2.

Rnd 3: ch, (3sc in ch-2-sp, fpsc around popcorn) 8 times, slst in initial sc. [24sc, 8fpsc]

Rnd 4: *slst in next st, sk next st, 5dc in fpsc, sk next st**, rep from * to ** 7 times, slst in initial slst. [40dc, 8slst]

Fasten off **Colour 45**.

Join **Colour 17** around first dc of any 5-dc group with a bphdc. This counts as first bphdc in Rnd 5.

Rnd 5: *bphdc around each of 5dc sts, sc over Rnd 4 slst and in corresponding st of Rnd 3**, rep from * to ** 7 times, slst in initial bphdc. [40bphdc, 8sc]

Fasten off **Colour 17**.

Join **Colour 21** in any sc of Rnd 5 with a standing dc. This counts as first dc in Rnd 6.

Rnd 6: *7dc in sc, sk next 2 sts, slst in next st, sk 2 sts**, rep from * to ** 7 times, slst in initial dc. [56dc, 8slst]

Fasten off **Colour 21**.

Join **Colour 27** in first dc of any 7dc-group in Rnd 6 with a bphdc. This counts as first bphdc in Rnd 7.

Rnd 7: *bphdc around each of 7dc sts, sc over Rnd 6 slst and in Rnd 5 st**, rep from * to ** 7 times, slst in initial bphdc. [56bphdc, 8sc]

Fasten off **Colour 27**.

Join **Colour 1** in any sc with a standing tr. This counts as first tr in Rnd 8. All sts in this rnd are made in BLO.

Rnd 8: *(tr, ch, tr, ch, tr, ch, tr, ch2, tr, ch, tr, ch, tr) in sc, sk next 3 sts, sc in next st, hdc in next 2 sts, dc in next 3 sts, hdc in next 2 sts, sc in next st, sk next 3 sts**, rep from * to ** 3 times, slst in initial tr. [24tr, 12dc, 16hdc, 8sc, 16ch-1, 4ch-2]

Fasten off **Colour 1**.

Join **Colour 31** in any ch-2-sp of Rnd 8 with a standing dc. This counts as first dc in Rnd 9.

Rnd 9: *(2dc, ch2, 2dc) in ch-2-sp, (sk next st, 2dc in next ch-1 sp) twice, sk st, dc in next 9 sts, sk st, (2dc in next ch-1 sp, sk next st) twice, rep from * to ** 3 times, slst in first dc. [84dc, 4ch-2]

Fasten off **Colour 31**.

Join **Colour 39** in any ch-2-sp of Rnd 9 with a standing dc. This counts as first dc in Rnd 10.

Rnd 10: *(2hdc, ch2, 2hdc) in ch-2-sp, hdc in next 21 sts**, rep from * to ** 3 times, slst in initial hdc. [100hdc, 4ch-2]

Fasten off **Colour 39**.

SQUARE CHART

21	
1	
45	
17	
27	
31	
39	

21	
1	
45	
39	
31	
27	

SQUARE CHART

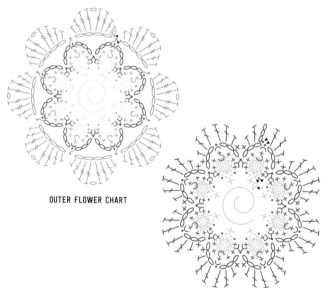

OUTER FLOWER CHART

INNER FLOWER CHART

INNER FLOWER

With a 4mm hook and **Colour 21**, make a magic ring.

Rnd 1: ch, work 8sc in ring, slst in first sc. [8sc]

Fasten off **Colour 21**.

Join **Colour 1** in any st of Rnd 1.

Rnd 2: *(slst, ch3, puff, ch3, slst) in each st around. [16ch3, 8 puffs, 16slst]

Fasten off **Colour 1**.

Join **Colour 45** in any st of Rnd 1 with a slst, placing the st to the right of puff from Rnd 2. This counts as first slst in Rnd 3.

Rnd 3: *slst in next Rnd 1 st {working over Rnd 2 slst}, 3sc in ch-3-sp, fpsc around puff, 3sc in ch-3-sp, slst in same Rnd 1 st {working over Rnd 2 slst}**, rep from * to ** 7 times. [48sc, 8fpsc, 16slst]

Fasten off **Colour 45**.

Join **Colour 39** in any fpsc of Rnd 3 with a slst. This counts as first slst in Rnd 4. All sts in this rnd are made in BLO:

Rnd 4: *slst in fpsc, ch3, sk 2 sts, slst in 2 sts across 2sc on either side of Rnd 3 slsts, ch3, sk 2 sts**, rep from * to ** 7 times, slst in initial slst. [16slst, 16ch-3]

Rnd 5: slst in next ch-3-sp, ch3, (dc, hdc, sc) in same sp, (sc, hdc, 2dc) in next ch-3-sp, *(2dc, hdc, sc) in next ch-3-sp, (sc, hdc, 2dc) in next ch-3-sp**, rep from * to ** 6 times. [32dc, 16hdc, 16sc]

Fasten off **Colour 39**.

OUTER FLOWER

Join **Colour 31** in any slst from Rnd 4 of inner flower with a bpslst. This counts as first bpslst in Rnd 6.

Rnd 6: (bpslst around slst from Rnd 4, ch4) 8 times, slst in initial bpslst. [8bpslst, 8ch-4]

Rnd 7: slst in next ch-4-sp, ch, *(hdc, dc, 2tr, ch, 2tr, dc, hdc) in ch-4-sp**, rep from * to ** 7 times, slst in first slst. [32tr, 16dc, 16hdc, 8ch-1]

Fasten off **Colour 31**.

SQUARE

Join **Colour 1** in any bpslst from Rnd 6 of outer flower with a bpslst. This counts as first bpslst in Rnd 8.

Rnd 8: (bpslst around Rnd 6 bpslst, ch5) 8 times, slst in initial bpslst. [8bpslst, 8ch-5]

Rnd 9: slst in next ch-5-sp, ch4, (2tr, ch3, 3tr) in same ch-5-sp, 3dc in next ch-5-sp, *(3tr, ch3, 3tr) in next ch-5-sp, 3dc in next ch-5-sp**, rep from * to ** twice, slst in fourth ch of initial ch4. [24tr, 12dc, 4ch-3]

Rnd 10: slst in next 2 sts, slst in next ch-3-sp, ch3, (2dc, ch2, 3dc) in same ch-3-sp, sk next 3 sts, (3dc in next st sp, sk next 3 sts) twice, *(3dc, ch2, 3dc) in next ch-3-sp, sk next 3 sts, (3dc in next st sp, sk next 3 sts) twice**, rep from * to ** twice, slst in third ch of initial ch3. [48dc, 4ch-2]

Rnd 11: slst in next 2 sts, slst in next ch-2-sp, ch3, (2dc, ch2, 3dc) in same ch-2-sp, sk next 3 sts, (3dc in next st sp, sk next 3 sts) 3 times, *(3dc, ch2, 3dc) in ch-2-sp, sk next 3 sts, (3dc in next st sp, sk next 3 sts) twice**, rep from * to ** 3 times, slst in third ch of initial ch3. [60dc, 4ch-2]

Rnd 12: slst in next 2 sts, slst in next ch-2-sp, ch3, (2dc, ch2, 3dc) in same ch-2-sp, sk next 3 sts, (3dc in next st sp, sk next 3 sts) 4 times, *(3dc, ch2, 3dc) in ch-2-sp, sk next 3 sts, (3dc in next st sp, sk next 3 sts) 4 times**, rep from * to ** twice. [72dc, 4ch-2]

Fasten off **Colour 1**.

Join **Colour 27** in any ch-2-sp of Rnd 12 with a standing hdc. This counts as first hdc in Rnd 13.

Rnd 13: *(2hdc, ch, 2hdc) in ch-2-sp, hdc in next 18 sts**, rep from * to ** 3 times. [88hdc, 4ch-1]

Fasten off **Colour 27**.

FLOWER PILLOW

SQUARE 1: BOTTOM LEFT

Follow instructions for Layered Flower to make 1 complete square, replacing **Colour 45** with **Colour 21**, **Colour 39** with **Colour 17**, **Colour 31** with **Colour 45** and **Colour 27** with **Colour 39**.

SQUARE 2: MIDDLE LEFT

Follow instructions for Layered Flower to make 1 complete square, replacing **Colour 45** with **Colour 27**, **Colour 39** with **Colour 31**, **Colour 31** with **Colour 39** and **Colour 27** with **Colour 45**.

SQUARE 3: TOP LEFT

Follow instructions for Layered Flower to make 1 complete square, replacing **Colour 39** with **Colour 17** and **Colour 31** with **Colour 21**.

SQUARE 4: BOTTOM CENTRE

Follow instructions for Layered Flower to make 1 complete square using original colours.

SQUARE 5: MIDDLE CENTRE

Follow instructions for Layered Flower to make 1 complete square, replacing **Colour 45** with **Colour 17**, **Colour 39** with **Colour 21**, **Colour 31** with **Colour 27** and **Colour 27** with **Colour 31**.

SQUARE 6: TOP CENTRE

Follow instructions for Layered Flower to make 1 complete square, replacing **Colour 45** with **Colour 31**, **Colour 31** with **Colour 45** and **Colour 27** with **Colour 17**.

SQUARE 7: BOTTOM RIGHT

Follow instructions for Layered Flower to make 1 complete square, replacing **Colour 45** with **Colour 31**, **Colour 39** with **Colour 27**, **Colour 31** with **Colour 21** and **Colour 27** with **Colour 17**.

SQUARE 8: MIDDLE RIGHT

Follow instructions for Layered Flower to make 1 complete square, replacing **Colour 45** with **Colour 39**, **Colour 39** with **Colour 45**, **Colour 31** with **Colour 17** and **Colour 27** with **Colour 21**.

SQUARE 9: TOP RIGHT

Follow instructions for Layered Flower to make 1 complete square, replacing **Colour 45** with **Colour 21**, **Colour 39** with **Colour 27** and **Colour 27** with **Colour 39**.

ASSEMBLY

Sew 9 squares together in a grid through BL of each pair of sts as shown to make panel.

BORDER

Join **Colour 1** in any corner ch-sp of 9-square panel with a standing hdc. This counts as first hdc in Rnd 1.

Rnd 1: *(2hdc, ch2, 2hdc) in corner ch-sp, (hdc in next 22 sts, hdc in next 2 ch-sp, hdc in next ch-2-sp) twice, hdc in next 22 sts**, rep from * to ** 3 times, slst in initial hdc. [296hdc, 4ch-2]

Rnd 2: slst in next st, slst in next ch-2-sp, ch3, (2dc, ch2, 3dc) in same ch-2-sp, sk next 2 sts, (3dc in next st, sk next 2 sts) 24 times, *(3dc, ch2, 3dc) in next ch-2-sp, sk next 2 sts, (3dc in next st, sk next 2 sts) 24 times**, rep from * to ** twice, slst in third ch of initial ch3. [312dc, 4ch-2]

Rnd 3: slst in next 2 sts, slst in next ch-2-sp, ch, (3hdc in ch-2-sp, hdc in next 78 sts) 4 times. [324hdc]

Fasten off **Colour 1**.

FINISHING

Sew panel to front of pre-made cushion cover to finish.

1	
45	
17	
21	
27	
31	
39	

20	
44	
45	
19	

SQUARE CHART

SQUARE

Starting with a 4mm hook and **Colour 20**, make a magic ring.

Rnd 1: ch3, 11dc in ring, slst in third ch of initial ch3. [12dc]

Fasten off **Colour 20**.

Join **Colour 44** in any st of Rnd 1. All sts in this rnd are made in BLO:

Rnd 2: ch3, dc in same st, 2dc in each st to end of rnd, slst in third ch of initial ch3. [24dc]

Fasten off **Colour 44**.

Join **Colour 45** in any st of Rnd 2. All sts in this rnd are made in BLO:

Rnd 3: ch3, dc in same st, dc in next st, *2dc in next st, dc in next st**, rep from * to ** to end of rnd, slst in third ch of initial ch3. [36dc]

Rnd 4: ch3, dc in same st, ch2, 2dc in next st, hdc in next 2 sts, sc in next 3 sts, hdc in next 2 sts, *2dc in next st, ch2, 2dc in next st, hdc in next 2 sts, sc in next 3 sts, hdc in next 2 sts**, rep from * to ** twice, join to third ch of starting ch with a slst. [16dc, 16 hdc, 12sc, 4ch-2]

Fasten off **Colour 45**.

Join **Colour 19** in any ch-2-sp of Rnd 4.

Rnd 5: (ch3, dc, ch2, 2dc) in ch-2-sp, dc in each st to next ch-2-sp, *(2dc, ch2, 2dc) in next ch-2-sp, dc in each st to next ch-2-sp**, rep from * to ** twice ending last rep at initial ch3, slst in third ch of initial ch3, slst in next st, slst in ch-2-sp. [60dc, 4ch-2]

Rnds 6-7: Rep Rnd 5. [92dc, 4ch-2]

Fasten off **Colour 19**.

Join **Colour 45** in any ch-2-sp of Rnd 7.

Rnd 8: ch, (sc, ch, sc) in first ch-2-sp, *sc in each st to next ch-2-sp, (sc, ch, sc) in ch-2-sp**, rep from * to ** to end of rnd omitting (sc, ch, sc) in last rep, slst to close rnd. [100sc, 4ch-1]

Fasten off **Colour 45**.

INNER PETALS

Join **Colour 44** in FL of Rnd 1 of square.

Rnd 1: sc in first st, *(hdc, 3dc, hdc) in next st, sc in next st**, rep from * to ** to end of rnd omitting sc in last rep, slst to close rnd. [6 petals, 6sc]

Fasten off **Colour 44**.

OUTER PETALS

Join **Colour 44** in FL of Rnd 2 of square.

Rnd 2: sc in first st, *(hdc, 2dc, hdc) in next st, sc in next st**, rep from * to ** to end of rnd omitting sc in last rep, slst to close rnd. [12 petals, 12sc]

Fasten off **Colour 44**.

INNER AND OUTER PETALS CHART

SQUARE

With a 4mm hook and **Colour 40**, make a magic ring.

Rnd 1: ch3, 11dc in ring, slst to close rnd. [12dc]

Fasten off **Colour 40**.

Join **Colour 48** between any 2 dc of Rnd 1.

Rnd 2: ch3, (1 puff, ch) between each pair of dc from last rnd, slst to close rnd. [12 puffs, 12ch-1]

Fasten off **Colour 48**.

Join **Colour 19** in any st of Rnd 2. In this rnd the ch-1-sps count as sts:

Rnd 3: *2sc in first st, sc in next st**, rep from * to ** to end of rnd, slst to join. [36sc]

All sts in this rnd are made in BLO:

Rnd 4: ch3, dc in same st, ch2, 2dc in next st, hdc in next 2 sts, sc in next 3 sts, hdc in next 2 sts, *2dc in next st, ch2, 2dc in next st, hdc in next 2 sts, sc in next 3 sts, hdc in next 2 sts**, rep from * to ** twice, slst in third ch of initial ch3, slst in next st, slst in next ch-2-sp. [16dc, 16hdc, 12sc, 4ch-2]

Rnd 5: (ch3, dc, ch2, 2dc) in ch-2-sp, dc in each st to next ch-2-sp, *(2dc, ch2, 2dc) in next ch-2-sp, dc in each st to next ch-2-sp**, rep from * to ** twice ending last rep at initial ch3, slst to third ch of initial ch3, slst in next st, slst to ch-2-sp. [60dc, 4ch-2]

Rnds 6-7: Rep Rnd 5. [92dc, 4ch-2]

Fasten off **Colour 19**.

Join **Colour 20** in any ch-2-sp of Rnd 7.

Rnd 8: ch, (sc, ch, sc) in first ch-2-sp, *sc in each st to next ch-2-sp, (sc, ch, sc) in ch-2-sp**, rep from * to ** to end of rnd omitting (sc, ch, sc) in last rep, slst to close rnd. [100sc, 4ch-1]

Fasten off **Colour 20**.

INNER PETALS

Join **Colour 20** in FL of any st in Rnd 3 of square.

Rnd 1: *(2sc in next st, ch, sk st) 4 times, sc in next st, ch**, rep from * to ** to end of rnd, slst to close rnd. [36sc, 20ch-1]

Fasten off **Colour 20**.

OUTER PETALS

Join **Colour 48** in any ch-1-sp of Rnd 1 of inner petals.

Rnd 1: *(sc, ch4) in next ch-1-sp, (sc, ch2) in next ch-1-sp**, rep from * to ** 9 times, slst in first sc. [10ch-4, 10ch-2]

Rnd 2: slst in ch-4-sp, 7dc in every ch-4-sp and sc in every ch-2-sp to end of rnd, slst to close rnd. [10 7-dc groups, 10sc]

Fasten off **Colour 48**.

Join **Colour 44** in any first dc of 7-dc groups in Rnd 2.

Rnd 3: sc in same st, sc in next 2 sts, *(sc, ch, sc) in next st, sc in next 3 sts, 1 spike st in next sc**, rep from * to ** to end of rnd, slst to close rnd. [8sc per petal, 1 spike st between each petal]

Fasten off **Colour 44**.

40	
48	
19	
20	
44	

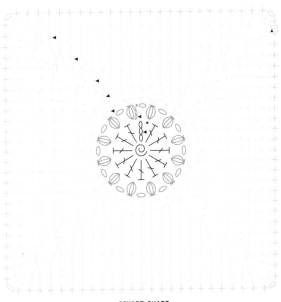

SQUARE CHART

INNER AND OUTER PETALS CHART

42
43
23

INNER FLOWER

With a 4mm hook and **Colour 42**, make a magic ring.

Rnd 1: ch3, 11dc in ring, slst to close rnd. [12dc]

Fasten off **Colour 42**.

Join **Colour 43** in any st of Rnd 1.

Rnd 2: *sc in first st, (hdc, 4dc, hdc) in next st, sc in next st**; rep from * to ** to end of rnd omitting sc in last rep. [6 petals, 6sc]

Fasten off **Colour 43**.

OUTER FLOWER

Join **Colour 42** in BL of any sc from Rnd 2 of inner flower. All sts in this rnd are made in BLO:

Rnd 3: *ch4, slst in next sc**, rep from * to ** 4 times, ch4. [6slst, 6ch-4]

Rnd 4: (sc, hdc, dc, 3tr, dc, hdc, sc) in each ch-4-sp to end of rnd, slst in first sc. [6 petals]

Fasten off **Colour 42**.

SQUARE

Join **Colour 42** in any sp between petals in Rnd 4 of outer flower. All sts in this rnd are made in BLO:

Rnd 5: ch5, sk 2 petals, slst to far side of second petal, ch5, slst to far side of third petal, ch5, sk 2 petals, slst to far side of fifth petal, ch5, slst to close rnd. [4ch-5]

Fasten off **Colour 42**.

Join **Colour 23** in any ch-5-sp of Rnd 5 with a standing dc.

Rnd 6: (2dc, ch2, 3dc) in same sp, *(3dc, ch2, 3dc) in next ch-5-sp**, rep from * to ** twice. [2 3dc-groups per side]

Rnd 7: slst in each st to corner ch-2-sp, (ch3, 2dc, ch2, 3dc) in same sp, 3dc in next ch-2-sp, *(3dc, ch2, 3dc) in corner ch-2-sp, 3dc in next ch-2-sp**, rep from * to ** to end of rnd, slst to close rnd. [3 3dc-groups per side]

Rnd 8: slst in each st to corner ch-2-sp, (ch3, 2dc, ch2, 3dc) in same sp, 3dc in sp between next 2 3dc-groups, *(3dc, ch2, 3dc) in corner ch-2-sp, 3dc in sp between next 2 3dc-groups**, rep from * to ** to end of rnd, slst to close rnd. [4 3dc-groups per side]

Rnds 9-11: Rep Rnd 8, adding 1 extra group of 3dc on each side of rnd. [7 3dc-groups per side]

Fasten off **Colour 23**.

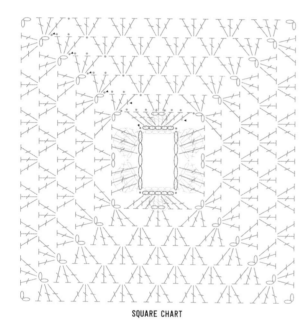

SQUARE CHART

OUTER FLOWER CHART

INNER FLOWER CHART

VIOLET WRIST WARMERS

MITTEN FRONT

Follow instructions for Violet to make 2 complete squares.

You can make mittens bigger or smaller by adding or reducing rnds.

MITTEN BACK

With a 4mm hook and **Colour 23**, make a magic ring,

Rnd 1: ch3, 2dc in ring, ch2, *3dc in ring, ch2**, rep from * to ** twice, slst in third ch of initial ch3. [12dc, 4ch-2]

Rnd 2: slst in next 2 sts, slst in ch-2-sp, (ch3, 2dc, ch2, 3dc) in ch-2-sp, *(3dc, ch2, 3dc) in next ch-2-sp**, rep from * to ** twice, slst in third ch of initial ch3. [2 3dc-groups per side]

Rnd 3: slst in next 2 sts, slst in ch-2-sp, (ch3, 2dc, ch2, 3dc) in ch-2-sp, 3dc in sp between next 2 3dc-groups, *(3dc, ch2, 3dc) in next ch-2-sp, 3dc in sp between next 2 3dc-groups, **, rep from * to ** twice, slst in third ch of initial ch3. [3 3dc-groups per side]

Rnds 4-7: Rep Rnd 3, adding 1 extra group of 3dc on each side of rnd. [7 3dc-group per side]

Fasten off **Colour 23**. Rep to make a total of 2 mitten backs.

ASSEMBLY

Place 1 mitten front on top of 1 mitten back, with RS facing, and slst squares together on 1 side.

Open out folded panel and join **Colour 43** to top corner.

Row 1: sc in each dc and ch-2-sp across both squares, ch, turn. [50sc]

Row 2: ch3, dc in each rem st across both squares, ch2, turn. [50dc]

Row 3: ch3, dc in BL of each rem st to end of row, ch2, turn. [50dc]

Row 4: ch, sc in each st to end of row. [50sc]

Fasten off **Colour 43**.

Fold mitten in half, with WS facing, and sew sides together, leaving a hole for thumb.

Join **Colour 43** to bottom corner of mitten, sc in each dc and ch-2-sp along bottom of mittens, and fasten off. [50sc]

Rep with other mitten front and back pieces to make second mitten.

DAISY

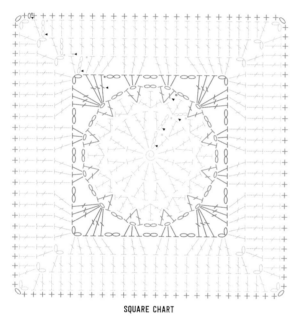

▨	20
▨	1
▨	27
▨	28
▨	44

SQUARE CHART

PETALS CHART

SQUARE

With a 4mm hook and **Colour 20**, make a magic ring.

Rnd 1: ch3, 11dc in ring, slst to end of rnd. [12dc]

Fasten off **Colour 20**.

Join **Colour 1** in BL of any st of Rnd 1 with a standing dc. This counts as first dc in Rnd 2. All sts in this rnd are made in BLO:

Rnd 2: 2dc in each st to end of rnd, slst to close rnd. [24dc]

Rnd 3: (ch3, 2dc) in sp between 2dc-groups, 3dc between each 2dc-group from Rnd 2 to end of rnd, slst to close rnd. [36dc]

Fasten off **Colour 1**.

Join **Colour 27** between any 3dc-group of Rnd 3 with a standing dc. This counts as first dc in Rnd 4.

Rnd 4: (dc, ch, dc) in same sp, ch2, *(dc, ch, dc) in next sp between 3dc-groups, ch2**, rep from * to ** 10 times, slst in first dc. [24dc, 12ch-2-sp, 12ch-1]

Fasten off **Colour 27**.

Join **Colour 28** in any ch-1-sp of Rnd 4 with a standing dc. This counts as first dc in Rnd 5.

Rnd 5: *3dc, ch2, 3dc in same sp, ch2, 3hdc in next ch-1-sp, ch2, 3hdc in next ch-1-sp, ch2**, rep from * to ** 3 times, slst in first dc. [24dc, 24hdc, 16ch-2]

Fasten off **Colour 28**.

Join **Colour 44** in ch-2-sp of Rnd 5.

Rnd 6: (ch3, dc, ch2, 2dc) in ch-2-sp, dc in each st to next ch-2-sp, *(2dc, ch2, 2dc) in ch-2-sp, dc in each st to next ch-2-sp**, rep from * to ** twice, slst to close rnd. [60dc, 4ch-2]

Rnd 7: slst in next dc, slst in ch-2-sp, rep Rnd 6. [76dc, 4ch-2]

Fasten off **Colour 28**.

Join **Colour 1** in any ch-2-sp of Rnd 7.

Rnd 8: Rep Rnd 6. [92dc, 4ch-2]

Fasten off **Colour 1**.

Join **Colour 27** in any ch-2-sp of Rnd 8.

Rnd 9: ch, (sc, ch, sc) in ch-2-sp, *sc in each st to next ch-2-sp, (sc, ch, sc) in ch-2-sp**, rep from * to ** to end of rnd omitting (sc, ch, sc) in last rep, slst to close rnd. [100sc, 4ch-1]

Fasten off **Colour 27**.

PETALS

Join **Colour 1** in FL of any st in Rnd 1 of square.

Rnd 1: *(sc, hdc, 2dc) in same st, (2dc, hdc, sc) in next st**, rep from * to ** to end of rnd, slst in first sc. [6 petals]

Fasten off **Colour 1**.

FLOWERS

90

FLOWER

With a 4mm hook and **Colour 45**, make a magic ring.

Rnd 1: work beginning popcorn in ring, ch2, (popcorn, ch2) 5 times, slst in first popcorn. [6 popcorns, 6ch-2]

Fasten off **Colour 45**.

Join **Colour 17** in any ch-2-sp of Rnd 1 with a standing dc. This counts as first dc in Rnd 2.

Rnd 2: (5dc in ch-2-sp, fpslst around popcorn) 6 times. [30dc, 6fpslst]

Fasten off **Colour 17**.

Join **Colour 21** in third dc of any 5dc-group from Rnd 2 with a slst. This counts as first slst in Rnd 3.

Rnd 3: (slst in third dc of 5dc-group, ch8) 6 times, slst to close rnd. [6slst, 6ch-8]

Rnd 4: slst in next ch-8-sp, ch, (13sc in ch-8-sp, sk slst) 6 times, slst in first sc. [78sc]

Fasten off **Colour 21**.

Join **Colour 27** in FL of last sc of any 13sc-group from Rnd 4. All sts in this rnd are made in FLO:

Rnd 5: *slst in last sc of 13sc-group, (slst in next st, sk next st, 5hdc in next st, sk next st) 3 times**, rep from * to ** 5 times. [90hdc, 24slst]

Fasten off **Colour 27**.

SQUARE

Join **Colour 31** in BL of seventh sc of any 13sc-group from Rnd 4 with a standing bpsc. This counts as first sc in Rnd 6. All sts in this rnd are made in BL of Rnd 4 sts:

Rnd 6: *sc in seventh sc of 13sc-group, ch6, sk 5 sts, sc2tog across next 2 sts, ch6, sk 5 sts**, rep from * to ** 5 times, slst in initial slst. [6sc, 6sc2tog, 12ch-6]

Rnd 7: slst in next ch-6-sp, ch, (9sc in ch-6-sp) 12 times, slst in first sc. [108sc]

Fasten off **Colour 31**.

Join **Colour 1** in fifth sc of any 9sc-group from Rnd 7 with a standing tr. This counts as first st in Rnd 8.

Rnd 8: *(2tr, ch3, 2tr) in fifth sc of 9sc-group, ch4, sk 8 sts, sc in next st, ch6, sk 8 sts, sc in next st, ch4, sk 8 sts**, rep from * to ** 3 times, slst in first tr. [16tr, 8sc, 4ch3, 8ch4, 4ch-6]

Fasten off **Colour 1**.

Join **Colour 39** in any ch-3-sp of Rnd 8 with a standing hdc. This counts as first hdc in Rnd 9.

Rnd 9: *(2hdc, ch2, 2hdc) in ch-3-sp, hdc in next 2 sts, 5hdc in next ch-4-sp, hdc in next st, 7hdc in next ch-6-sp, hdc in next st, 5hdc in next ch-4-sp, hdc in next 2 sts**, rep from * to ** 3 times. [108hdc, 4ch-2]

Fasten off **Colour 39**.

SQUARE CHART

45	
17	
21	
27	
31	
1	
39	

FLOWER CHART

■	45
■	14

INNER ROSE

With a 4mm hook and Colour 45, ch5.

Rnd 1: *(dc, ch) in fifth ch from hook**, rep from * to ** 6 times, slst to close rnd. [8dc, 8ch-1-sp]

Rnd 2: (ch2, 2dc, hdc) in first ch-1-sp, (hdc, 2dc, hdc) in each rem ch-1-sp to end of rnd, slst to close rnd. [8 petals]

Fasten off **Colour 45**.

OUTER ROSE

Join **Colour 45** in last st of Rnd 2 of inner rose. This rnd is worked on WS.

Rnd 3: slst halfway up each st to middle st of first petal, *ch3, slst halfway up middle st of next petal**, rep from * to ** to end of rnd. [8ch-3]

This rnd is worked on RS in ch-3-sps from Rnd 3:

Rnd 4: (ch2, 5dc hdc) in first ch-3-sp, (hdc, 5dc, hdc) in each rem ch-3-sp to end of rnd, slst to close rnd. [8 petals]

This rnd is worked on WS:

Rnd 5: slst halfway up each st to middle st of first petal from Rnd 4, ch4, *slst halfway up middle st of next petal, ch4**, rep from * to ** to end of rnd, slst to close rnd. [8ch-4]

Fasten off **Colour 45**.

SQUARE

Join **Colour 14** in any ch-4-sp of Rnd 5 of outer rose.

Rnd 1: (ch3, 2dc, ch2, 3dc) in first ch-4-sp, *3dc in next ch-4-sp, (3dc, ch2, 3dc) in next ch-4-sp**, rep from * to ** twice, 3dc in last ch-4-sp, slst to close rnd. [36dc, 4ch-2]

Rnd 2: slst in next 2 sts, slst in ch-2-sp, (ch3, 2dc, ch2, 3dc) in same ch-2-sp, *3dc in sp between 3dc-group to next corner sp, (3dc, ch2, 3dc) in next ch-2-sp**, rep from * to ** twice, 3dc in sp between 3dc-groups to end, slst to close rnd. [48dc, 4ch-2]

Rnd 3: Rep Rnd 2. [60dc, 4ch-2]

Rnds 4-5: slst in each st to ch-2-sp, slst in ch-2-sp, (ch3, dc, ch2, 2dc) in corner sp, *dc in each st to next corner sp, (2dc, ch2, 2dc) in corner sp**, rep from * to ** to end of rnd, slst to close rnd omitting last (2dc, ch2, 2dc). [92dc, 4ch-2]

Fasten off **Colour 14**.

SQUARE CHART

OUTER ROSE CHART

INNER ROSE CHART

SQUARE

With a 4mm hook and **Colour 2**, make a magic ring.

Rnd 1: ch3, 11dc in ring, slst to close rnd. [12dc]

Rnd 2: ch3, *1 puff in space between 2 dc, ch, skip 1 dc**, rep from * to ** to end, slst to close rnd. [12 puffs, 12ch-1]

Rnd 3: slst into ch-1-sp, (ch3, 2dc) in same sp, ch, sk 1 puff, *3dc in ch-1-sp, ch, sk 1 puff**, rep from * to ** to end, slst to close rnd. [36dc, 12ch-1]

Fasten off **Colour 2**.

Join **Colour 21** in any st of Rnd 3.

Rnd 4: ch, sc in each dc and ch-1-sp to end of rnd, slst to close rnd. [48sc]

Fasten off **Colour 21**.

Join **Colour 19** in BL of any st of Rnd 4. All sts in this rnd are made in BLO:

Rnd 5: ch3, dc in same st, *ch2, 2dc in next st, dc in next st, hdc in next 2 sts, sc in next 4 sts, hdc in next 2 sts, dc in next st, 2dc in next st**, rep from * to ** 3 times omitting final 2dc on last side, slst to close rnd. [24dc, 16hdc, 16sc, 4ch-2]

Rnd 6: slst in next st, slst in ch-2-sp, (ch3, dc, ch2, 2dc) in ch-2-sp, dc in each st to next ch-2-sp, *(2dc, ch2, 2dc) in next ch-2-sp, dc in each st to next ch-2 sp**, rep from * to ** twice ending last rep at starting ch, slst to close rnd. [72dc, 4ch-2]

Rnd 7: Rep Rnd 6. [88dc, 4ch-2]

Fasten off **Colour 19**.

PETALS

Join **Colour 21** to FL of Rnd 4 of square.

Rnd 1: ch3, dc in same st, *ch3, skip 1 st, 2dc in next st, ch, skip 1 st, 2dc in next st**, rep from * to * to end of rnd omitting last 2dc, slst to close rnd. [48dc, 12ch-1, 12ch-3]

Rnd 2: slst in next st, slst in ch-3-sp, (ch3, 2dc, ch2, 3dc) in same ch-3-sp, sc in ch-1-sp, *(3dc, ch2, 3dc) in ch-3-sp, sc in ch-1-sp**, rep from * to ** to end, slst to close rnd. [12 petals, 12sc]

Fasten off **Colour 21**.

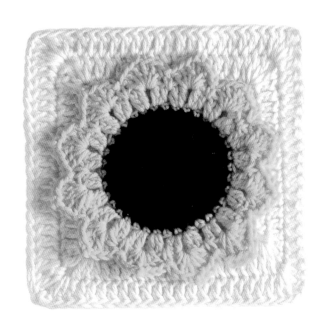

2	■
21	▨
19	▨

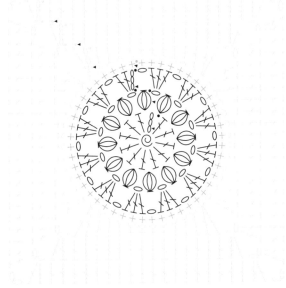

SQUARE CHART

PETALS CHART

■	45
■	17
■	21
■	27
■	31
■	1
■	39

SQUARE CHART

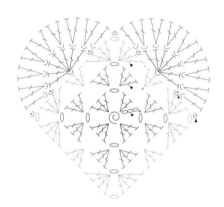

HEART CHART

HEART

With a 4mm hook and **Colour 45**, make a magic ring.

Rnd 1: ch3, 2dc, ch, (3dc, ch) 3 times in ring, slst to close rnd. [12dc, 4ch]

Fasten off **Colour 45**.

Join **Colour 17** in any ch-1-sp of Rnd 1 with a standing dc. This counts as first dc in Rnd 2.

Rnd 2: *(3dc, ch, 3dc) in ch-1-sp, sk next 3 sts**, rep from * to ** 3 times, slst to close rnd. [24dc, 4ch-1]

Fasten off **Colour 17**.

Join **Colour 21** in any ch-1-sp of Rnd 2 with a standing dc. This counts as first dc in Rnd 3.

Rnd 3: *(4dc, ch, 4dc) in ch-1-sp, sk next 3 sts, 3dc in next st sp, sk next 3 sts**, rep from * to ** 3 times, slst to close rnd. [48dc, 4ch-2]

Fasten off **Colour 21**.

Place stitch marker in seventh dc of first (4dc, ch, 4dc) and again in seventh dc of next (4dc, ch, 4dc).

Join **Colour 27** in FL of st where first stitch marker was placed. All sts in this rnd are made in FLO:

Rnd 4: slst in same st, sk next 2 sts, 7dc in next st, sk next 2 sts, slst in next st. [7dc, 2slst]

Fasten off and rejoin **Colour 27** in st where second stitch marker was placed.

Rep Rnd 4. Fasten off **Colour 27**.

Join **Colour 31** in FL of Rnd 3, in corner ch that is closest to first Rnd 4 slst. Work slsts in this rnd in FLO:

Rnd 5: *slst in ch, sk next 2 sts, dc in slst, 2dc in next 7 sts, dc in slst, sk next 2 sts**, rep from * to ** once, slst in next ch. [32dc, 3slst]

Fasten off **Colour 31**.

SQUARE

Join **Colour 1** in BL of second dc from any Rnd 3 3dc-group of heart with a standing tr. This counts as the first tr in Rnd 6. All sts in this rnd are made in BLO.

Rnd 6: *(3tr, ch2, 3tr) in st, sk next 2 sts, 3dc in next st, sk next 2 sts, 3hdc in ch, sk next 2 sts, 3dc in next st, sk next 2 sts**, rep from * to ** 3 times, slst to close rnd. [24tr, 24dc, 12hdc, 4ch-2]

Rnd 7: slst in next 2 sts, slst in next ch-2-sp, ch3, (2dc, ch2, 3dc) in same sp, sk next 3 sts, (3dc in next st sp, sk next 3 sts) 4 times, *(3dc, ch2, 3dc) in ch-2-sp, sk next 3 sts, (3dc in next st sp, sk next 3 sts) 4 times**, rep from * to ** twice, slst to close rnd. [72dc, 4ch-2]

Rnd 8: slst in next 2 sts, slst in next ch-2-sp, ch3, (2dc, ch2, 3dc) in same sp, sk next 3 sts, (3dc in next st sp, sk next 3 sts) 5 times, *(3dc, ch2, 3dc) in ch-2-sp, sk next 3 sts, (3dc in next st sp, sk next 3 sts) 5 times**, rep from * to ** twice, slst to close rnd. [84dc, 4ch-2]

Fasten off **Colour 1**.

Join **Colour 39** in any ch-2-sp of Rnd 8 with a standing hdc. This counts as first hdc in Rnd 9.

Rnd 9: *(2hdc, ch2, 2hdc) in ch-2-sp, hdc in next 21 sts**, rep from * to ** 3 times, slst to close rnd. [100hdc, 4ch-2]

Fasten off **Colour 39**.

HEART

With a 4mm hook and **Colour 48**, make a magic ring.

Rnd 1: ch3, 11dc in ring, slst in FL of third ch of initial ch3. [12dc]

All sts in this rnd are made in FLO:

Rnd 2: ch3, (tr, dc) in next st, 3dc in next st, hdc in next st, (hdc, sc) in next st, sc in next st, (sc, ch, sc) in next st, sc in next st, (sc, hdc) in next st, hdc in next st, 3dc in next st, (dc, tr) in next st, ch2, slst in slst. [2tr, 8dc, 4hdc, 6sc, 1ch-3, 1ch-2]

Fasten off **Colour 48**.

SQUARE

Join **Colour 45** in BL of first st from Rnd 1 of heart with a standing dc. This counts as first dc in Rnd 3. All sts in this rnd are made in BL of Rnd 1 sts:

Rnd 3: 2dc in each st to end of rnd, slst to close rnd. [24dc]

Rnd 4: ch2, hdc in same st, hdc in next st, (2hdc in next st, hdc in next st) 11 times, slst to close rnd. [36hdc]

Fasten off **Colour 45**.

Join **Colour 19** in first st made in Rnd 4.

Rnd 5: *sc in st, ch2, sk next st, (dc, ch2, dc) in next st, ch2, sk next st**, rep from * to ** 8 times. [18dc, 9sc, 27ch-2]

Fasten off **Colour 19**.

Join **Colour 38** in ch-2-sp from last (dc, ch2, dc) made in Rnd 5.

Rnd 6: ch3, *popcorn in ch-2-sp, ch, sk next st, dc in next ch-2-sp, ch, dc in next st, ch, dc in next ch-2-sp, ch, sk next st**, rep from * to ** 8 times, slst to close rnd. [27dc, 9 popcorns, 36ch-1]

Fasten off **Colour 38**.

Join **Colour 19** in the first ch-1-sp after any popcorn in Rnd 6 with a standing tr. This counts as first tr in Rnd 7. All sts in this rnd are made in ch-sp only:

Rnd 7: *(2tr, ch2, 2tr) in ch-sp, 2dc in next 3 ch-sp, (dc, hdc) in next ch-sp, (hdc, dc) in next ch-sp, 2dc in next 3 ch-sp**, rep from * to ** 3 times, slst to close rnd. [16tr, 56dc, 8hdc, 4ch-2]

Fasten off **Colour 19**.

Join **Colour 48** in any ch-2-sp of Rnd 7 with a standing hdc. This counts as first hdc in Rnd 8.

Rnd 8: *(2hdc, ch2, 2hdc) in ch-2-sp, hdc in next 20 sts**, rep from * to ** 3 times. [96hdc, 4ch-2]

Fasten off **Colour 48**.

Join **Colour 45** in any ch-2-sp.

Rnd 9: ch, *(sc, ch2, sc) in ch-2-sp, sc in next 24 sts**, rep from * to ** 3 times. [104sc, 4ch-2]

Fasten off **Colour 45**.

48	
45	
19	
38	

SQUARE CHART

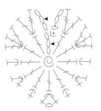

HEART CHART

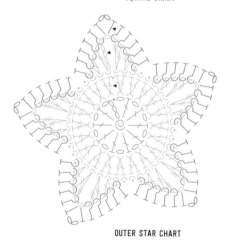

■	13
■	17
■	21
■	27
■	1
■	36
■	39

SQUARE CHART

OUTER STAR CHART

INNER STAR CHART

INNER STAR

With a 4mm hook and **Colour 13**, make a magic ring.

Rnd 1: ch4, (dc, ch) 9 times, slst in third ch of initial ch4. [10dc, 10ch]

Place stitch marker in BL of third ch of initial ch4. All sts in this rnd are made in FLO:

Rnd 2: *slst in next ch-sp, sk st, (hdc, dc, ch, dc, hdc) in next ch-sp, sk st**, rep from * to ** 4 times, slst to close rnd. [10dc, 10hdc, 5ch-1]

Fasten off **Colour 13**.

Join **Colour 17** in any ch-1-sp of Rnd 2 with an sc. This counts as first sc in Rnd 3. Sk all slsts in this rnd.

Rnd 3: *(sc, ch2, sc) in ch-1-sp, bpsc around each of next 4 sts**, rep from * to ** 4 times. [10sc, 20bpsc, 5ch-2]

Fasten off **Colour 17**.

OUTER STAR

Join **Colour 21** in st where stitch marker was placed in Rnd 1 of inner star with a standing dc. This counts as first dc in Rnd 4. All sts in this rnd are made in BL of Rnd 1 sts:

Rnd 4: (2dc in st, 2dc in next ch st) 10 times, slst in FL of initial dc. [40dc]

Place stitch marker in BL of initial dc. All sts in this rnd are made in FLO:

Rnd 5: ch5, tr in same st, (dc, hdc) in next st, sc in next st, slst in next 2 sts, sc in next st, (hdc, dc) in next st, (tr, dtr) in next st, ch, *(dtr, tr) in next st, (dc, hdc) in next st, sc in next st, slst in next 2 sts, sc in next st, (hdc, dc) in next st, (tr, dtr) in next st, ch**, rep from * to ** 3 times. [10dtr, 10tr, 10dc, 10hdc, 10sc, 10slst, 5ch-1]

Fasten off **Colour 21**.

Join **Colour 27** in any ch-sp of Rnd 5 with a standing hdc. This counts as first hdc in Rnd 6.

Rnd 6: *(hdc, ch2, hdc) in ch-1-sp, bphdc around each of next 5 sts, sk 2 sts, bpdc around each of next 5 sts**, rep from * to ** 4 times. [50bphdc, 10hdc, 5ch-2]

Fasten off **Colour 27**.

SQUARE

Join **Colour 1** in st where stitch marker was placed in Rnd 4 of outer star with a standing hdc. This counts as first hdc in Rnd 7. All sts in this rnd are made in BL of Rnd 4 sts:

Rnd 7: hdc in st, hdc in next st, dc in next st, *(tr, ch2, tr) in next st, dc in next st, hdc in next 2 sts, sc in next 3 sts, hdc in next 2 sts, dc in next st**, rep from * to ** twice, (tr, ch2, tr) in next st, dc in next st, hdc in next 2 sts, sc in next 3 sts, slst to close rnd. [8tr, 8dc, 16hdc, 12sc, 4ch-2]

Rnd 8: slst in next 3 sts, slst in ch-2-sp, ch3, (dc, ch2, 2dc) in ch-2-sp, dc in next 11 sts, *(2dc, ch2, 2dc) in next ch-2-sp, dc in next 11 sts**, rep from * to ** twice, slst to close rnd. [60dc, 4ch-2]

Rnd 9: slst in next st, slst in ch-2-sp, ch3, (dc, ch2, 2dc) in ch-2-sp, dc in next 15 sts, *(2dc, ch2, 2dc) in next ch-2-sp, dc in next 15 sts**, rep from * to ** twice, slst to close rnd. [76dc, 4ch-2]

Rnd 10: slst in next st, slst in ch-2-sp, ch, *(sc, ch2, sc) in ch-2-sp, sc in next 19 sts**, rep from * to ** 3 times. [84sc, 4ch-2]

Fasten off **Colour 1**.

Join **Colour 36** in any ch-2-sp with a standing hdc. This counts as first hdc in Rnd 11.

Rnd 11: *(2hdc, ch2, 2hdc) in ch-2-sp, hdc in next 21 sts**, rep from * to ** 3 times. [100hdc, 4ch-2]

Fasten off **Colour 36**.

Join **Colour 39** in any ch-2-sp with a standing hdc. This counts as first hdc in Rnd 12.

Rnd 12: *(2hdc, ch2, 2hdc) in ch-2-sp, bphdc around each of next 25 sts**, rep from * to ** 3 times. [16hdc, 100bphdc, 4ch-2]

Fasten off **Colour 39**.

SQUARE

With a 3mm hook and **Colour 4**, make a magic ring.

Rnd 1: ch3, 11dc in ring, slst to close rnd. [12dc]

Rnd 2: ch2, hdc in same st, 2hdc in each st to end of rnd, slst to close rnd. [24hdc]

Fasten off **Colour 4**.

Join **Colour 39** in first st made in Rnd 2 with a standing hdc. This counts as first hdc in next rnd.

Rnd 3: 2hdc in st, hdc in next st, (2hdc in next st, hdc in next st) 5 times, fasten off **Colour 39** and join **Colour 4**, (2hdc in next st, hdc in next st) 6 times, slst to close rnd. [36hdc]

Fasten off **Colour 4**.

Join **Colour 36** in first st made in Rnd 3 with a standing hdc. This counts as first hdc in next rnd.

Rnd 4: hdc in st, hdc in next st, 2hdc in next st, (hdc in next 2 sts, 2hdc in next st) 5 times, fasten off **Colour 36** and join **Colour 4**, (hdc in next 2 sts, 2hdc in next st) 6 times, slst to close rnd. [48hdc]

Fasten off **Colour 4**.

Join **Colour 27** in first st made in Rnd 4 with a standing hdc. This counts as first hdc in next rnd.

Rnd 5: 2hdc in st, hdc in next 3 sts, (2hdc in next st, hdc in next 3 sts) 5 times, fasten off **Colour 27** and join **Colour 4**, (2hdc in next st, hdc in next 3 sts) 6 times, slst to close rnd. [60hdc]

Fasten off **Colour 4**.

Join **Colour 21** in first st made in Rnd 5 with a standing hdc. This counts as first hdc in next rnd.

Rnd 6: hdc in st, hdc in next 3 sts, 2hdc in next st, (hdc in next 4 sts, 2hdc in next st) 5 times, fasten off **Colour 21** and join **Colour 4**, (hdc in next 4 sts, 2hdc in next st) 6 times, slst to close rnd. [72hdc]

Fasten off **Colour 4**.

Join **Colour 17** in first st made in Rnd 6 with a standing hdc. This counts as first hdc in next rnd.

Rnd 7: 2hdc in st, hdc in next 5 sts, (2hdc in next st, hdc in next 5 sts) 5 times, fasten off **Colour 17** and join **Colour 4**, (2hdc in next st, hdc in next 5 sts) 6 times, slst to close rnd. [84hdc]

Fasten off **Colour 4**.

Join **Colour 13** in first st made in Rnd 7 with a standing hdc. This counts as first hdc in next rnd.

Rnd 8: hdc in st, hdc in next 5 sts, 2hdc in next st, (hdc in next 6 sts, 2hdc in next st) 5 times, fasten off **Colour 13** and join **Colour 4**, (hdc in next 6 sts, 2hdc in next st) 6 times, slst to close rnd. [96hdc]

Rnd 9: ch, sc in same st, sc in next 2 sts, hdc in next 4 sts, dc in next 3 sts, tr in next 2 sts, ch2, *tr in next 2 sts, dc in next 3 sts, hdc in next 4 sts, sc in next 6 sts, hdc in next 4 sts, dc in next 3 sts, tr in next 2 sts, ch2**, rep from * to ** twice, tr in next 2 sts, dc in next 3 sts, hdc in next 4 sts, sc in next 3 sts, slst in initial sc. [16tr, 24dc, 32hdc, 24sc, 4ch-2]

Rnd 10: ch3, dc in next 11 sts, *(2dc, ch2, 2dc) in ch-2-sp, dc in next 24 sts**, rep from * to ** twice, dc in next 12 sts. [112dc, 4ch-2]

Fasten off **Colour 4**.

Join **Colour 1** in any ch-2-sp of Rnd 10.

Rnd 11: ch, *(sc, ch2, sc) in ch-2-sp, sc in next 28 sts**, rep from * to ** 3 times. [120sc, 4ch-2]

Fasten off **Colour 4**.

CLOUDS

With a 4mm hook and **Colour 1**, ch6.

Rnd 1: sc in second ch from hook, sc in next 3 ch, 3sc in next ch, turn to work on other side of foundation ch, sc in next 3 ch, 2sc in next ch, slst in initial sc. [12sc]

Rnd 2: 4hdc in next st, (slst in next st, 4hdc in next st) 5 times. [24hdc, 6slst]

Fasten off **Colour 1**. Rep to make a total of 2 clouds.

Attach the clouds to the bottom of each end of the rainbow.

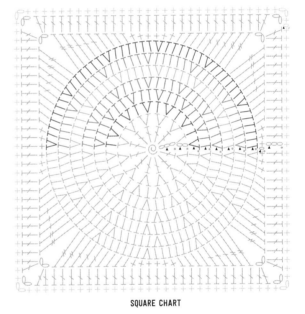

4	
39	
36	
27	
21	
17	
13	
1	

SQUARE CHART

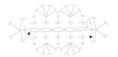

CLOUD CHART

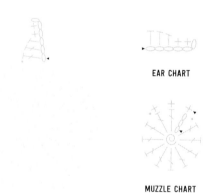

SQUARE CHART

HORN CHART

EAR CHART

MUZZLE CHART

FLOWER CHART

Colour key:
- 1
- 42
- 20
- 40
- 44
- 12
- 2
- 19

SQUARE

With a 4mm hook and **Colour 1**, make a magic ring,

Rnd 1: ch3, 11dc in ring, slst to close rnd. [12dc]

Rnd 2: ch3, dc in same st, 2dc in each st to end of rnd, slst to close rnd. [24dc]

Rnd 3: ch3, dc in same st, dc in next st, *2dc in next st, dc in next st**, rep from * to ** to end of rnd, slst to close rnd. [36dc]

Fasten off **Colour 1**.

Join **Colour 42** in any st of Rnd 3. All sts in this rnd are made in BLO:

Rnd 4: ch3, dc in same st, ch2, 2dc in next st, hdc in next 2 sts, sc in next 3 sts, hdc in next 2 sts, *2dc in next st, ch2, 2dc in next st, hdc in next 2 sts, sc in next 3 sts, hdc in next 2 sts**, rep from * to ** twice, slst to close rnd. [16dc, 16hdc, 12sc, 4ch-2]

Rnd 5: slst in next st, slst in ch-2-sp, (ch3, 1dc, ch2, 2dc) in ch-2-sp, dc in each st to next ch-2-sp, *(2dc, ch2, 2dc) in next ch-2-sp, dc in each st to next ch-2-sp**, rep from * to ** twice ending last rep at starting ch, slst to close rnd. [60dc, 4ch-2]

Rnds 6-7: Rep Rnd 5. [92dc, 4ch-2]

Fasten off **Colour 42**.

MUZZLE

With **Colour 1**, make a magic ring.

Rnd 1: ch3, 11dc in ring, slst to close rnd. [12dc]

Rnd 2: sc in next 3 sts, slst in same st as last sc. [3sc]

Fasten off **Colour 1**.

EARS

With **Colour 1**, ch6.

Row 1: sc in second ch from hook, sc, hdc in next 3 ch. [3hdc, 2sc]

Fasten off **Colour 1**. Rep to make a total of 2 ears

HORN

Join **Colour 20** in top of Rnd 3 of square.

Rnd 1: ch6, sc in second ch from hook, sc, hdc, dc in next 2 sts, sk st, slst to next st. [2dc, 1hdc, 2sc]

Fasten off **Colour 20**.

FLOWERS

With **Colour 40**, ch5, slst in first st to make a ring.

Rnd 1: ch, (dc, slst in ring) 5 times. [5 petals]

Fasten off **Colour 40**. Rep to make a total of 3 flowers, with one each in **Colour 40**, **Colour 44** and **Colour 12**.

FINISHING

Attach muzzle to unicorn's face and stitch ears on either side of horn.

Stitch flowers to top of head between ears as shown.

Embroider eyes and nostrils onto head with **Colour 2**.

Make small tassels with **Colour 19**. and attach on either side of unicorn's face.

SQUARE

With a 4mm hook and **Colour 20**, make a magic ring.

Rnd 1: ch3, 11dc in ring, slst to close rnd. [12dc]

Rnd 2: ch3, dc in same st, 2dc in each st to end of rnd, slst to close rnd. [24dc]

Rnd 3: ch3, dc in same st, dc in next st, *2dc in next st, dc in next st**, rep from * to ** to end of rnd, slst to close rnd. [36dc]

Fasten off **Colour 20**.

Join **Colour 2** in any st of Rnd 3. All sts in this rnd are made in BLO:

Rnd 4: ch3, dc in same st, ch2, 2dc in next st, hdc in next 2 sts, sc in next 3 sts, hdc in next 2 sts, *2dc in next st, ch2, 2dc in next st, hdc in next 2 sts, sc in next 3 sts, hdc in next 2 sts**, rep from * to ** twice, slst to close rnd. [16dc, 16hdc, 12sc, 4ch-2]

Fasten off **Colour 2**.

Join **Colour 35** in any ch-2-sp of Rnd 4.

Rnd 5: (ch3, dc, ch2, 2dc) in ch-2-sp, dc in each st to next ch-2-sp, *(2dc, ch2, 2dc) in next ch-2-sp, dc in each st to next ch-2-sp**, rep from * to ** twice, slst to close rnd. [60dc, 4ch-2]

Rnds 6-7: Rep Rnd 5. [92dc, 4ch-2]

Fasten off **Colour 35**.

CIRCLE

With **Colour 2**, ch3.

Rnd 1: 5hdc in third ch from hook, slst to close rnd. [6hdc]

Rnd 2: ch2, hdc in same st, 2hdc in every st to end of rnd, slst to close rnd. [12hdc]

Rnd 3: ch2, hdc in same st, *hdc in next st, 2hdc in next st**, rep from * to ** to last st, hdc in last st, slst to close rnd. [18hdc]

Rnd 4: ch2, hdc in same st, *hdc in next 2 sts, 2hdc in next st**, rep from * to ** to last 2 sts, hdc in last 2 sts, slst to close rnd. [24hdc]

Rnd 5: ch2, hdc in same st, *hdc in next 3 sts, 2hdc in next st**, rep from * to ** to last 3 sts, hdc in last 3 sts, slst to close rnd. [30hdc]

STAR

With **Colour 35**, ch2.

Rnd 1: 10hdc in second ch from hook, slst to close rnd. [10hdc]

Rnd 2: *ch4, slst in second ch from hook, sc in next ch, hdc in next ch, sk next st from Rnd 1, slst in next st**, rep from * to ** 4 times. [5 points]

Fasten off **Colour 35**.

Stitch star onto circle, and stitch circle onto square as shown.

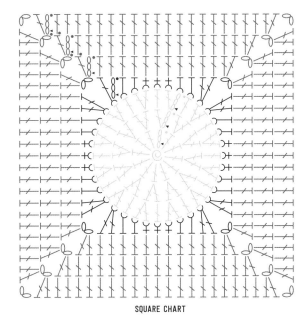

20

2

35

SQUARE CHART

STAR CHART

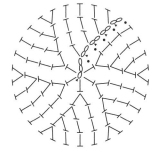

CIRCLE CHART

SQUARE

With a 4mm hook and **Colour 11**, make a magic ring.

Rnd 1: ch3, 11dc in ring, slst to close rnd. [12dc]

Rnd 2: ch3, dc in same st, 2dc in each st to end of rnd, slst to close rnd. [24dc]

Rnd 3: ch3, dc in same st, dc in next st, *2dc in next st, dc in next st**, rep from * to ** to end of rnd, slst to close rnd. [36dc]

Fasten off **Colour 11**.

Join **Colour 44** in any st of Rnd 3. All sts in this rnd are made in BLO:

Rnd 4: ch3, dc in same st, ch2, 2dc in next st, hdc in next 2 sts, sc in next 3 sts, hdc in next 2 sts, *2dc in next st, ch2, 2dc in next st, hdc in next 2 sts, sc in next 3 sts, hdc in next 2 sts**, rep from * to ** twice, slst to close rnd. [16dc, 16hdc, 12sc, 4ch-2]

Rnd 5: slst in next st, slst in ch-2-sp, (ch3, dc, ch2, 2dc) in ch-2-sp, dc in each st to next ch-2-sp, *(2dc, ch2, 2dc) in next ch-2-sp, dc in each st to next ch-2-sp**, rep from * to ** twice, slst to close rnd. (60dc, 4ch-2]

Rnds 6-7: Rep Rnd 5. [92dc, 4ch-2]

Fasten off **Colour 44**.

Join **Colour 11** in any ch-2-sp of Rnd 7.

Rnd 8: ch, *(sc, ch, sc) in ch-2-sp, sc in each st to next ch-2-sp**, rep from * to ** 3 times ending last rep at initial ch, slst to close rnd. [100sc, 4ch-2]

Fasten off **Colour 11**.

EDGING AND EARS

Join **Colour 11** yarn in FL of left-hand corner in Rnd 3 of square. All sts in this rnd are made in FLO:

Rnd 1: ch, sc in same st, ch, sc, 8dc in same st, (sc, ch) in next 25 sts, 8dc in next st, (sc, ch) in each st to end of rnd. [2 8dc-groups, 34dc, 32ch-1]

Fasten off **Colour 11**.

NOSE

With **Colour 9** ch4, 9dc in fourth ch from hook, slst to join.

Fasten off **Colour 9**. Stitch nose onto teddy's face.

With **Colour 2**, embroider details onto nose and 2 small eyes onto teddy's face above nose.

■	11
▨	44
▨	9
■	2

SQUARE CHART

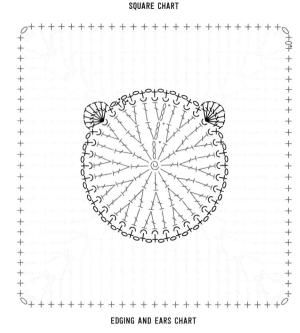

EDGING AND EARS CHART

NOSE CHART

DIAMOND

With a 4mm hook and **Colour 45**, make a magic ring.

Rnd 1: ch3, 2dc in ring, ch2, *3dc, ch2**, rep from * to ** twice, slst to close rnd. [12dc, 4ch-2]

Fasten off **Colour 45**.

Join **Colour 44** in any ch-2-sp of Rnd 1 with a standing hdc. This counts as first hdc in next rnd.

Rnd 2: *(hdc, ch2, hdc) in ch-2-sp, hdc in next 3 sts**, rep from * to ** 3 times, slst to close rnd. [20hdc, 4ch-2]

Fasten off **Colour 44**.

Join **Colour 17** in any ch-2-sp of Rnd 2 with a standing dc. This counts as first dc in next rnd.

Rnd 3: *(3dc, ch2, 3dc) in ch-2-sp, sk next 2 sts, 3dc in next st, sk next 2 sts**, rep from * to ** 3 times, slst to close rnd. [36dc, 4ch-2]

Fasten off **Colour 17**.

Join **Colour 49** in any ch-2-sp of Rnd 3 with a standing hdc. This counts as first hdc in next rnd.

Rnd 4: *(hdc, ch, hdc) in ch-2-sp, hdc in next 9 sts**, rep from * to ** 3 times, slst to close rnd. [44hdc, 4ch-1]

Fasten off **Colour 49**.

Join **Colour 21** in FL of any ch st with a standing dc. This counts as first dc in next rnd. All sts in this rnd are made in FL of Rnd 4 sts:

Rnd 5: *(3dc, ch2, 3dc) in ch-1-sp, sk next 2 sts, (3dc in next st, sk next 2 sts) 3 times**, rep from * to ** 3 times, slst to close rnd. [60dc, 4ch-2]

Fasten off **Colour 21**.

Join **Colour 20** in any ch-2-sp of Rnd 5.

Rnd 6: ch, *(sc, ch, sc) in ch-2-sp, bpsc around each of next 15 sts**, rep from * to ** 3 times, slst to close rnd. [60bpsc, 8sc, 4ch-1]

Fasten off **Colour 20**.

SQUARE

Join **Colour 27** in BL of sixth hdc of Rnd 4 of diamond on any side with a standing tr. This counts as first tr in next rnd. All sts in this rnd are made in BL of Rnd 4 sts:

Rnd 7: (3tr, ch2, 3tr) in st, sk next 2 sts, 3dc in next st, sk next 2 sts, 3hdc in next ch-1-sp, sk next 2 sts, 3dc in next st, sk next 2 sts, *(3tr, ch2, 3tr) in st, sk next 2 sts, 3dc in next st, sk next 2 sts, 3hdc in next ch-1-sp, sk next 2 sts, 3dc in next st, sk next 2 sts**, rep from * to ** twice, slst to close rnd. [24tr, 24dc, 12hdc, 4ch-2]

Rnd 8: slst in next 2 sts, slst in next ch-2-sp, ch, *(sc, ch2, sc) in ch-2-sp, sc in next 15 sts**, rep from * to ** 3 times, slst to close rnd. [68sc, 4ch-2]

Fasten off **Colour 27**.

Join **Colour 31** in in any ch-2-sp of Rnd 8 with a standing dc. This counts as first dc in next rnd.

Rnd 9: *(3dc, ch2, 3dc) in ch-2-sp, sk next 2 sts, (3dc in next st, sk next 2 sts) 5 times**, rep from * to ** 3 times, slst to close rnd. [84dc, 4ch-2]

Fasten off **Colour 31**.

Join **Colour 39** in any ch-2-sp of Rnd 9 with a standing hdc. This counts as first hdc in next rnd.

Rnd 10: *(2hdc, ch2, 2hdc) in ch-2-sp, hdc in next 21 sts**, rep from * to ** 3 times, slst to close rnd. [100hdc, 4ch-2]

Fasten off **Colour 39**.

Join **Colour 38** in any ch-2-sp of Rnd 10 with a standing hdc. This counts as first hdc in next rnd.

Rnd 11: *(2hdc, ch2, 2hdc) in ch-2-sp, bphdc in next 25 sts**, rep from * to ** 3 times, slst to close rnd. [16hdc, 100bphdc, 4ch-2]

Fasten off **Colour 38**.

SQUARE CHART

45	
44	
17	
49	
21	
20	
27	
31	
39	
38	

DIAMOND CHART

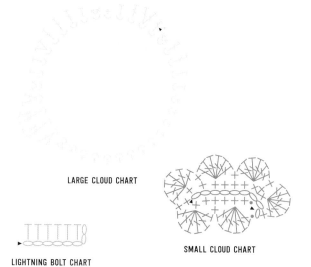

SQUARE

With a 4mm hook and **Colour 3**, make a magic ring.

Rnd 1: ch3, 11dc in ring, slst to close rnd. [12dc]

Rnd 2: ch3, dc in same st, 2dc in each st to end of rnd, slst to close rnd. [24dc]

Rnd 3: ch2, hdc in same st, *hdc in next st, 2hdc in next st**, rep from * to ** to last st, hdc in last st, slst to close rnd. [36hdc]

Fasten off **Colour 3**.

Join **Colour 32** in any st of Rnd 3. All sts in this rnd are made in BLO:

Rnd 4: ch3, dc in same st, ch2, 2dc in next st, hdc in next 2 sts, sc in next 3 sts, hdc in next 2 sts, *2dc in next st, ch2, 2dc in next st, hdc in next 2 sts, sc in next 3 sts, hdc in next 2 sts**, rep from * to ** twice, slst to close rnd. [16dc, 16hdc, 12sc, 4ch-2]

Rnd 5: slst in next st, slst in ch-2-sp, (ch3, dc, ch2, 2dc) in ch-2-sp, dc in each st to next ch-2-sp, *(2dc, ch2, 2dc) in next ch-2-sp, dc in each st to next ch-2-sp**, rep from * to ** twice ending last rep at initial ch3, slst to close rnd. [60dc, 4ch-2]

Rnds 6-7: Rep Rnd 5. [92dc, 4ch-2]

Fasten off **Colour 32**.

LARGE CLOUD

Join **Colour 3** in FL of top right-hand corner in Rnd 3 of square with a standing dc. This counts as first dc in next rnd.

Rnd 1: dc, 2dc in next st, dc, hdc, sc, 2sc in next st, hdc, dc in next 3 sts, 2hdc in next st, hdc in next 2 sts, 2sc in next st, 2dc in next st, 2tr in next 2 sts, 2dc in next st, 2sc in next st, sc in next 12 sts, hdc in next 2 sts, dc in next 2 sts, 2sc in next st, slst to close rnd. [46]

Fasten off **Colour 3**.

LIGHTNING BOLT

With **Colour 21**, ch8.

Row 1: hdc in third ch from hook, hdc in each st to end of row. [6hdc]

Fasten off **Colour 21**. Rep to make a total of 2 lightning bolts.

Stitch lightning bolts across large cloud as shown.

SMALL CLOUD

With **Colour 5**, ch8.

Rnd 1: 3sc in second ch from hook, sc in next 5 sts, 3sc in last st, turn to work on other side of foundation ch, sc in next 5 sts, slst in first sc to close rnd.

Rnd 2: ch, sc in same st, *6dc in next st, sc in next st, 6dc in next st, sk next st, sc in next st, sk next st, 6dc in next st, sc in next st**, rep from * to ** to end of rnd omitting final sc, slst to close rnd.

Fasten off **Colour 5**.

Attach small cloud on top of lightning.

3	
32	
5	
21	

SQUARE CHART

LARGE CLOUD CHART

LIGHTNING BOLT CHART

SMALL CLOUD CHART

SQUARE

With a 4mm hook and **Colour 1**, make a magic ring.

Rnd 1: ch4, (3dc, ch) twice, 2dc, slst in BL of third ch of initial ch4. [12dc, 4ch-1]

All sts in this rnd are made in BL of Rnd 1 sts:

Rnd 2: slst in next ch-1-sp, ch3, (dc, ch, 2dc) in ch-1-sp, dc in next 3 sts, *(2dc, ch, 2dc) in ch-1-sp, dc in next 3 sts**, rep from * to ** twice, slst in BL of third ch of initial ch3. [28dc, 4ch-1]

All sts in this rnd are made in BL of Rnd 2 sts:

Rnd 3: slst in next st, slst in next ch-1-sp, ch3, (dc, ch, 2dc) in ch-1-sp, dc in next 7 sts, *(2dc, ch, 2dc) in ch-1-sp, dc in next 7 sts**, rep from * to ** twice, slst in BL of third ch of initial ch3. [44dc, 4ch-1]

All sts in this rnd are made in BL of Rnd 3 sts:

Rnd 4: slst in next st, slst in next ch-1-sp, ch3, (dc, ch, 2dc) in ch-1-sp, dc in next 11 sts, *(2dc, ch, 2dc) in ch-1-sp, dc in next 11 sts**, rep from * to ** twice, slst in BL of third ch of initial ch3. [60dc, 4ch-1]

All sts in this rnd are made in BL of Rnd 4 sts:

Rnd 5: slst in next st, slst in next ch-1-sp, ch3, (dc, ch, 2dc) in ch-1-sp, dc in next 15 sts, *(2dc, ch, 2dc) in ch-1-sp, dc in next 15 sts**, rep from * to ** twice, slst in BL of third ch of initial ch3. [76dc, 4ch-1]

All sts in this rnd are made in BL of Rnd 5 sts:

Rnd 6: slst in next st, slst in next ch-1-sp, ch3, (dc, ch, 2dc) in ch-1-sp, dc in next 19 sts, *(2dc, ch, 2dc) in ch-1-sp, dc in next 19 sts**, rep from * to ** twice, slst in BL of third ch of initial ch3. [92dc, 4ch-1]

All sts in this rnd are made in BL of Rnd 6 sts:

Rnd 7: slst in next st, slst in next ch-1-sp, ch, *(sc, ch, sc) in ch-1-sp, sc in next 23 sts**, rep from * to ** 3 times, slst to close rnd. [100 sc, 4ch-1]

Fasten off **Colour 1**.

RIDGES

Join **Colour 39** in FL of any ch-1-sp in Rnd 1 of square. All sts in this rnd are made in FL of Rnd 1 sts:

Rnd 8: *(sc, ch, sc) in ch-1-sp, sc in next 3 sts**, rep from * to ** 3 times. [20sc, 4ch-1]

Fasten off **Colour 39**.

Join **Colour 31** in FL of any ch in Rnd 2 of square. All sts in this rnd are made in FL of Rnd 2 sts:

Rnd 9: *(sc, ch, sc) in ch-1-sp, sc in next 7 sts**, rep from * to ** 3 times. [36sc, 4ch-1]

Fasten off **Colour 31**.

Join **Colour 27** in FL of any ch in Rnd 3 of square. All sts in this rnd are made in FL of Rnd 3 sts:

Rnd 10: *(sc, ch, sc) in ch-1-sp, sc in next 11 sts**, rep from * to ** 3 times. [52sc, 4ch-1]

Fasten off **Colour 27**.

Join **Colour 21** in FL of any ch in Rnd 4 of square. All sts in this rnd are made in FL of Rnd 4 sts:

Rnd 11: *(sc, ch, sc) in ch-1-sp, sc in next 15 sts**, rep from * to ** 3 times. [68sc, 4ch-1]

Fasten off **Colour 21**.

Join **Colour 17** in FL of any ch in Rnd 5 of square. All sts in this rnd are made in FL of Rnd 5 sts:

Rnd 12: *(sc, ch, sc) in ch-1-sp, sc in next 19 sts**, rep from * to ** 3 times. [84sc, 4ch-1]

Fasten off **Colour 17**.

Join **Colour 13** in FL of any ch in Rnd 6 of square. All sts in this rnd are made in FL of Rnd 6 sts:

Rnd 13: *(sc, ch, sc) in ch-1-sp, sc in next 23 sts**, rep from * to ** 3 times. [100sc, 4ch-1]

Fasten off **Colour 13**.

1	
39	
31	
27	
21	
17	
13	

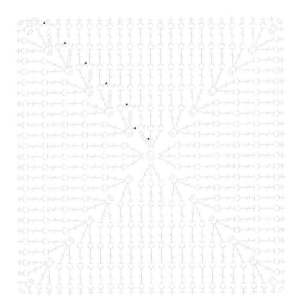

SQUARE CHART

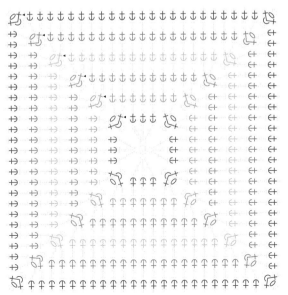

RIDGES CHART

BOBBLE

1
21
49
17
45

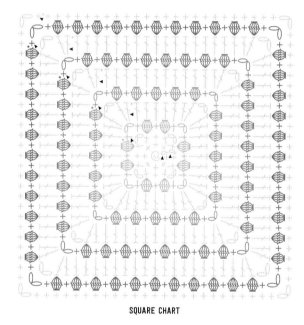

SQUARE CHART

SQUARE

With a 3.5mm hook and **Colour 1**, make a magic ring.

Rnd 1: ch, work 8sc in ring, slst to close rnd. [8sc]

Rnd 2: ch, (sc, ch2, sc) in same st, sc in next st, *(sc, ch2, sc) in next st, sc in next st**, rep from * to ** twice, slst to close rnd. [12sc, 4ch-2]

Fasten off **Colour 1**.

Join **Colour 21** in any ch-2-sp of Rnd 2. This rnd is worked on WS:

Rnd 3: *(sc, ch2, sc) in ch-2-sp, bobble in next st, sc in next st, bobble in next st**, rep from * to ** 3 times, slst to close rnd. [12sc, 8 bobbles, 4ch-2]

Fasten off **Colour 21**.

Join **Colour 1** in any ch-2-sp of Rnd 3 with a standing dc. This counts as first dc in next rnd.

Rnd 4: *(2dc, ch2, 2dc) in ch-2-sp, dc in next 5 sts**, rep from * to ** 3 times, slst to close rnd. [36dc, 4ch-2]

Fasten off **Colour 1**.

Join **Colour 49** in any ch-2-sp of Rnd 4. This rnd is worked on WS:

Rnd 5: *(sc, ch2, sc) in ch-2-sp, (bobble in next st, sc in next st) 4 times, bobble in next st**, rep from * to ** 3 times, slst to close rnd. [24sc, 20 bobbles, 4ch-2]

Fasten off **Colour 49**.

Join **Colour 1** in any ch-2-sp of Rnd 5 with a standing dc. This counts as first dc in next rnd.

Rnd 6: *(2dc, ch2, 2dc) in ch-2-sp, dc in next 11 sts**, rep from * to ** 3 times, slst to close rnd. [60dc, 4ch-2]

Fasten off **Colour 1**.

Join **Colour 17** in any ch-2-sp of Rnd 6. This rnd is worked on WS:

Rnd 7: *(sc, ch2, sc) in ch-2-sp, (bobble in next st, sc in next st) 7 times, bobble in next st**, rep from * to ** 3 times, slst to close rnd. [36sc, 32 bobbles, 4ch-2]

Fasten off **Colour 17**.

Join **Colour 1** in any ch-2-sp of Rnd 7 with a standing dc. This counts as first dc in next rnd.

Rnd 8: *(2dc, ch2, 2dc) in ch-2-sp, dc in next 17 sts**, rep from * to ** 3 times, slst to close rnd. [84dc, 4ch-2]

Fasten off **Colour 1**.

Join **Colour 45** in any ch-2-sp of Rnd 8. This rnd is worked on WS:

Rnd 9: *(sc, ch2, sc) in ch-2-sp, (bobble in next st, sc in next st) 10 times, bobble in next st**, rep from * to ** 3 times, slst to close rnd. [48sc, 44 bobbles, 4ch-2]

Fasten off **Colour 45**.

Join **Colour 1** in any ch-2-sp of Rnd 9.

Rnd 10: *(sc, ch2, sc) in ch-2-sp, sc in next 23 sts**, rep from * to ** 3 times, slst to close rnd. [100sc, 4ch-2]

Fasten off **Colour 1**.

SQUARE

With a 4mm hook and **Colour 1**, make a magic ring.

Rnd 1: ch3, 11dc in ring, slst in BL of third ch of initial ch3. [12dc]

All sts in this rnd are made in BLO:

Rnd 2: ch2, hdc in same st, (2hdc in next st) 11 times, slst to close rnd. [24hdc]

Fasten off **Colour 1**.

Join **Colour 41** in any st of Rnd 2 with a standing hdc. This counts as first hdc in next rnd. All sts in this rnd are made in BLO:

Rnd 3: *hdc in st, hdc in next st, dc in FL of Rnd 1 st**, rep from * to ** 11 times, slst to close rnd. [12dc, 24hdc]

Fasten off **Colour 41**.

Join **Colour 36** in any dc of Rnd 3 with a standing dc. This counts as first dc in next rnd. All sts in this rnd are made in BLO:

Rnd 4: *dc in dc, dc in next st, tr in FL of Rnd 2 st, dc in next st**, rep from * to ** 11 times, slst to close rnd. [12tr, 36dc]

Fasten off **Colour 36**.

Join **Colour 27** in any tr of Rnd 4 with a standing hdc. This counts as first hdc in next rnd. All sts in this rnd are made in BLO:

Rnd 5: *hdc in tr, hdc in next 2 sts, fptr around Rnd 3 dc, hdc in next st**, rep from * to ** 11 times, slst to close rnd. [12fptr, 48hdc]

Fasten off **Colour 27**.

Join **Colour 21** in any fptr of Rnd 5 with a standing dc. This counts as first dc in next rnd. All sts in this rnd are made in BLO:

Rnd 6: *dc in fptr, dc in next 2 sts, fptr around Rnd 4 tr, dc in next 2 sts**, rep from * to ** 11 times, slst to close rnd. [12fptr, 60dc]

Fasten off **Colour 21**.

Join **Colour 17** in any fptr of Rnd 6 with a standing tr. This counts as first tr in next rnd. All sts in this rnd are made in BLO:

Rnd 7: *(tr, ch2, tr) in fptr, tr in next st, dc in next 2 sts, hdc in next 3 sts, sc in next 5 sts, hdc in next 3 sts, dc in next 2 sts, tr in next st**, rep from * to ** 3 times, slst to close rnd. [16tr, 16dc, 24hdc, 20sc, 4ch-2]

Fasten off **Colour 17**.

Join **Colour 13** in any ch-2-sp of Rnd 7 with a standing dc. This counts as first dc in next rnd.

Rnd 8: *(2dc, ch2, 2dc) in ch-2-sp, dc in next 6 sts, fptr around Rnd 6 fptr, sk next st, dc in next 2 sts, fpdtr around Rnd 5 fptr, sk next st, dc in next 2 sts, fptr around Rnd 6 fptr, sk next st, dc in next 6 sts**, rep from * to ** 3 times, slst to close rnd. [4fpdtr, 8fptr, 80dc, 4ch-2]

Fasten off **Colour 13**.

Join **Colour 1** in any ch-2-sp of Rnd 8. All sts in this rnd are made in BLO:

Rnd 9: *(sc, ch2, sc) in ch-2-sp, sc in next 23 sts**, rep from * to ** 3 times, slst to close rnd. [100sc, 4ch-2]

Fasten off **Colour 1**.

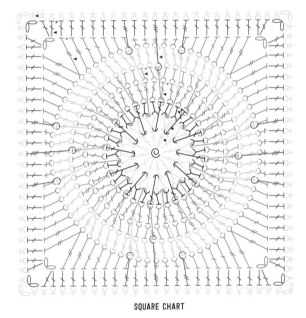

SQUARE CHART

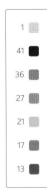

1	
41	
36	
27	
21	
17	
13	

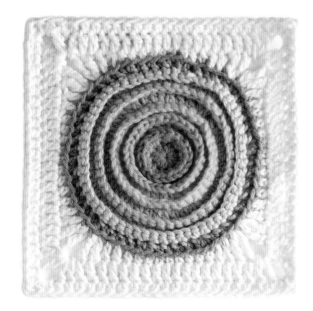

45
17
21
27
31
39
1

SQUARE CHART

SQUARE

With a 4mm hook and **Colour 45**, make a magic ring.

Rnd 1: ch2, 9hdc in ring, slst in FL of second ch of initial ch2. [10hdc]

All sts in this rnd are made in FL of Rnd 1 sts:

Rnd 2: ch, 2sc in same st, (2sc in next st) 9 times, slst to close rnd. [20sc]

Fasten off **Colour 45**.

Join **Colour 17** in BL of any Rnd 1 st with a standing dc. This counts as first dc in next rnd. All sts in this rnd are made in BL of Rnd 1 sts:

Rnd 3: 2dc in each st to end of rnd, slst in FL of initial dc. [20dc]

All sts in this rnd are made in FL of Rnd 3 sts:

Rnd 4: ch, 2sc in same st, sc in next st, (2sc in next st, sc in next st) 9 times, slst to close rnd. [30sc]

Fasten off **Colour 17**.

Join **Colour 21** in BL of any Rnd 3 st with a standing dc. This counts as first dc in next rnd. All sts in this rnd are made in BL of Rnd 3 sts:

Rnd 5: 2dc in st, dc in next st, (2dc in next st, dc in next st) 9 times, slst in FL of initial dc. [30dc]

All sts in this rnd are made in FL of Rnd 5 sts:

Rnd 6: ch, 2sc in same st, sc in next 2 sts, (2sc in next st, sc in next 2 sts) 9 times, slst to close rnd. [40sc]

Fasten off **Colour 21**.

Join **Colour 27** in BL of any Rnd 5 st with a standing dc. This counts as first dc in next rnd. All sts in this rnd are made in BL of Rnd 5 sts:

Rnd 7: 2dc in st, dc in next 2 sts, (2dc in next st, dc in next 2 sts) 9 times, slst in FL of initial dc. [40dc]

All sts in this rnd are made in FL of Rnd 7 sts:

Rnd 8: ch, 2sc in same st, sc in next 3 sts, (2sc in next st, sc in next 3 sts) 9 times, slst to close rnd. [50sc]

Fasten off **Colour 27**.

Join **Colour 31** in BL of any Rnd 7 st with a standing dc. This counts as first dc in next rnd. All sts in this rnd are made in BL of Rnd 7 sts:

Rnd 9: 2dc in st, dc in next 3 sts, (2dc in next st, dc in next 3 sts) 9 times, slst in FL of initial dc. [50dc]

All sts in this rnd are made in FL of Rnd 9 sts:

Rnd 10: ch, 2sc in same st, sc in next 4 sts, (2sc in next st, sc in next 4 sts) 9 times. [60sc]

Fasten off **Colour 31**.

Join **Colour 39** in BL of any Rnd 9 st with a standing hdc. This counts as first hdc in next rnd. All sts in this rnd are made in BL of Rnd 9 sts:

Rnd 11: 2hdc in st, hdc in next 4 sts, (2hdc in next st, hdc in next 4 sts) 9 times, slst to close rnd. [60hdc]

Fasten off **Colour 39**.

Join **Colour 1** in BL of any Rnd 11 st with a standing tr. This counts as first tr in next rnd. All sts in this rnd are made in BL of Rnd 11 sts:

Rnd 12: 2tr in st, ch2, 2tr in next st, dc in next 2 sts, hdc in next 3 sts, sc in next 3 sts, hdc in next 3 sts, dc in next 2 sts, *2tr in next st, ch2, 2tr in next st, dc in next 2 sts, hdc in next 3 sts, sc in next 3 sts, hdc in next 3 sts, dc in next 2 sts**, rep from * to ** twice, slst in initial tr. [16tr, 16dc, 24hdc, 12sc, 4ch-2]

Rnd 13: slst in next st, slst in ch-2-sp, ch3, (dc, ch2, 2dc) in same ch-2-sp, dc in next 17 sts, *(2dc, ch2, 2dc) in ch-2-sp, dc in next 17 sts**, rep from * to ** twice, slst to close rnd. [84dc, 4ch-2]

Rnd 14: slst in next st, slst in ch-2-sp, ch2, (hdc, ch2, 2hdc) in same ch-2-sp, hdc in next 21 sts, *(2hdc, ch2, 2hdc) in ch-2-sp, hdc in next 21 sts**, rep from * to ** twice, slst to close rnd. [100hdc, 4ch-2]

Fasten off **Colour 1**.

SQUARE

With a 4mm hook and **Colour 48**, make a magic ring.

Rnd 1: ch3, 2dc in ring, ch2, (3dc, ch2) 3 times, slst to close rnd. [12dc, 4ch-2]

Fasten off **Colour 48**.

Join **Colour 45** in any ch-2-sp of Rnd 1 with a standing dc. This counts as first dc in next rnd.

Rnd 2: *(2dc, ch2, 2dc) in ch-2-sp, ch, sk next st, 3-dc-popcorn in next st, ch, sk next st**, rep from * to ** 3 times, slst to close rnd. [16dc, 4 popcorn, 4ch-2, 8ch-1]

Fasten off **Colour 45**.

Join **Colour 1** in any ch-2-sp of Rnd 2 with a standing hdc. This counts as first hdc in next rnd. In this rnd, sk all ch-1-sp:

Rnd 3: *(2hdc, ch2, 2hdc) in ch-2-sp, hdc in next 2 sts, fptr around skipped st from Rnd 1, fphdc around popcorn, fptr around skipped st from Rnd 1, hdc in next 2 sts**, rep from * to ** 3 times, slst to close rnd. [8fptr, 32hdc, 4fphdc, 4ch-2]

Fasten off **Colour 1**.

Join **Colour 22** in any ch-2-sp of Rnd 3 with a standing dc. This counts as first dc in next rnd.

Rnd 4: *(2dc, ch2, 2dc) in ch-2-sp, dc in next st, ch, sk next st, 3-dc-popcorn in next st, ch, sk next st, dc in next 3 sts, ch, sk next st, 3-dc-popcorn in next st, ch, sk next st, dc in next st**, rep from * to ** 3 times, slst to close rnd. [36dc, 8 popcorn, 4ch-2, 16ch-1]

Fasten off **Colour 22**.

Join **Colour 1** in any ch-2-sp of Rnd 4 with a standing hdc. This counts as first hdc in next rnd. In this rnd, sk all ch-1-sp:

Rnd 5: *(2hdc, ch2, 2hdc) in ch-2-sp, hdc in next 3 sts, (fptr around skipped st from Rnd 3, fphdc around popcorn, fptr around skipped st from Rnd 3, hdc in next 3 sts) twice**, rep from * to ** 3 times, slst to close rnd. [16fptr, 52hdc, 8 fphdc, 4ch-2]

Fasten off **Colour 1**.

Join **Colour 31** in any ch-2-sp of Rnd 5 with a standing dc. This counts as first dc in next rnd.

Rnd 6: *(2dc, ch2, 2dc) in ch-2-sp, dc in next st, ch, sk next st, 3-dc-popcorn in next st, ch, sk next st, (dc in next 4 sts, ch, sk next st, 3-dc-popcorn in next st, ch, sk next st) twice, dc in next st**, rep from * to ** 3 times, slst to close rnd. [56dc, 12 popcorns, 4ch-2, 24ch-1]

Fasten off **Colour 31**.

Join **Colour 1** in any ch-2-sp of Rnd 6 with a standing hdc. This counts as first hdc in next rnd. In this rnd, sk all ch-1-sp:

Rnd 7: *(2hdc, ch2, 2hdc) in ch-2-sp, hdc in next 3 sts, (fptr around skipped st from Rnd 5, fphdc around popcorn, fptr around skipped st from Rnd 5, hdc in next 4 sts) twice, fptr around skipped st from Rnd 5, fphdc around popcorn, fptr around skipped st from Rnd 5, hdc in next 3 sts**, rep from * to ** 3 times, slst to close rnd. [24fptr, 72hdc, 12fphdc, 4ch-2]

Fasten off **Colour 1**.

Join **Colour 45** in any ch-2-sp of Rnd 7.

Rnd 8: *(sc, ch2, sc) in ch-2-sp, sc in next 27 sts**, rep from * to ** 3 times, slst to close rnd. [116sc, 4ch-2]

Fasten off **Colour 45**.

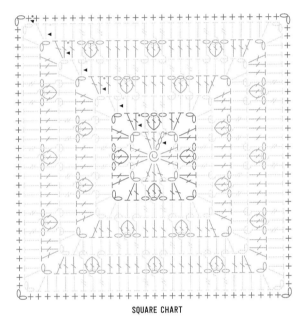

SQUARE CHART

48	
45	
1	
22	
31	

SQUARE CHART

■	45
■	13
▦	17
▨	21
▦	27
▥	31
■	39
▦	1

SQUARE

With a 4mm hook and **Colour 45**, make a magic ring.

Rnd 1: work beginning popcorn in ring, ch2, (3-dc-popcorn, ch2) 3 times, slst to close rnd. [4 popcorns, 4ch-2]

Fasten off **Colour 45**.

Join **Colour 13** in any ch-2-sp of Rnd 1 with a standing dc. This counts as first dc in next rnd.

Rnd 2: *(3dc, ch2, 3dc) in ch-2-sp**, rep from * to ** 3 times, slst to close rnd. [24dc, 4ch-2]

Fasten off **Colour 13**.

Join **Colour 17** in any ch-2-sp of Rnd 2 with a standing dc. This counts as first dc in next rnd.

Rnd 3: *(3dc, ch2, 3dc) in ch-2-sp, ch, sk next 3 sts, 3-dc-popcorn in st sp, ch, sk next 3 sts**, rep from * to ** 3 times, slst to close rnd. [24dc, 4 popcorns, 4ch-2, 8ch-1]

Fasten off **Colour 17**.

Join **Colour 21** in any ch-2-sp of Rnd 3 with a beginning popcorn. This counts as first 3-dc-popcorn in next rnd.

Rnd 4: *(3-dc-popcorn, ch2, 3-dc-popcorn) in ch-2-sp, ch, sk next 3 sts, 3dc in next ch-1-sp, sk popcorn, 3dc in next ch-1-sp, ch, sk next 3 sts**, rep from * to ** 3 times, slst to close rnd. [24dc, 8 popcorns, 4ch-2, 8ch-1]

Fasten off **Colour 21**.

Join **Colour 27** in any ch-2-sp of Rnd 4 with a standing hdc. This counts as first hdc in next rnd.

Rnd 5: *3hdc in ch-2-sp, sk popcorn, 3dc in next ch-1-sp, sk next 3 sts, (3tr, ch3, 3tr) in next st sp, sk next 3 sts, 3dc in next ch-1-sp, sk popcorn**, rep from * to ** 3 times, slst to close rnd. [24tr, 24dc, 12hdc, 4ch-3]

Fasten off **Colour 27**.

Join **Colour 31** in any ch-3-sp of Rnd 5 with a standing dc. This counts as first dc in next rnd.

Rnd 6: *(3dc, ch2, 3dc) in ch-2-sp, ch, sk next 3 sts, 3-dc-popcorn in st sp, ch, sk next 3 sts, 3dc in st sp, sk next 3 sts, 3dc in st sp, ch, sk next 3 sts, 3-dc-popcorn in st sp, ch, sk next 3 sts**, rep from * to ** 3 times, slst to close rnd. [48dc, 8 popcorns, 4ch-2, 16ch-1]

Fasten off **Colour 31**.

Join **Colour 39** in any ch-2-sp of Rnd 6 with a standing hdc. This counts as first hdc in next rnd.

Rnd 7: *(2hdc, ch2, 2hdc) in ch-2-sp, hdc in next 3 sts, hdc in next ch-1-sp, fphdc around popcorn, hdc in next ch-1-sp, hdc in next 6 sts, hdc in next ch-1-sp, fphdc around popcorn, hdc in next ch-1-sp, hdc in next 3 sts**, rep from * to ** 3 times, slst to close rnd. [80hdc, 8fphdc, 4ch-2]

Fasten off **Colour 39**.

Join **Colour 1** in any ch-2-sp of Rnd 7.

Rnd 8: *(sc, ch2, sc) in ch-2-sp, sc in next 22 sts**, rep from * to ** 3 times, slst to close rnd. [96sc, 4ch-2]

Fasten off **Colour 1**.

SQUARE

With a 4mm hook and **Colour 45**, make a magic ring.

Rnd 1: ch3, 2dc in ring, ch2, (3dc, ch2) 3 times, slst to close rnd. [12dc, 4ch-2]

Fasten off **Colour 45**.

Join **Colour 13** any ch-2-sp of Rnd 1 with a standing hdc. This counts as first hdc in next rnd.

Rnd 2: *(2hdc, ch2, 2hdc) in ch-2-sp, fpdc around each of next 3 sts, (2hdc, ch2, 2hdc) in next ch-2-sp, bpdc around each of next 3 sts**, rep from * to ** once, slst to close rnd. [16hdc, 6fpdc, 6bpdc, 4ch-2]

Fasten off **Colour 13**.

Join **Colour 17** in first ch-2-sp made in Rnd 2 with a standing hdc. This counts as first hdc in next rnd.

Rnd 3: *(hdc, ch2, hdc) in ch-2-sp, bpdc around each of next 7 sts, (hdc, ch2, hdc) in next ch-2-sp, fpdc around each of next 7 sts**, rep from * to ** once, slst to close rnd. [8hdc, 14fpdc, 14bpdc, 4ch-2]

Fasten off **Colour 17**.

Join **Colour 21** in first ch-2-sp made in Rnd 3 with a standing hdc. This counts as first hdc in next rnd.

Rnd 4: *(2hdc, ch2, 2hdc) in ch-2-sp, fpdc around each of next 9 sts, (2hdc, ch2, 2hdc) in next ch-2-sp, bpdc around each of next 9 sts**, rep from * to ** once, slst to close rnd. [16hdc, 18fpdc, 18bpdc, 4ch-2]

Fasten off **Colour 21**.

Join **Colour 27** in first ch-2-sp made in Rnd 4 with a standing hdc. This counts as first hdc in next rnd.

Rnd 5: *(hdc, ch2, hdc) in ch-2-sp, bpdc around each of next 13 sts, (hdc, ch2, hdc) in next ch-2-sp, fpdc around each of next 13 sts**, rep from * to ** once, slst to close rnd. [8hdc, 26fpdc, 26bpdc, 4ch-2]

Fasten off **Colour 27**.

Join **Colour 31** in first ch-2-sp made in Rnd 5 with a standing hdc. This counts as first hdc in next rnd.

Rnd 6: *(2hdc, ch2, 2hdc) in ch-2-sp, fpdc around each of next 15 sts, (2hdc, ch2, 2hdc) in next ch-2-sp, bpdc around each of next 15 sts**, rep from * to ** once, slst to close rnd. [16hdc, 30fpdc, 30bpdc, 4ch-2]

Fasten off **Colour 31**.

Join **Colour 39** in first ch-2-sp made in Rnd 6 with a standing hdc. This counts as first hdc in next rnd.

Rnd 7: *(hdc, ch2, hdc) in ch-2-sp, bpdc around each of next 19 sts, (hdc, ch2, hdc) in next ch-2-sp, fpdc around each of next 19 sts**, rep from * to ** once, slst to close rnd. [8hdc, 38fpdc, 38bpdc, 4ch-2]

Fasten off **Colour 39**.

Join **Colour 45** in first ch-2-sp made in Rnd 7 with a standing hdc. This counts as first hdc in next rnd.

Rnd 8: *(2hdc, ch2, 2hdc) in ch-2-sp, fpdc around each of next 21 sts, (2hdc, ch2, 2hdc) in next ch-2-sp, bpdc around each of next 21 sts**, rep from * to ** once, slst to close rnd. [16hdc, 42fpdc, 42bpdc, 4ch-2]

Fasten off **Colour 45**.

Join **Colour 1** in any ch-2-sp of Rnd 8 with a standing hdc. This counts as first hdc in next rnd.

Rnd 9: *(sc, ch2, sc) in ch-2-sp, sc in next 25 sts**, rep from * to ** 3 times, slst to close rnd. [116sc, 4ch-2]

Fasten off **Colour 1**.

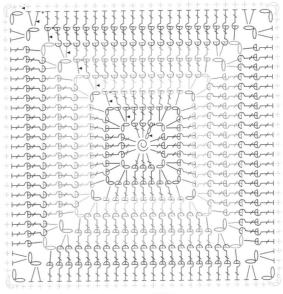

SQUARE CHART

45	
13	
17	
21	
27	
31	
39	
1	

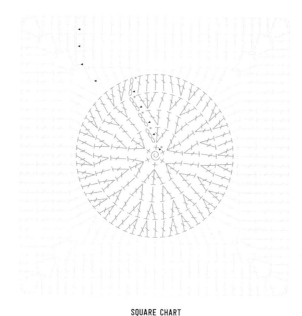

SQUARE CHART

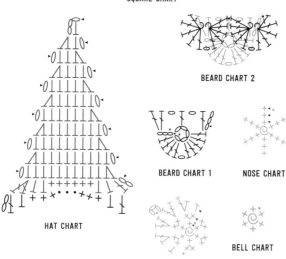

HAT CHART

BEARD CHART 2

BEARD CHART 1

NOSE CHART

EAR CHART

BELL CHART

Colours:
9
3
25
15
22
11
2

SQUARE

With a 2.75mm hook and **Colour 9**, make a magic ring.

Rnd 1: 6sc, slst to close rnd. [6sc]

Rnd 2: ch3, 3dc in each of next 5 sts, 2dc in last st, slst to close rnd. [18dc]

Rnd 3: ch3, dc in next st, (dc in next st, 2dc in next st) 8 times. slst to close rnd. [26dc]

Rnd 4: ch3, (2dc in next 2 sts, dc in next st) 8 times, 3dc in last st, slst to close rnd. [44dc]

Rnd 5: ch3, (2dc in next 2 sts, dc in next 2 sts) 10 times, dc in last 3 sts, slst to close rnd. [64dc]

Fasten off **Colour 9**. Join **Colour 3** in any Rnd 5 st with a standing tr.

Rnd 6: (ch2, tr) in same st, *tr in next st, dc in next 2 sts, hdc in next 2 sts, sc in next 5 sts, hdc in next 2 sts, dc in next 2 sts, tr in next st, (tr, ch2, tr) in same st**, rep from * to ** 3 times omitting (tr, ch2, tr) in last rep, slst to close rnd. [68, 4ch-2]

Rnd 7: slst in ch-2-sp, ch3, (dc, ch2, 2dc) in ch-2-sp, *dc in next 17 sts, (2dc, ch2, 2dc) in ch-2-sp**, rep from * to ** 3 times omitting (2dc, ch2, 2dc) in last rep, slst to close rnd. [84dc, 4ch-2]

Rnd 8: ch3, dc in next st, *(2dc, ch3, 2dc) in ch-2-sp, dc in next 21 sts**, rep from * to ** 3 times omitting last 2dc in last rep, slst to close rnd. [100dc, 4ch-3]

Rnd 9: ch3, dc in next 3 sts, *(2dc, ch3, 2dc) in ch-3-sp, dc in next 25 sts**, rep from * to ** 3 times omitting last 4dc in last rep, slst to close rnd. [116dc, 4ch-3]

Fasten off **Colour 3**.

NOSE

With **Colour 9**, make a magic ring.

Rnd 1: 6sc, slst to close rnd. [6sc]

Rnd 2: sc in each st to end. [6sc]

Rnd 3: sc in each st to end, slst to close rnd. [6sc]

Fasten off **Colour 9**. Stuff lightly and attach to centre of square.

Stitch nose to centre of square. Embroider eyes on either side of nose with **Colour 2**. Embroider mouth along outer edge of Rnd 3 of square with **Colour 15**.

HAT

With **Colour 25**, ch3.

Row 1: hdc in third ch from hook, ch. [2hdc]

Row 2: turn, hdc in next st, 2hdc in last st, ch. [3hdc]

Row 3: turn, hdc in each st to last st, 2hdc in last st, ch. [4hdc]

Rows 4-11: Rep Row 3. [12hdc]

Row 12: ch, dc in same st, hdc in next 2 sts, sc in next 6 sts, hdc in next 2 sts, 2dc in last st. [13]

Fasten off **Colour 25**. Join **Colour 15** in last st of Row 12.

Row 13: ch2, dc in same st, hdc in next st, sc in next 3 sts, slst in next 3 sts, sc in next 3 sts, hdc in next st, dc in last st. [13]

Fasten off **Colour 15**.

Stitch hat in place on top of elf's head. Fold top of hat down and secure in place as shown.

EARS

With **Colour 9**, make a magic ring.

Rnd 1: 6sc, slst to close rnd. [6sc]

Rnd 2: 2sc in each st to end. [12sc]

Rnd 3: hdc in next st, (hdc, dc) in next st, (2dc, picot, 2dc) in next st, (dc, hdc) in next st, hdc in next st, slst in next st to end rnd. [10, picot]

Fasten off **Colour 9**. Rep to make a total of 2 ears.

Stitch ears on either side of hat.

BELL

With **Colour 22**, make a magic ring.

Rnd 1: 6sc, slst to close rnd. [6sc]

Fasten off **Colour 22**. Stitch bell to tip of hat.

BEARD

With **Colour 11**, ch5, slst to make ring.

Rnd 1: ch3, 4dc in ring, ch, 5dc in ring. [1 beard loop]

This rnd sets up posts for next row of beard loops:

Rnd 2: ch3, dc in same st, ch, dc in ring sp from Rnd 1, ch, 2dc in third ch of ch3 from Rnd 1. [2 double posts, 1 single post]

Rnd 3: 5bpdc around first dc-post from Rnd 2, ch, 5dc around next dc-post, slst in single dc-post, 5bpdc around first dc-post, ch, 5dc around next dc-post. [2 beard loops]

Fasten off **Colour 11**. Attach beard to bottom of elf's head.

SQUARE

With a 4mm hook and **Colour 42**, make a magic ring.

Rnd 1: ch3, 11dc in ring, slst to close rnd. [12dc]

Rnd 2: ch3, dc in same st, 2dc in each st to end of rnd, slst to close rnd. [24dc]

Rnd 3: ch3, dc in same st, dc in next st, *2dc in next st, dc in next st**, rep from * to ** to end of rnd, slst to close rnd. [36dc]

Fasten off **Colour 42**.

Join **Colour 19** in any st of Rnd 3. All sts in this rnd are made in BLO:

Rnd 4: ch3, dc in same st, ch2, 2dc in next st, hdc in next 2 sts, sc in next 3 sts, hdc in next 2 sts, *2dc in next st, ch2, 2dc in next st, hdc in next 2 sts, sc in next 3 sts, hdc in next 2 sts**, rep from * to ** twice, slst to close rnd. [16dc,16hdc, 12sc, 4ch-2]

Rnd 5: slst in next st, slst in ch-2-sp, (ch3, dc, ch2, 2dc) in ch-2-sp, dc in each st to next ch-2-sp, *(2dc, ch2, 2dc) in next ch-2-sp, dc in each st to next ch-2-sp**, rep from * to ** twice, slst to close rnd. [60dc, 4ch-2]

Rnds 6-7: Rep Rnd 5. [92dc, 4ch-2]

Fasten off **Colour 19**.

Join **Colour 32** in any ch-2-sp of Rnd 7.

Rnd 8: *(sc, ch, sc) in ch-2-sp, sc in each st to next ch-2-sp**, rep from * to ** 3 times, slst to close rnd. [100sc, 4ch-1]

Fasten off **Colour 32**.

CUPCAKE CASE

With **Colour 11**, ch11.

Row 1: dc in fourth ch from hook, dc in each st to end of row, ch2, turn. [9dc]

Row 2: 2dc in first st, dc in next 7 sts, 2dc in last st, ch2, turn. [11dc]

Row 3: dc in each st to end of row, ch2, turn. [11dc]

Row 4: 2dc in first st, dc in next 9 sts, 2dc in last st. [13dc]

Fasten off **Colour 11**.

Join **Colour 42** in last st of Row 4.

Row 5: sc in each st to end of row, ch, turn. [13sc]

Row 6: sc in first st, *3hdc in next st, sc in next st**, rep from * to ** to end of row. [18hdc, 7sc]

Fasten off **Colour 42**.

CANDLE

With **Colour 45**, ch6.

Row 1: sc in second ch from hook, sc in each st to end. [5sc]

Row 2: ch, sc in each st to end. [5sc]

Row 3: As Row 2. [5sc]

Fasten off **Colour 45**.

FLAME

With **Colour 22**, ch2.

Rnd 1: (sc, hdc, dc, hdc, sc) in second ch from hook, pull tight, slst to close rnd. [5]

Fasten off **Colour 22**.

FINISHING

Embroider sprinkles onto top of cupcake with **Colours 32**, **45** and **20**.

Stitch candle and flame on top of cupcake.

Stitch cupcake case to square as shown.

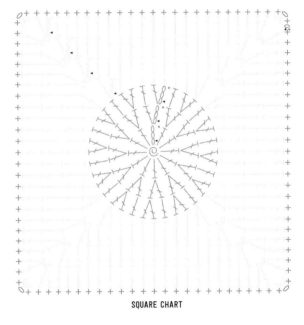

42	
19	
32	
11	
45	
22	
20	

SQUARE CHART

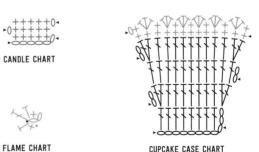

CANDLE CHART

FLAME CHART

CUPCAKE CASE CHART

10	
12	
16	
8	
11	
2	
22	
15	

INNER FEATHERS

With a 2.75mm hook and **Colour 10**, make a magic ring.

Rnd 1: 6sc, slst to close rnd. [6sc]

Rnd 2: ch3, 3dc in each of next 5 sts, 2dc in last st, slst to close rnd. [18dc]

Rnd 3: ch3, dc in next st, (dc in next st, 2dc in next st) 8 times, slst to close rnd. [26dc]

All sts in this rnd are made in FLO of Rnd 3:

Rnd 4: ch, *sk 1 st, 5dc-shell in next st, sk st, sc in next st**, rep from * to ** 4 times. [5 shells, 6sc]

Fasten off **Colour 10**.

CENTRE FEATHERS

Join **Colour 12** with a standing dc in BL at start of first shell from Rnd 4. All sts in this rnd are made in BLO of Rnd 3:

Rnd 5: (2dc in next st, 2dc in next st, dc in next st) 8 times, 3dc in last st, slst to close rnd. [44dc]

All sts in this rnd are made in FLO of Rnd 5:

Rnd 6: ch, (sk st, 5dc in next, sk st, sc in next st) 9 times. [9 shells, 10sc]

Fasten off **Colour 12**.

OUTER FEATHERS

Join **Colour 16** with a standing dc in BL at start of first shell from Rnd 6. All sts in this rnd are made in BLO of Rnd 5:

Rnd 7: (2dc in next 2 sts, dc in next 2 sts) 10 times, dc in last 3 sts, slst to close rnd. [64dc]

All sts in this rnd are made in FLO of Rnd 7:

Rnd 8: ch, (sk st, 5dc in next st, sk st, sc in next st) 14 times. [14 shells, 15sc]

Fasten off **Colour 16**.

SQUARE

Join **Colour 8** with a standing tr in BL of Rnd 7, between 9th and 10th shells counting from right.

Rnd 9: (ch2, tr) in same st, *tr in next st, dc in next 2 sts, hdc in next 2 sts, sc in next 5 sts, hdc in next 2 sts, dc in next 2 sts, tr in next st, (tr, ch2, tr) in next st**, rep from * to ** 3 times omitting (tr, ch2, tr) in last rep, slst to close rnd. [68, 4ch-2]

Rnd 10: slst in ch-2-sp, ch3, (dc, ch2, 2dc) in ch-2-sp, *dc in next 17 sts, (2dc, ch2, 2dc) in ch-2-sp**, rep from * to ** 3 times omitting (2dc, ch2, 2dc) in last rep, slst to close rnd. [84dc, 4ch-2]

Rnd 11: ch3, dc in next st, *(2dc, ch3, 2dc) in ch-2-sp, dc in next 21 sts**, rep from * to ** 3 times omitting last 2dc in last rep, slst to close rnd. [100dc, 4ch-3]

Rnd 12: ch3, dc in next 3 sts, *(2dc, ch3, 2dc) in ch-3-sp, dc in next 25 sts**, rep from * to ** 3 times omitting last 4dc in last rep. [116dc, 4ch-3]

Fasten off **Colour 8**.

SQUARE CHART

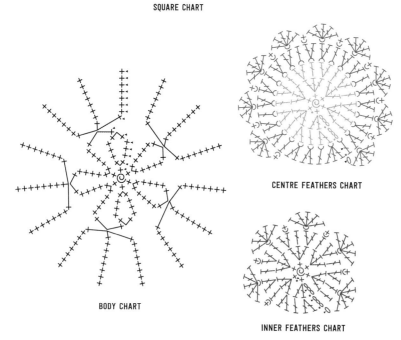

BODY CHART

CENTRE FEATHERS CHART

INNER FEATHERS CHART

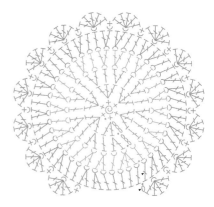

OUTER FEATHERS CHART

BODY

With **Colour 11**, make a magic ring.

Rnd 1: 6sc in ring. [6sc]

Rnd 2: 2sc in each st to end. [12sc]

Rnd 3-5: sc in each st to end. [12sc]

Rnd 6: (sc2tog, sc in next 4 sts) twice. [10sc]

Rnd 7: sc2tog to end of rnd. [5sc]

Rnd 8: 3sc in each st to end. [15sc]

Rnds 9-15: sc in each st to end of rnd. [15sc]

Flatten open end of turkey body and hold both sides together, sc through both sides.

Fasten off **Colour 11**.

FINISHING

Embroider eyes onto turkey's head with **Colour 2**.

Embroider a beak and two feet onto turkey with **Colour 22**.

Cut a length of **Colour 15**, approx 15cm long. Secure on back of body and thread from back to front in corner of beak. Insert needle back into same hole and slowly pull yarn through to back to form a loop. When loop is correct size, hold it firmly and secure on back of turkey's body.

Stitch body onto square, leaving head loose.

SQUARE

With a 4mm hook and **Colour 14**, ch27.

Row 1: (RS) sc in second ch from hook, sc in next 25 ch, turn. [26sc]

Row 2: ch, sc in each st to end of row, turn. [26sc]

Row 3: ch, sc in each st to end of row, turn. [26sc]

Rows 4-11: (Rep Rows 2-3) 4 times. [26sc]

Fasten off **Colour 14**.

Join **Colour 2** at end of Row 11. All sts in this row are made in FLO:

Row 12: (WS) ch, sc in each st to end of row, turn. [26sc]

Rows 13-16: ch, sc in each st to end of row, turn. [26sc]

Fasten off **Colour 2**.

Join **Colour 14** at end of Row 16. All sts in this row are made in BLO:

Row 17: (RS) ch, sc in each st to end of rnd, turn. [26sc]

Row 18: ch, sc in each st to end of rnd, turn. [26sc]

Row 19: ch, sc in each st to end of rnd, turn. [26sc]

Rows 20-28: Rep Row 19. [26sc]

Fasten off **Colour 14**.

Join **Colour 1** in last st made in Row 28.

Rnd 1: sc in st, ch2, *work 26sc evenly down side, ch2, sc in next 26 sts, ch2**, rep from * to ** twice, sc in next 25 sts, slst in initial sc. [104sc, 4ch-2]

Rnd 2: slst in next ch-2-sp, ch2, (hdc, ch2, 2hdc) in same ch-2-sp, hdc in next 26 sts, *(2hdc, ch2, 2hdc) in next ch-2-sp, hdc in next 26 sts**, rep from * to ** twice, slst to close rnd. [120hdc, 4ch-2]

Fasten off **Colour 1**.

BUCKLE

With **Colour 22**, ch14, slst in first ch to make a loop.

Rnd 1: ch, 2hdc in same ch, ch, 2hdc in next ch, hdc in next 2 ch, 2hdc in next ch, ch, 2hdc in next ch, hdc in next ch, 2hdc in next ch, ch, 2hdc in next ch, hdc in next 2 ch, 2hdc in next ch, ch, 2hdc in next ch, hdc in next ch. [22hdc, 4ch-1]

Fasten off **Colour 22**.

Sew beginning ch of buckle onto centre of square.

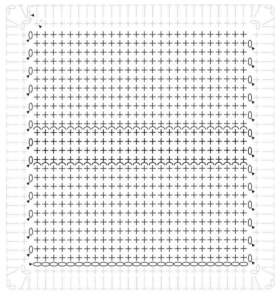

SQUARE CHART

14	■
2	■
1	▦
22	▦

BUCKLE CHART

■	10
■	25
■	11
■	15
░	8
■	2

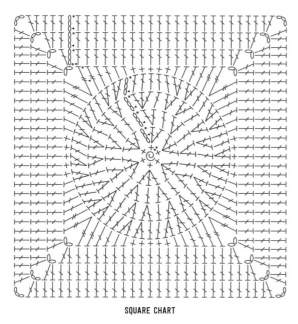

SQUARE CHART

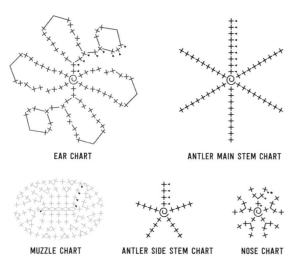

EAR CHART   ANTLER MAIN STEM CHART

MUZZLE CHART   ANTLER SIDE STEM CHART   NOSE CHART

SQUARE

With a 2.75mm hook and **Colour 10**, make a magic ring.

Rnd 1: 6sc, slst to close rnd. [6sc]

Rnd 2: ch3, 3dc in each of next 5 sts, 2dc in last st, slst to close rnd [18dc]

Rnd 3: ch3, dc in next st, (dc in next st, 2dc in next st) 8 times, slst to close rnd. [26dc]

Rnd 4: ch3, (2dc in next st, 2dc in next st, dc in next st) 8 times, 3dc in last st, slst to close rnd. [44dc]

Rnd 5: ch3, (2dc in next 2 sts, dc in next 2 sts) 10 times, dc in last 3 sts, slst to close rnd. [64dc]

Fasten off **Colour 10**.

Join **Colour 25** in any st of Rnd 5 with a standing tr.

Rnd 6: (ch2, tr) in same st, *tr in next st, dc in next 2 sts, hdc in next 2 sts, sc in next 5 sts, hdc in next 2 sts, dc in next 2 sts, tr in next st, (tr, ch2, tr) in next st**, rep from * to ** 3 times omitting (tr, ch2, tr) in last rep, slst to close rnd. [68dc, 4ch-2]

Rnd 7: slst in ch-2-sp, ch3, (dc, ch2, 2dc) in ch-2-sp, *dc in next 17 sts, (2dc, ch2, 2dc) in ch-2-sp**, rep from * to ** 3 times omitting (2dc, ch2, 2dc) in last rep, slst to close rnd. [84dc, 4ch-2]

Rnd 8: ch3, dc in next st, *(2dc, ch3, 2dc) in ch-2-sp, dc in next 21 sts**, rep from * to ** 3 times omitting last 2dc in last rep, slst to close rnd. [100dc, 4ch-3]

Rnd 9: ch3, dc in next 3 sts, *(2dc, ch3, 2dc) in ch-3-sp, dc in next 25 sts**, rep from * to ** 3 times omitting last 4dc in last rep, slst to close rnd. [116dc, 4ch-3]

Fasten off **Colour 25**.

ANTLER MAIN STEM

With **Colour 11**, make a magic ring.

Rnd 1: 6sc in ring. [6sc]

Rnds 2-9: sc in each st to end. [6sc]

Fasten off **Colour 11**. Rep to make a total of 2 main stems.

Stuff lightly and stitch open end of main stem closed.

ANTLER SIDE STEM

With **Colour 11**, make a magic ring.

Rnd 1: 5sc in ring. [5sc]

Rnds 2-4: sc in each st to end. [5sc]

Fasten off **Colour 11**. Rep to make a total of 2 side stems.

Stuff lightly and attach 1 side stem about half way up each main stem to create 2 antlers.

NOSE

With **Colour 15**, make a magic ring.

Rnd 1: 5sc in ring. [5sc]

Rnd 2: 2sc in each st to end. [10sc]

Rnd 3: sc in each st to end, slst to close rnd. [10sc]

Fasten off **Colour 15**.

MUZZLE

With **Colour 8**, ch5.

Rnd 1: sk first ch, sc in next 3 ch, 3sc in last ch, turn to work on other side of foundation ch, sc in next 3 ch, 3sc in next ch. [12sc]

Rnd 2: sc in next 4 sts, 2sc in next 2 sts, sc in next 4 sts, 2sc in next 2 sts. [16sc]

Rnd 3: (sc in next st, 2sc in next st) 8 times. [24sc]

Rnd 4: (sc in next st, 2sc in next st) 12 times. [36sc]

Fasten off **Colour 8**.

EARS

With **Colour 10**, make a magic ring.

Rnd 1: 6sc in ring. [6sc]

Rnd 2: sc in each st to end. [6sc]

Rnd 3: (2sc in next st, sc in next 2 sts) twice. [8sc]

Rnd 4: sc in each st to end. [8sc]

Rnd 5: (2sc in next st, sc in next 3 sts) twice. [10sc]

Rnd 6: sc in each st to end. [10sc]

Rnd 7: (2sc in next st, sc in next 4 sts) twice. [12sc]

Rnd 8: sc in each st to end. [12sc]

Rnd 9: sc2tog to end of rnd. [6sc]

Fasten off **Colour 10**. Rep to make a total of 2 ears.

FINISHING

Stitch muzzle and nose in place on square.

Embroider eyes on either side of muzzle (on outer edge of Rnd 2 of square) with **Colour 2**.

Fold each ear in half lengthways and stitch through bottom of ear to hold shaping.

Attach antlers to top of head, approx 9 sts apart.

Stitch ears in place, one below each antler.

SQUARE

With a 2.75mm hook and **Colour 40**, ch16.

Row 1: sk 2 ch, hdc in next st, hdc in each st to end of row. [14]

Rows 2-12: ch, hdc in each st to end of row. [14hdc]

The rest of the square is worked in rnds:

Rnd 13: ch2, sc in same st, sc in each sc along top of square, (ch2, sc) in corner, *turn work 90° to right and work along next side of square, sc 12 sts evenly along edge, (sc, ch2, sc) in corner st**, rep from * to ** once omitting last corner, slst in first corner to close. [56sc, 4ch-2]

Fasten off **Colour 40**.

Join **Colour 38** in any ch-2-sp of Rnd 13 with a standing dc. This counts as first dc in next rnd.

Rnd 14: *(dc, ch2, dc) in ch-2-sp, dc in BL of next 14 sts**, rep from * to ** 3 times, slst to close rnd. [64dc, 4ch-2]

Rnd 15: slst in ch-2-sp, ch3, (dc, ch2, 2dc) in ch-2-sp, *dc in next 16 sts, (2dc, ch2, 2dc) in ch-2-sp**, rep from * to ** 3 times, omitting last (2dc, ch2, 2dc), slst to close rnd. [80dc, 4ch-2]

Rnd 16: ch3, dc in next st, *(2dc, ch2, 2dc) in ch-2-sp, dc in next 20 sts**, rep from * to ** 3 times omitting last 2 sts, slst to close rnd. [96dc, 4ch-2]

Rnd 17: ch3, dc in next 3 sts, *(2dc, ch3, 2dc) in ch-2-sp, dc in next 24 sts**, rep from * to ** 3 times omitting last 4 sts, slst to close rnd. [112dc, 4ch-3]

Fasten off **Colour 38**.

RIBBON DETAILS

Ribbon detail around present is created using surface crochet:

With **Colour 1**, make a slip knot.

Holding yarn at back of work, insert hook (from front to back) into stitch where you would like to start surface crochet (halfway across each side of square).

Place slip knot onto hook and draw it to front of work, so loop is at front and working yarn remains at back.

Insert hook in next st, pull up a loop and work a slst.

Continue to work slst across present.

Fasten off **Colour 1**. Rep for second row of detail.

BOW

With **Colour 1**, ch22, slst into first ch to join into ring.

Rnd 1: sc in each st to end of rnd, making sure not to twist ring. It is helpful to use a stitch marker to mark beginning of rnd. [22]

Rnd 2: (slst in next 3 sts, sc in BL of next 8 sts) twice. [22]

Rnds 3-5: Rep Rnd 2, slst in next st. [22]

Fasten off **Colour 1**.

The slsts will have created a narrowing in 2 sides of ring. Press these sides together and wrap yarn tail tightly around bow. Use both of yarn tail to secure shape of bow.

Attach bow to top of present on square.

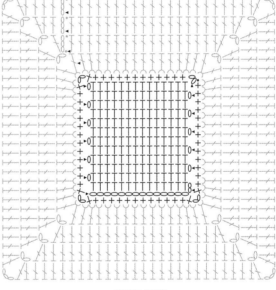

1	
38	
40	

SQUARE CHART

BOW CHART

SQUARE CHART

HOLLY LEAF CHART

	1
	26
	15
	28

SQUARE

With a 2.75mm hook and **Colour 1**, make a magic ring.

Rnd 1: 6sc, slst to close rnd. [6sc]

Rnd 2: ch3, 3dc in each of next 5 sts, 2dc in last st, slst to close rnd. [18dc]

Rnd 3: ch3, dc in next st, (dc in next st, 2dc in next st) 8 times, slst to close rnd. [26dc]

Fasten off **Colour 1**.

Join **Colour 26** in any st of Rnd 3 with a standing 3-dc-puff. This counts as first 3-dc-puff in next rnd.

Rnd 4: 3-dc-puff in same st, (ch2, 3-dc-puff in next st) 25 times, ch2, slst in first puff of rnd to close. [26 3-dc-puffs, 26ch-2-sp]

Rnd 5: slst in next ch-2-sp, ch3, *(4-dc-popcorn, ch2) in ch-2-sp**, rep from * to ** 6 times omitting last ch on last popcorn, join and change to **Colour 15**, (4-dc-popcorn, ch2) in next 2 ch-2-sp omitting last ch of last popcorn, change to **Colour 26**, (4-dc-popcorn, ch2) in next 6 ch-2-sp omitting last ch on last popcorn, change to **Colour 15**, (4-dc-popcorn, ch2) in next 2 ch-2-sp omitting last ch of last popcorn, change to **Colour 26**, (4-dc-popcorn, ch2) in next 7 ch-2-sp omitting last ch on last popcorn, change to **Colour 15**, (4-dc-popcorn, ch2) in each of last 2 ch-2-sp, slst to close rnd. [26 4-dc-popcorns, 26ch-2-sp]

Fasten off **Colours 26** and **15**.

Join **Colour 1** in in any ch-2-sp of Rnd 5 with a standing tr. In this rnd, note that you may be working in a ch-2-sp which is also considered a st for this rnd.

Rnd 6: (ch2, tr) in same st, *tr in next st, 2dc in next st, 2hdc in next st, sc in next 5 sts, hdc in next 2 sts, 2dc in next st, tr in next st, (tr, ch2, tr) in next st**, rep from * to ** 3 times omitting (tr, ch2, tr) in last rep, slst to close rnd. [68, 4ch-2]

Rnd 7: slst in ch-2-sp, ch3, (dc, ch2, 2dc) in ch-2-sp, *dc in next 17 sts, (2dc, ch2, 2dc) in ch-2-sp**, rep from * to ** 3 times omitting (2dc, ch2, 2dc) in last rep, slst to close rnd. [84dc, 4ch-2]

Rnd 8: ch3, dc in next st, *(2dc, ch3, 2dc) in ch-2-sp, dc in next 21 sts**, rep from * to ** 3 times omitting last 2dc in last rep, slst to close rnd. [100dc, 4ch-3]

Rnd 9: ch3, dc in next 3 sts, *(2dc, ch3, 2dc) in ch-3-sp, dc in next 25 sts**, rep from * to ** 3 times omitting last 4dc in last rep, slst to close rnd. [116dc, 4ch-3]

Fasten off **Colour 1**.

HOLLY LEAVES

With **Colour 28**, ch6.

Row 1: slst in the second ch from hook, (sc in next st, picot, slst in next st) twice, ch, turn to work on other side of foundation ch, (slst in next st, sc in next st, picot) twice, slst in last st, ch. [4sc, 6slst, 2 picot]

Fasten off **Colour 28**. Rep to make a total of 6 holly leaves.

Stitch holly leaves in place on square as shown.

SQUARE

With a 2.75mm hook and Colour 3, make a magic ring.

Rnd 1: ch3, 2dc, ch2, (3dc, ch2) 3 times, pull tight, slst to close rnd. [12dc, 4ch-2]

Rnd 2: ch3 , dc in next 2 sts, *(2dc, ch2, 2dc) in ch-2-sp, dc in next 3 sts**, rep from * to ** 3 times, omitting last 3dc, slst to close rnd. [28dc, 4ch-2]

Fasten off and rejoin Colour 3 in any ch-2-sp of Rnd 2 with a standing dc.

Rnd 3: (dc, ch2, 2dc) in same sp, *sk st, dc in next 2 sts, join and change to Colour 48, 5dc in next st, change to Colour 3, dc in next 2 sts, sk st, (2dc, ch2, 2dc) in ch-2-sp**, rep from * to ** 3 times omitting last (2dc, ch2, 2dc), slst to close rnd. [52dc, 4ch-2]

Fasten off Colours 3 and 48.

Join Colour 3 in any ch-2-sp of Rnd 3 with a standing dc.

Rnd 4: (ch2, dc) in same sp, *sk st, dc in next 3 sts, join and change to Colour 20, fpdc around next 5 sts, change to Colour 3, dc in next 3 sts, sk st, (dc, ch2, dc) in ch-2-sp**, rep from * to ** 3 times omitting last (dc, ch2, dc), slst to close rnd. [52dc, 4ch-2]

Fasten off Colour 20.

Rnd 5: slst in ch-2-sp, ch3, (dc, ch2, 2dc) in same sp, *sk st, dc in next 3 sts, join and change to Colour 34, dc5tog over fpdc from previous rnd, ch, change to Colour 3, dc in next 3 sts, sk st, (2dc, ch2, 2dc) in ch-2-sp**, rep from * to ** 3 times omitting last (2dc, ch2, 2dc), slst to close rnd. [44dc, 4ch, 4ch-2]

Fasten off Colour 34.

Rnd 6: ch3, sk st, (2dc, ch2, 2dc) in ch-2-sp, *sk st, dc in next st, join and change to Colour 49, 5dc in next st, change to Colour 3, dc in next 2 sts, dc in top of egg, sk ch, dc in next 2 sts, change to Colour 49, 5dc in next st, change to Colour 3, dc in next st, sk st, (2dc, ch2, 2dc) in ch-2-sp**, rep from * to ** 3 times omitting last (2dc, ch2, 2dc) and dc, slst to close rnd. [84dc, 4ch-2]

Fasten off Colour 49.

Rnd 7: slst in next 2 sts, slst in ch-2-sp, (ch3, dc, ch2, 2dc) in ch-2-sp, *sk st, dc in next 2 sts, join and change to Colour 38, fpdc in next 5 sts, change to Colour 3, dc in next 5 sts, change to Colour 38, fpdc in next 5 sts, change to Colour 3, dc in next 2 sts, sk st, (2 dc, ch2, 2dc) in ch-2-sp**, rep from * to ** 3 times omitting last (2 dc, ch2, 2dc), slst to close rnd. [92dc, 4ch-2]

Fasten off Colour 38.

Rnd 8: slst in next st, slst in ch-2-sp, (ch3, dc, ch3, 2dc) in ch-2-sp, *dc in next 4 sts, join and change to Colour 23, dc5tog, ch, change to Colour 3, dc in next 5 sts, change to Colour 23, dc5tog, ch, change to Colour 3, dc in next 4 sts, (2dc, ch3, 2dc) in ch-2-sp**, rep from * to ** 3 times omitting (2dc, ch3, 2dc), slst to close rnd. [76dc, 4ch-3, 8ch]

Fasten off Colour 23.

Rnd 9: ch3, dc in next st, *(2dc, ch2, 2dc) in ch-3 sp, dc in next 6 sts, 2dc in top of egg, sk ch, dc in next 5 sts, 2dc in top of egg, sk ch, dc in next 6 sts**, rep from * to ** 3 times omitting last 2dc, slst to close rnd. [100dc, 4ch-2]

Fasten off Colour 3.

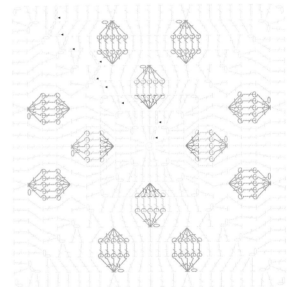

SQUARE CHART

3	
48	
20	
34	
49	
38	
23	

SQUARE

With a 2.75mm hook and **Colour 37**, make a magic ring.

Rnd 1: 6sc, slst to close rnd. [6sc]

Rnd 2: ch3, 3dc in each of next 5 sts, 2dc in last st, slst to close rnd. [18dc]

Rnd 3: ch3, dc in next st, (dc in next st, 2dc in next st) 8 times, slst to close rnd. [26dc]

Rnd 4: ch3, (2dc in next st, 2dc in next st, dc in next st) 8 times, 3dc in last st, slst to close rnd. [44dc]

Fasten off **Colour 37**.

Join **Colour 3** in any st of Rnd 4 with a standing dc.

Rnd 5: (2dc in next 2 sts, dc in next 2 sts) 10 times, dc in last 3 sts, slst to close rnd. [64dc]

Rnd 6: ch6, tr in same st, *tr in next st, dc in next 2 sts, hdc in next 2 sts, sc in next 5 sts, hdc in next 2 sts, dc in next 2 sts, tr in next st, (tr, ch2, tr) in next st**, rep from * to ** 3 times omitting (tr, ch2, tr) in last rep, slst to close rnd. [68, 4ch-2]

Rnd 7: slst in ch-2-sp, ch3, (dc, ch2, 2dc) in ch-2-sp, *dc in next 17 sts, (2dc, ch2, 2dc) in ch-2-sp**, rep from * to ** 3 times omitting (2dc, ch2, 2dc) in last rep, slst to close rnd. [84dc, 4ch-2]

Rnd 8: ch3, dc in next st, *(2dc, ch3, 2dc) in ch-2-sp, dc in next 21 sts**, rep from * to ** 3 times omitting last 2dc in last rep, slst to close rnd. [100dc, 4ch-3]

Rnd 9: ch3, dc in next 3 sts, *(2dc, ch3, 2dc) in ch-3-sp, dc in next 25 sts**, rep from * to ** 3 times omitting last 4dc in last rep, slst to close rnd. [116dc, 4ch-3]

Fasten off **Colour 3**.

BAUBLE

With **Colour 37**, make a magic ring.

Rnd 1: 6sc, slst to close rnd. [6sc]

Rnd 2: 2sc in each st to end of rnd, slst to close rnd. [12sc]

Rnd 3: *sc in next st, 2sc in next st**, rep from * to ** to end of rnd, slst to close rnd. [18sc]

Rnd 4: *2sc in next st, sc in next 2 sts**, rep from * to ** to end of rnd, slst to close rnd. [24sc]

Rnd 5: *sc in next 3 sts, 2sc in next st**, rep from * to ** to end of rnd, slst to close rnd. [30sc]

Rnd 6: *2sc in next st, sc in next 4 sts**, rep from * to ** to end of rnd, slst to close rnd. [36sc]

Rnd 7: *sc in next 5 sts, 2sc in next st**, rep from * to ** to end of rnd, slst to close rnd. [42sc]

Rnd 8: 2sc in next st, sc in each st to end of rnd, 2sc in last st. [44sc]

Rnds 9-10: sc in each st to end of rnd, slst to close rnd. [44sc]

Fasten off **Colour 37**.

Embroider a snowflake onto bauble with **Colour 1** as shown.

HANGER

With **Colour 5**, make a magic ring.

Rnd 1: 4sc, pull tight, slst to close rnd. [4sc]

Rnd 2: 2sc in each st to end of rnd, slst to close rnd. [8sc]

Rnd 3: sc in BL of each st to end of rnd, slst to close rnd. [8sc]

Rnd 4: sc in each st to end of rnd, slst to close rnd. [8sc]

Fasten off **Colour 5**.

FINISHING

Pin bauble onto centre of square and attach, stitching through BL of bauble and outer edge of Rnd 4 of square. Leave a gap of approx 5cm, lightly stuff bauble and stitch gap closed.

Cut a length of **Colour 22** approx 20cm long and secure to inside of hanger. Using a yarn needle, pull yarn through centre of Rnd 1 of hanger, insert needle back into same hole and slowly draw yarn back down until you reach desired length of loop. Secure yarn inside hanger and fasten off **Colour 22**.

Stitch hanger on top of bauble.

■	37
□	3
▨	1
▦	5
▩	22

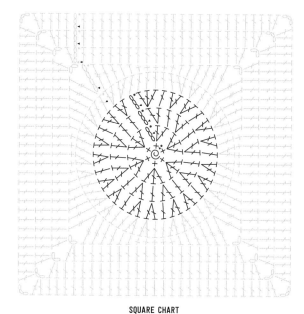

SQUARE CHART

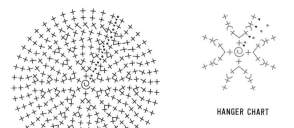

BAUBLE CHART

HANGER CHART

TREE

With a 4mm hook and **Colour 25**, ch18.

Row 1: sc in second ch from hook, sc in each ch to end, ch, turn. [17sc]

Row 2: sk first st, sc in each st to end of row, ch, turn. [16sc]

Row 3: sk first st, sc in each st to end of row, ch turn. [15sc]

Rows 4-15: Rep Row 3. [3sc]

Fasten off **Colour 25**.

TRUNK

Join **Colour 11** in eighth st from the left side at bottom of tree.

Row 1: sc in same st, sc in next 2 sts, ch, turn. [3sc]

Rows 2-3: Rep Row 1 omitting last turning ch. [3sc]

Fasten off **Colour 11**.

SQUARE

With **Colour 19**, make a magic ring.

Rnd 1: ch3, 2dc in ring, ch2, (3dc in ring, ch2) 3 times, slst in third ch of initial ch3. [12dc]

Rnd 2: ch3, *dc in each st to next ch-2-sp, (2dc, ch2, 2dc) in ch-2-sp**, rep from * to ** to last ch-2-sp, slst in third ch of initial ch3. [28dc, 4ch-2]

Rnd 3: ch3, *dc in each st to next ch-2-sp, (2dc, ch2, 2dc) in ch-2-sp**, rep from * to ** to last ch-2-sp, dc in rem sts to complete rnd, slst in third ch of initial ch3. [44dc, 4ch-2]

Rnd 4: Rep Rnd 3. [60dc, 4ch-2]

Join and crochet through bottom of Christmas tree and into one side of square in this rnd:

Rnd 5: ch3, *dc in each st to next ch-2-sp, (2dc, ch2, 2dc) in ch-2-sp**, rep from * to ** to last ch-2-sp, dc in rem sts to complete rnd, slst in third ch of initial ch3. [76dc, 4ch-2]

Rnd 6: Rep Rnd 3. [92dc, 4ch-2]

Fasten off **Colour 19**.

Join **Colour 5** in any st of Rnd 6.

Rnd 7: ch, *sc in each st to corner sp**, (sc, ch, sc) in corner sp**, rep from * to ** to complete rnd, sc in rem sts, slst to close rnd. [100sc, 4ch-1]

Fasten off **Colour 5**.

BAUBLES

With **Colour 19**, ch2,

Rnd 1: 6sc in second ch from hook, slst to join. [6sc]

Fasten off **Colour 19**. Rep to make a total of 2 baubles in **Colour 19** and 3 baubles in **Colour 5**.

Stitch all baubles onto tree as shown, and stitch tree to square.

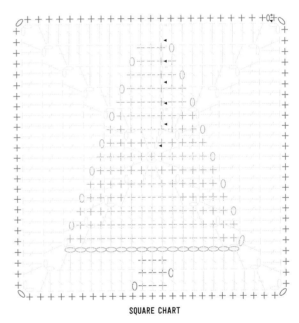

25	
11	
19	
5	

SQUARE CHART

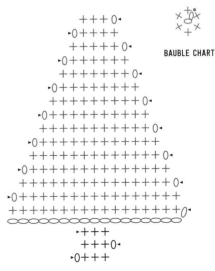

BAUBLE CHART

TREE AND TRUNK CHART

THE SKILLS

STITCH BASICS

In this section you'll find instructions and diagrams for all of the stitches and techniques featured in this book. Refer to the front of the book (see How to Use This Book) for more information on the terminology, symbols and abbreviations used for these patterns.

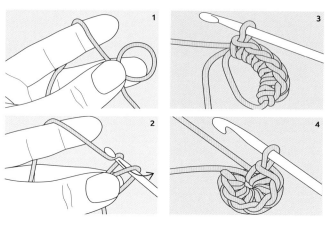

MAGIC RING

With the tail end of the yarn hanging down, make a loop and hold it securely between two fingers (1). Insert the hook into the loop and pull the yarn through (2), make a chain stitch to secure, and begin making stitches inside the loop (3). When you have finished pull the tail to tighten the loop (4). Slip st into the first stitch to join.

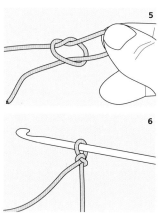

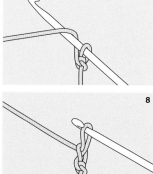

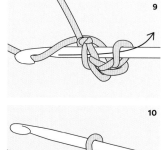

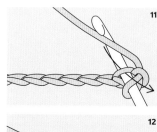

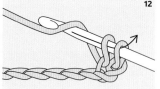

SLIP KNOT

Make a loop with the tail end of the yarn hanging down. Insert the hook or your fingers into the loop and pull the working yarn through (5). Pull to tighten and place onto hook (6).

CHAIN

Place the yarn over the hook (7) and pull through the loop (8).

SLIP STITCH

Insert the hook into the stitch, place the yarn over the hook (9) and pull through both the stitch and loop on the hook (10).

SINGLE CROCHET

Insert the hook into the stitch, place the yarn over the hook and pull through the stitch so that two loops are on the hook (11). Place the yarn over the hook again and pull through both loops on the hook (12).

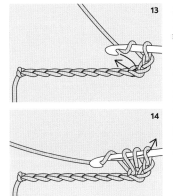

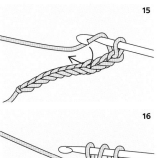

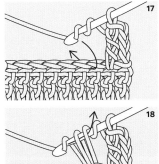

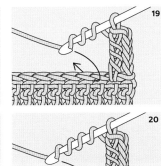

HALF DOUBLE CROCHET

Place the yarn over the hook and insert the hook into the stitch (13). Yarn over and pull up a loop, so that three loops are now on the hook. Yarn over and pull the yarn through all three loops on the hook (14).

DOUBLE CROCHET

Place the yarn over the hook and insert the hook into the stitch (15). Yarn over and pull through the stitch, so that three loops are left on the hook (16). Yarn over and pull through the first two loops on the hook, so that two loops are left on the hook. Yarn over and pull through the remaining two loops.

TREBLE CROCHET

Wrap the yarn over the hook twice and insert the hook into the stitch (17). Yarn over and pull through the stitch. Yarn over and pull through the first two loops on the hook, so that there are three loops left on the hook (18). Yarn over and pull through the first two loops on the hook again, so that there are two loops left on the hook. Yarn over again and pull through the remaining two loops.

DOUBLE TREBLE CROCHET

Follow the same process as the treble crochet, but wrap the yarn three times over the hook before inserting it into the stitch (19). Yarn over and pull through 2 loops each time, until you have 1 loop left on your hook.

TRIPLE TREBLE CROCHET

Follow the same process as the treble crochet, but wrap the yarn four times over the hook before inserting it into the stitch (20). Yarn over and pull through 2 loops each time, until you have 1 loop left on your hook.

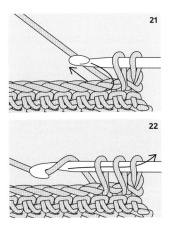

SINGLE CROCHET 2 TOGETHER

Insert the hook into the first stitch, place the yarn over the hook and pull a loop through the stitch, two loops are now on the hook (21). Insert the hook into the second stitch, place the yarn over the hook and pull a loop through the stitch, three loops are now on the hook (22). Place the yarn over the hook and pull through all three loops on the hook.

SINGLE CROCHET 3 TOGETHER

Follow the instructions for single crochet 2 together until there are three loops on the hook (22), now insert the hook into the third stitch, place the yarn over the hook and pull a loop through the stitch, four loops are now on the hook. Place the yarn over the hook and pull through all four loops on the hook.

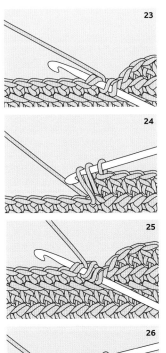

HALF DOUBLE CROCHET 2 TOGETHER

Place the yarn over the hook and insert the hook into the first stitch (23). Place the yarn over again and pull a loop through the stitch, three loops are now on the hook (24). Place the yarn over the hook and insert the hook into the second stitch (25). Yarn over the hook and pull through the stitch, five loops are now on the hook (26). Yarn over and pull through all five loops on the hook.

HALF DOUBLE CROCHET 5 TOGETHER

Follow the instructions for half double crochet 2 together until there are five loops on the hook (26), now *place the yarn over the hook and insert the hook into the third stitch, place the yarn over the hook and pull a loop through the stitch, seven loops are now on the hook; repeat from * into the fourth and fifth stitch in the same way, ten loops are now on the hook. Place the yarn over the hook and pull through all ten loops on the hook.

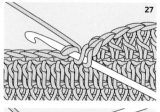

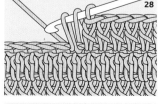

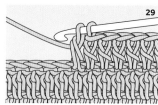

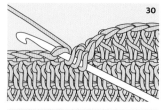

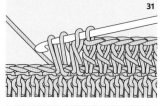

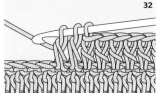

DOUBLE CROCHET 2 TOGETHER

Place the yarn over the hook and insert the hook into the first stitch (27). Yarn over and pull a loop through the stitch, three loops are now on the hook (28). Yarn over and pull through the first two loops on the hook, two loops are now on the hook (29). Yarn over and insert the hook into the second stitch (30). Yarn over and pull through the stitch, four loops are now on the hook (31). Yarn over and pull through the first two loops on the hook, three loops are now on the hook (32). Yarn over and pull through all three loops on the hook.

DOUBLE CROCHET 4 TOGETHER

Follow the instructions for double crochet 2 together up until the final yarn over (32), now *place the yarn over the hook and insert the hook into the third stitch, place the yarn over the hook and pull a loop through the stitch, five loops are now on the hook, yarn over and pull through the first two loops on the hook, four loops are now on the hook. Repeat from * into the fourth stitch, you should now have five loops on the hook. Place the yarn over the hook and pull through all five loops on the hook.

DOUBLE CROCHET 5 TOGETHER

Follow the instructions for double crochet 4 together up until the last yarn over, now place the yarn over the hook and insert the hook into the fifth stitch, place the yarn over the hook and pull a loop through the stitch, seven loops are now on the hook, yarn over and pull through the first two loops on the hook, you should now have six loops on the hook. Place the yarn over the hook and pull through all six loops on the hook.

TRIPLE TREBLE CROCHET 2 TOGETHER

Wrap the yarn four times over the hook and insert into the first stitch, yarn over and pull through the stitch, five loops are on the hook, (yarn over and pull through two loops) three times, two loops are left on the hook, yarn over the hook four times and insert the hook into the second stitch, yarn over and pull through the stitch, six loops are now on the hook, (yarn over and pull through two loops) three times, three loops are left on the hook, yarn over and pull through all three loops on the hook.

TECHNIQUES

STANDING SC

Place a slip knot on the hook, insert hook into stitch, yarn over and pull up a loop, yarn over and pull through both loops on hook

STANDING HDC

Place a slip knot on the hook, yarn over, insert hook into stitch, yarn over and pull up a loop, yarn over and pull through all three loops on hook

STANDING DC

Place a slip knot on the hook, yarn over, insert hook into stitch, yarn over and pull up a loop, yarn over and pull through first two loops, yarn over and pull through last two loops

STANDING TR

Place a slip knot on the hook, yarn over twice, insert hook into stitch, yarn over and pull up a loop, yarn over and pull through two loops three times.

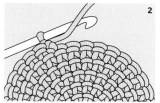

RIGHT / WRONG SIDE

When crocheting in rounds it is important to be able to distinguish which side of the crocheted piece is the right side. This is especially true when you are asked to work in the front or back loops of a stitch.
On the right or front side there are little 'V's that appear (1). The wrong or back side has horizontal lines which are called back bumps or back bars (2).

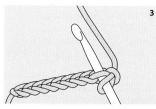

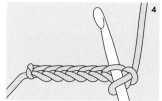

FRONT LOOP

The front loop of a stitch is the loop closest to you. If the crochet pattern says to work in front loops only (FLO) you will work your stitches into just this front loop (3).

BACK LOOP

The back loop is the loop furthest away from you. If the crochet pattern says to work in back loops only (BLO) you will work your stitches into just this back loop (4).

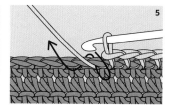

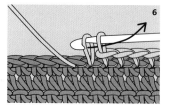

FRONT POST SLIP STITCH

Working on the WS, insert the hook around the post of the stitch, from front to back and up to the front again (5), yarn over and pull up a loop (6), then pull that loop all the way through.

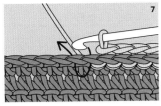

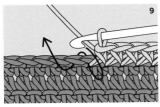

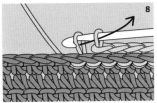

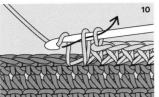

BACK POST SLIP STITCH

Working on the RS, insert the hook around the post of the stitch, from back to front, then out the back again (7), yarn over and pull up a loop, then pull that loop all the way through (8).

FRONT POST SINGLE CROCHET

Insert the hook from front to back to front around the post of the stitch (9). Yarn over and pull up a loop, yarn over and pull yarn through 2 loops on the hook (10).

FRONT POST HALF DOUBLE CROCHET

Place the yarn over the hook and insert the hook from front to back to front around the post of the stitch. Yarn over and pull up a loop, 3 loops are now on the hook. Yarn over and pull the yarn through all 3 loops on the hook.

FRONT POST DOUBLE CROCHET

Work as for Double Crochet inserting the hook from front to back to front around the post of the stitch instead of into it.

FRONT POST TREBLE CROCHET

Work as for Treble Crochet inserting the hook from front to back to front around the post of the stitch instead of into it.

FRONT POST DOUBLE TREBLE CROCHET

Work as for Double Treble Crochet inserting the hook from front to back to front around the post of the stitch instead of into it.

FRONT POST TRIPLE TREBLE CROCHET

Work as for Triple Treble Crochet inserting the hook from front to back to front around the post of the stitch instead of into it.

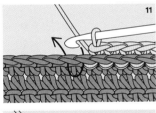

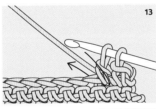

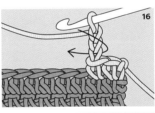

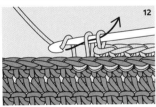

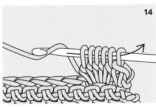

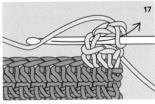

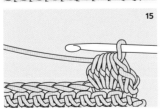

BACK POST SINGLE CROCHET

Insert the hook from back to front to back around the post of the stitch (11). Yarn over and pull up a loop, yarn over and pull yarn through 2 loops on the hook (12).

BACK POST HALF DOUBLE CROCHET

Work as for Half Double Crochet inserting the hook from back to front to back around the post of the stitch instead of into it.

BACK POST DOUBLE CROCHET

Work as for Double Crochet inserting the hook from back to front to back around the post of the stitch instead of into it.

BOBBLE STITCH

* Yarn over, insert the hook into the stitch, yarn over and pull up a loop. Yarn over and pull through 2 loops. (13). Continue from * in the same stitch until you have a total of 6 loops on your hook (14). Yarn over and pull through all 6 loops at once (15).

PICOT STITCH

Ch3, insert the hook from right to left under the front loop and bottom vertical bar of previously made chain (16), yarn over and pull through all loops on the hook (17).

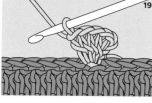

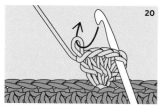

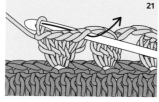

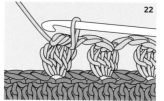

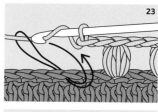

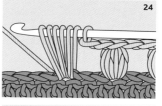

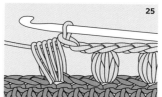

LOOP STITCH

Wrap the yarn from front to back over the index finger of the hand holding the yarn. Insert the hook into the next stitch, yarn over and pull through the stitch. With the loop still on your finger, yarn over and pull it through the two loops on the hook.

PUFF STITCH

Yarn over and insert into the stitch, yarn over and pull up a long loop (23), (yarn over and insert into the same stitch, yarn over and pull up a long loop) twice more (24), yarn over and pull through all seven loops on hook (25), ch to close puff.

For a 3-dc-puff, (yarn over and insert into stitch, yarn over and pull up a loop, yarn over and pull through two loops) three times, yarn over and pull through all four loops on hook, ch to close puff.

For a 5-dc-puff, work as for a 3-dc-puff working the repeated section five times. The final yarn over will be through six loops.

For a 7-dc-puff, work as for a 3-dc-puff working the repeated section seven times. The final yarn over will be through eight loops.

BEGINNING POPCORN STITCH

For a 5-dc-popcorn, pull the yarn through the stitch and make a chain to join, then ch3 (18), 4dc in same st (19), remove the hook from the loop and insert hook from front to back through the top of initial ch-3, replace the loop onto the hook (from the last dc), yarn over and pull through both loops on the hook (20).

POPCORN STITCH

Work desired number of stitches in same st (e.g. for 2-dc-popcorn, work 2dc, and for 5-dc-popcorn, work 5dc), remove hook from last dc and insert it, from front to back, in top of first dc of popcorn st, insert hook in loop from last dc, yarn over and pull through both loops on the hook (21 and 22).

SPIKE STITCH

Insert the hook into the indicated stitch, pull up a loop to the height of the working row, yarn over and pull through both loops on the hook.

FINISHING

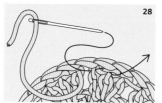

JOINING YARN

Insert the hook into the indicated stitch, wrap the yarn around the hook and pull it through the stitch, yarn over the hook and pull through to secure (26).

FASTENING OFF

Cut the yarn and pull the yarn tail through the last loop on your hook.

INVISIBLE FASTEN OFF

When you fasten off invisibly you get a smooth even edge. Cut the yarn and pull the yarn tail through the last stitch. Thread the yarn tail onto a yarn needle, insert the needle, from front to back, into the next stitch. Now insert the needle back into the same stitch that the yarn tail is coming out of, but into the back loop only, and pull gently (27). Weave the tail end into the wrong side of the fabric and cut the excess (28).

WEAVING IN ENDS

Using a tapestry needle, weave all loose yarn ends through the back of your work into stitches of the same colour where possible. Keep checking the right side to ensure they do not show through too much. Pull slightly once complete before cutting fairly close to the final position.

BLOCKING

Pin your items to size using rust-proof pins and steam lightly with an iron. Do not touch your work with the iron but hover over it giving blasts of steam. Leave to dry completely before removing the pins.

DESIGNERS

CAITIE MOORE

www.thoresbycottage.com
@thoresbycottage

Caitie is the maker, crafter and crochet designer behind the blog and online store Thoresby Cottage. She lives in the beautiful city of Cape Town, South Africa with her family and fur-friend, Lily Buttons. With a background in science and zoology, much of the inspiration for her whimsical amigurumi and home décor is drawn from the colors and shapes found in nature.

Caitie's patterns appear on the following pages in this book: 17, 18, 19, 20, 21, 22, 23, 26, 27, 30, 31, 33, 36, 37, 38, 40, 41, 44, 45, 46, 47, 48, 52, 53, 57, 60, 62, 64, 71, 72, 75, 76, 79, 110, 112, 113, 114, 115, 116, 118.

CELINE SEMAAN

www.craftycc.com
@crafty_cc

Celine is a crochet designer based in Australia. She loves to create modern and bright crochet projects, and is well known for this signature style. She will avoid the camera at all costs, so you're very unlikely to see a photo of her. However, she has a 6 year old cat named Archie who occasionally makes an appearance on her Instagram feed.

Celine's patterns appear on the following pages in this book: 10, 28, 32, 39, 51, 54, 55, 56, 59, 67, 78, 80, 81, 82, 83, 84, 85, 91, 94, 95, 96, 97, 101, 103, 104, 105, 106, 107, 108, 109, 117.

SHARNA MOORE

www.sharnamoore123.wixsite.com/
crochet
@sweet_sharna

Sharna studied textiles at college and has always been an avid crafter. Her passion for crochet has grown significantly over the years, so it felt very natural for her to start designing her own patterns and sharing them on social media. She finds inspiration everywhere, especially during springtime with all of the pretty coloured blossoms in the air.

Sharna's patterns appear on the following pages in this book: 11, 12, 13, 14, 15, 16, 24, 25, 29, 34, 35, 42, 43, 49, 50, 58, 61, 63, 65, 66, 68, 69, 70, 73, 74, 77, 86, 87, 88, 89, 90, 92, 93, 98, 99, 100, 102, 111, 119.

THANKS

The publisher and designers would like to thank Love Crafts for kindly supplying the yarn used for all of the granny squares and projects shown in this book.

www.lovecrafts.com

A DAVID AND CHARLES BOOK
© David and Charles, Ltd 2019

David and Charles is an imprint of David and Charles, Ltd
Suite A, Tourism House, Pynes Hill, Exeter, EX2 5WS

ISBN-13: 9781446307434 paperback
ISBN-13: 9781446378298 EPUB
ISBN-13: 9781446378281 PDF

This book has been printed on paper from approved suppliers and made from
pulp from sustainable sources.

Printed in the UK by Page Bros for:
David and Charles, Ltd
Suite A, Tourism House, Pynes Hill, Exeter, EX2 5WS

20 19 18 17 16 15 14 13 12

Content Director: Ame Verso
Senior Commissioning Editor: Sarah Callard
Managing Editor: Jeni Hennah
Project Editor: Carol Ibbetson
Design Manager: Anna Wade
Designer: Ali Stark
Photographer: Jason Jenkins
Charts and Illustrations: Kuo Kang Chen
Production Manager: Beverley Richardson

David and Charles publishes high-quality books on a wide range of subjects.
For more information visit www.davidandcharles.com.

Share your makes with us on social media using #dandcbooks and follow us on
Facebook and Instagram by searching for @dandcbooks.

Layout of the digital edition of this book may vary depending on reader
hardware and display settings.